THE COLLEGE OF LAW BRISTOL
BS1 6HG
D1389826

The College of Law, Bristol
R01267

Intellectual Property and the Limits of Antitrust

NEW HORIZONS IN COMPETITION LAW AND ECONOMICS

Series Editors: Steven D. Anderman, *Department of Law, University of Essex, UK* and Rudolph J.R. Peritz, *New York Law School, USA*

This series has been created to provide research based analysis and discussion of the appropriate role for economic thinking in the formulation of competition law and policy. The books in the series will move beyond studies of the traditional role of economics – that of helping to define markets and assess market power – to explore the extent to which economic thinking can play a role in the formulation of legal norms, such as abuse of a dominant position, restriction of competition and substantial impediments to or lessening of competition. This in many ways is the *new horizon* of competition law policy.

US antitrust policy, influenced in its formative years by the Chicago School, has already experienced an expansion of the role of economic thinking in its competition rules. Now the EU is committed to a greater role for economic thinking in its Block Exemption Regulations and Modernisation package as well as possibly in its reform of Article 82. Yet these developments still raise the issue of the *extent* to which economics should be adopted in defining the public interest in competition policy and what role economists should play in legal argument. The series will provide a forum for research perspectives that are critical of an unduly-expanded role for economics as well as those that support its greater use.

Titles in the series include:

Antitrust, Patents and Copyright
EU and US Perspectives
Edited by François Lévêque and Howard Shelanski

Innovation Markets and Competition Analysis
EU Competition Law and US Antitrust Law
Marcus Glader

Competition Law and Patents
A Follow-on Innovation Perspective in the Biopharmaceutical Industry
Irina Haracoglou

Antitrust and Regulation in the EU and US
Legal and Economic Perspectives
Edited by François Lévêque and Howard Shelanski

Competition Law, Innovation and Antitrust
An Analysis of Tying and Technological Integration
Hedvig Schmidt

Intellectual Property and the Limits of Antitrust
A Comparative Study of US and EU Approaches
Katarzyna Czapracka

Intellectual Property and the Limits of Antitrust

A Comparative Study of US and EU Approaches

Katarzyna Czapracka

Associate, White & Case LLP, Belgium

NEW HORIZONS IN COMPETITION LAW AND ECONOMICS

Edward Elgar

Cheltenham, UK • Northampton, MA, USA

Published by
Edward Elgar Publishing Limited
The Lypiatts
15 Lansdown Road
Cheltenham
Glos GL50 2JA
UK

Edward Elgar Publishing, Inc.
William Pratt House
9 Dewey Court
Northampton
Massachusetts 01060
USA

A catalogue record for this book is available from the British Library

Library of Congress Control Number: 2009936744

ISBN 978 1 84720 925 2

Typeset by Cambrian Typesetters, Camberley, Surrey
Printed and bound by MPG Books Group, UK

Contents

Acknowledgements

My deepest gratitude goes to my teachers and advisors. The Chair of my JSD Committee, Professor Petros C. Mavroidis, has been a great source of inspiration since the beginning of my studies at Columbia Law School. The ideas and comments of Professor Harvey J. Goldschmid challenged my thinking and broadened my horizons. I would also like to thank the editors of the New Horizons in Law and Economics series for their comments and suggestions, which have been really helpful. All remaining mistakes are mine.

The cut-off date for the book has been a moving target, but I have attempted to cover the developments through the end of 2008.

The text draws on the JSD thesis I defended at Columbia School of Law in 2007. The opinions expressed are strictly personal.

Introduction

Application of antitrust rules to intellectual property (IP) has always been a perplexing subject. It has recently gained importance in the context of new technologies and the associated market developments. Over the past few years, the US and EU antitrust enforcers have taken steps to reevaluate their approach to IP rights and to tackle the related issues concerning application of the antitrust rules in high-tech sectors of the economy. In the US the Federal Trade Commission (FTC) and the Department of Justice (DOJ) held months-long hearings focusing on the intersection of antitrust and IP laws in 2002 and published two reports on the topic. Both IP and high-technology industries were among the issues addressed in the 2007 report published by the Antitrust Modernization Commission. The agencies have also brought a number of high-profile cases involving information technology (IT) industries and IP rights, including *Microsoft*,[1] *Intel*[2] and *Rambus*.[3] Moreover, the Supreme Court addressed issues of vital importance to the antitrust and intellectual property intersection in the *Illinois Tool*[4] and *Trinko*[5] cases.

Equally fundamental developments have taken place on the other side of the Atlantic. In the spring of 2004, the European Commission adopted a new Technology Transfer Block Exemption Regulation[6] and ruled that Microsoft's refusal to provide interoperability information to its rivals constituted an abuse of a dominant position. In 2005, the Commission adopted a ground-breaking decision in the *AstraZeneca* case[7] – the first case in which EU competition law has been applied to an alleged misuse of the patent system and the procedures for marketing pharmaceuticals. In the same year, the Commission published

1 *U.S. v. Microsoft Corp.*, 253 F.3d 34 (D.C. Cir. 2001).

2 *In the Matter of Intel Corporation*, Docket No. 9288, available at: http://www.ftc.gov/os/adjpro/d9288/index.shtm.

3 *In the Matter of Rambus Incorporated*, Docket No. 9302, available at: http://www.ftc.gov/os/adjpro/d9302/index.shtm.

4 *Illinois Tool Works Inc. v. Independent Ink, Inc.*, 126 St. Ct. 1281 (2006).

5 *Verizon Communications Inc. v. Law Offices of Curtis v. Trinko*, LLP, 540 U.S. 398 (2004). Although the case does not involve IP rights, it is of vital importance for cases involving a refusal to license IP rights.

6 Commission Regulation No. 772/2004 of 27 April 2004 on the application of Article 81(3) of the Treaty to categories of technology transfer agreements, OJ (L 123) 11 (2004).

7 Commission Decision in COMP/37.507 – Generics/AstraZeneca (2005).

the *Article 82 Discussion Paper*, which outlined the Commission's views on the assessment of unilateral conduct involving intellectual property rights under competition laws.[8] In 2007, the Court of First Instance (CFI) delivered the long- awaited judgment in the *Microsoft* case, upholding the Commission's position on Microsoft's obligations to share interoperability information with its competitors,[9] and the Commission also issued a statement of objections in a first case involving an alleged patent ambush. The pharmaceutical sector inquiry launched by the Commission in 2008 targeted patent settlements between generic and brand name pharmaceutical companies.[10] Many of these recent cases involved a direct conflict between IP rights and antitrust laws, where the ordered remedies deprived the right holders of exclusivity either by imposing licensing obligations or by limiting their ability to enforce their rights.

The recent developments highlight a growing divergence between the EU and US antitrust enforcers over the approach to the application of antitrust rules to IP rights. This is so even though there is a broad analytical consensus as to the economic principles governing the application of antitrust rules to IP rights. It is equally accepted on both sides of the Atlantic that IP rights do not create monopolies, that IP and antitrust rules have the common objective of stimulating innovation and economic growth, and that IP rights need to be treated with some level of deference so that antitrust enforcement does not undermine the objectives of IP policy. It also appears that in both jurisdictions the antitrust authorities focus on dynamic competition and incentives to innovate.

---

[8] *See* European Commission, Directorate General for Competition, *DG Competition Discussion Paper on the Application of Article 82 of the Treaty to Exclusionary Abuses*, 19 Dec. 2005, http://europa.eu.int/comm/competition/antitrust/others/discpaper2005.pdf (*Article 82 Discussion Paper*). In December 2008, following the public consultations the Commission adopted *Guidance on the Commission's Enforcement Priorities in Applying Article 82 EC Treaty to Abusive Exclusionary Conduct by Dominant Undertaking*, Communication from the Commission, COM (2008). The new document, much shorter than the Discussion Paper, does not elaborate on the Commission's approach to IP and interoperability information.

[9] Case T-201/04, *Microsoft Corp. v. Commission* (*Microsoft* judgment), 2007 E.C.R. II-3601.

[10] *See* DG Competition Staff Working Paper, *Pharmaceutical Sector Inquiry Preliminary Report*, 28 Nov. 2008, at http://ec.europa.eu/competition/sectors/pharmaceuticals/inquiry/exec_summary_en.pdf. The Report does not identify wrongdoing of individual companies or provide guidance on the compatibility of certain behavior with EU competition law, but concludes that brand name companies engaged in practices that delayed market entry of generic medicines and possibility limited innovation in the pharmaceutical sector. The Commission announced public consultations to consider steps to address these issues.

This book strives to offer a better understanding of the roots of the differences in the application of antitrust principles to IP rights. It focuses on unilateral conduct and on cases where antitrust remedies deprive the right owner of exclusivity, the core of an IP right. This area merits special attention for two reasons. First, it is the source of the greatest differences in the approaches of EU and US antitrust enforcers to IP rights. Second, it is the area where the application of antitrust rules to IP rights can have the direst consequences for the right holders.

Whereas the scope of antitrust laws has been shrinking in the United States, EU competition law has been consistently used to regulate a number of issues that are considered to be outside the scope of the Sherman Act. In the United States, unilateral conduct involving exercise of a valid IP right can hardly give rise to liability under antitrust rules and antitrust authorities have been reluctant to intervene in what is perceived to be the sphere of IP policy. In contrast, the EU antitrust enforcers have been much more active than their US counterparts in addressing the consequences of what they perceive as imperfect IP laws, thus reshaping the substantive standards for IP protection. In a few cases involving difficult questions relating to the scope of IP rights, the Commission and the EU courts have ruled that, in limited circumstances, a dominant company may violate Article 82 by refusing to license a valid IP right to its competitors. Allocation of the burden of proof is also significant. For example, in the recent *Microsoft* ruling, the CFI required that the dominant company submit evidence showing that compulsory licensing would have 'a significant negative impact on its incentives to innovate' in order to justify its refusal to share its IP with competitors.[11] At the same time, it appears that the Court was satisfied that a compulsory license would stimulate follow-on innovation on the basis of less concrete evidence than was required in previous compulsory licensing cases.

One reason for these divergences is that EU and US courts assess market power and its abuse quite differently. Monopolization under §2 of the Sherman Act and an abuse of a dominant position under Article 82 of the EC Treaty comprise two elements: possession of market power and anticompetitive conduct. Yet, there are major differences between the EU and US rules relating, for example, to the definition of dominance, the assessment of what constitutes anticompetitive conduct, and the requirement of a causal link between maintenance of monopoly power and anticompetitive conduct. Whereas §2 of the Sherman Act is designed to protect competition by prohibiting the acquisition or maintenance of 'monopoly power', Article 82 is used to regulate the actions of companies in 'dominant positions'. One of the principles repeated in EU

---

[11] *Microsoft* judgment, ¶697.

case law is that dominant companies have a 'special responsibility' not to impair competition in the market. The EU antitrust enforcers have been receptive to the idea that monopolists may be required to provide certain services or share the essential inputs which they control. They advocate a relatively wide scope for antitrust intervention in cases involving unilateral refusals to deal, including refusals to license IP rights and to provide interoperability information. By contrast, the US Supreme Court questioned the merit of 'enforced sharing' in the *Trinko* case and set a very narrow scope for antitrust scrutiny of unilateral refusals to deal.[12] In the United States, there is a more general reluctance towards regulating the future conduct of companies with market power as it is perceived to potentially have a chilling effect on beneficial, procompetitive activities.

The transatlantic differences relating to the assessment of market dominance are only a partial explanation for the clashes over IP rights. An equally important issue is the application of antitrust laws to market distortions resulting from a government action. In unregulated markets, competition enforcement may remedy specific market failures. In regulated markets, competition law may also be used to address externalities created by regulatory activity. Patents, copyrights, trademarks, trade secrets and other forms of IP give their owners some exclusivity over the particular use and expression of a piece of information. The relation between antitrust law and regulation that may disrupt competitive processes is vital for the antitrust analysis of anticompetitive concerns resulting from IP rights. The differences in the approaches taken by the EU and US antitrust enforcers to these issues are even greater than those relating to the scrutiny of companies exercising their market power. The Sherman Act is generally inapplicable to actions by a state operating in its sovereign capacity or to private conduct approved and supervised by a state as a matter of state policy. In contrast, EU competition law has been used to curb anticompetitive policies at the national level and to erode the position of national monopolies. The roles of competition law and industrial policy have never been clearly delineated and the European Commission has been using competition law to promote industrial policy goals. Laws of the Member States may be and have been challenged as anticompetitive. This is also the case with IP laws, which are still largely regulated at the national level. Some commentators have interpreted the EU compulsory licensing decisions as a means to deal with what was considered an 'aberrant' national IP right.

Just as with state action, the use of government process by private parties may give rise to competitive concerns. Again, there are significant differences as to how antitrust enforcers approach such conduct in the two jurisdictions.

---

12 *Trinko*, 540 U.S. at 408.

In the United States the Noerr-Pennington doctrine provides antitrust immunity to those who use genuine efforts to influence public officials. Persons who seek action from any branch of the state or federal government by using administrative procedures or bringing a court action are immune from antitrust scrutiny, unless their action is a mere 'sham' to cover an attempt to interfere directly with a competitor's business relationships. While the status of antitrust immunity for government petitioning is uncertain in the EU, the available case law suggests that EU antitrust enforcers are more likely to challenge such conduct than their US counterparts. This has important consequences for the antitrust scrutiny of acquisition and enforcement of IP rights.

As mentioned above, the most common §2 challenges in the United States against IP owners involve allegations that their rights are invalid or improperly enforced. But the scope of antitrust scrutiny in such cases is rather limited, because these claims are very narrowly crafted and require a high burden of proof. To prevail on a *Walker Process* claim, for example, the antitrust plaintiff must show an intentional fraud on the Patent Office, causation, and other elements of a §2 violation. Similarly, an action to enforce an invalid IP right can be challenged under §2 only if it is objectively baseless, which requires showing that no reasonable litigant could realistically expect success on the merits.

In *AstraZeneca,* the European Commission suggests a lower standard of antitrust liability in cases involving acquisition or enforcement of IP rights In this case, the Commission alleged that AstraZeneca abused its dominant position by giving misleading information to several national patent offices in order to extend patent protection for one of its drugs. The Commission advanced the view that it is sufficient that the dominant company knowingly provides 'misleading' information; it did not allege that AstraZeneca's conduct was a 'sham' or amounted to fraud. Notably, the patent cases initiated by AstraZeneca's conduct were referred to the ECJ for clarification of the applicable EU regulations. The lack of clarity in applicable laws was no excuse. The Commission's position seems to be that a dominant company must refrain from exploiting uncertainties in applicable laws to preserve its exclusive rights. Moreover, the element of causation is not required to establish an abuse of Article 82, meaning that an act of petitioning may be abusive regardless of whether it would result in issuing an invalid patent. All in all, the AstraZeneca case suggests that acquisition and enforcement of IP rights will be subjected to greater antitrust scrutiny in the EU as compared with the US regime.

Application of antitrust rules to address imperfections in IP laws may offer significant advantages, especially given that IP policy makers often do not take due account of competition values. Still, it also has dangerous implications. Antitrust authorities are not always best positioned to create substantive standards for IP protection. Unduly restrictive antitrust rules may undermine the coherence of the IP system. In the pursuit of equilibrium between IP and antitrust law, European enforcers have embraced theories that may have led to a desirable outcome in a particular case but are unsuitable or too vague to serve as a general rule.

An example of such overeager antitrust enforcement is the application of antitrust laws to trade secrets. Both in the US and in the EU, 'federal' antitrust rules trump inconsistent trade secret laws adopted at the state level. Yet while the US antitrust authorities treat trade secrets with the same level of deference as IP rights, the European Commission does not. In the course of enforcing competition rules, the Commission adopted a definition of protectable trade secrets, asserted that they are not a form of property, and concluded that they do not merit the same level of protection as IP rights. In doing so, the Commission has been predominantly concerned with the need to ensure free competition and less with the companies' need to protect their valuable know-how. It has also ignored the basic principles of trade secret laws, thus undermining national trade secret protection measures.

It is crucial that the antitrust enforcers take due account of the applicable IP laws and clearly state the limiting principles, so that there is no doubt which conduct may be considered an antitrust violation. In this context, the recent decision of the Court of First Instance in the *Microsoft* case is particularly disappointing. The decision failed to clarify some of the important questions of law raised by the *Microsoft* case and further blurs the picture when it comes to the assessment of unilateral refusals to license under Article 82.

This book is organized as follows. The first chapter addresses the differences between the core EU and US antitrust principles crucial for the application of antitrust laws to IP rights, including the major differences between the monopolization offense and the abuse of dominance, the state action doctrine and the immunity for government petitioning, all of which are crucial to the understanding of the limits of antitrust intervention in the EU and in the US. The following chapters discuss examples of conduct involving IP rights that may amount to an antitrust violation in the two jurisdictions. The focus is on cases where antitrust enforcement affects the core of an IP right: refusals to license and anticompetitive acquisition or enforcement of IP rights. The last chapter describes cases where the antitrust laws were applied to trade secrets, showing how overeager antitrust intervention in the EU undermined national measures designed to protect trade secrets. Trade secrets merit a separate chapter also for another reason: the available case law suggests that the EU antitrust enforcers, unlike their US counterparts, apply different rules to trade secrets from those applied to other forms of IP.

Table of statutes

Table of cases

ADMINISTRATIVE DECISIONS

1. The roots of the transatlantic clashes*

This chapter explores the divergences between the EU and US antitrust laws with respect to the rules applicable to unilateral conduct and the antitrust treatment of market distortions resulting from a state action or private parties' petitioning for a state action. As explained in the Introduction, these rules are decisive for the treatment of unilateral conduct involving IP rights in the two jurisdictions. The discussion below is not meant as a comprehensive review of Article 82 and §2, the state action doctrine and the government petitioning immunity in the EU and in the United States. It is designed to offer some observations which are helpful in understanding how American and European antitrust enforcers approach competitive concerns resulting from the combination of IP and market power.

There are numerous ways in which dominant companies may unfairly use their market power to increase or maintain their market power and thereby disadvantage consumers. Market mechanisms are not always sufficient to ensure that dominant companies do not weaken competition and harm consumers, which is why §2 of the Sherman Act makes it illegal to 'monopolize' and Article 82 of the Treaty establishing the European Community prohibits an abuse of a dominant position. The key issue is how to distinguish between competition on merits, which is legal, even if it eliminates rivals of a dominant company, and conduct by private companies which limits competition and hurts consumer welfare.[1] Dissatisfaction with how the antitrust enforcers deal with distinguishing between illegal abuse of market power and legal means of competition has been common both in the EU[2] and in the

* Parts of this Chapter have previously been published in: Katarzyna Czapracka (2006), *Where Antitrust Ends and IP Begins*, 9 YALE J.L. & TECH. 44 (2007).

[1] Antitrust authorities on both sides of the Atlantic agree that, in principle, the ultimate objective of antitrust regulation is to enhance consumer welfare. *See, e.g., Reiter v. Sonotone Corp.*, 442 U.S. 330, 343 (1979) (the Congress designed the Sherman Act as a consumer welfare prescription) and the *Article 82 Discussion Paper*, ¶4 (The objective of Article 82 is the protection of competition on the market as a means of enhancing consumer welfare and of ensuring efficient allocation of resources).

[2] *See, e.g.*, John Temple Lang, *Anticompetitive Non-Pricing Abuses Under European and National Antitrust Law* in BARRY HAWK (ED.), FORDHAM CORPORATE L. INSTITUTE 235 (2003); Thomas Eilmansberger, *How to Distinguish Good from Bad*

United States.[3] In this context, the US Supreme Court adopted its 2004 *Trinko* decision,[4] which significantly limited the scope for antitrust intervention under §2 of the Sherman Act.[5] By contrast, the European Commission in the *Article 82 Discussion Paper*, published a year after the *Trinko* decision, restated the antitrust rules applicable to dominant companies and advocated a broad scope of antitrust regulation of dominant companies' unilateral conduct. That approach was essentially confirmed by the Court of First Instance in its *Microsoft*[6] judgment and in the Commission's *Article 82 Guidance* published in December 2008.[7] The *Trinko* decision and the *Microsoft* judgment are representative of the critical divergences relating to the elements of the monopolization offense and to the underlying philosophy of antitrust enforcement in the two jurisdictions.

Competition under Article 82 EC: In Search of Clearer and More Coherent Standards for Anti-Competitive Abuses, 42 COMMON MARKET L. REV. 129 (2005); Damien Geradin, *Limiting the Scope of Article 82 EC: What Can the EU Learn from the U.S. Supreme Court's Judgment in Trinko in the Wake of Microsoft, IMS, and Deutsche Telekom?*, 41 COMMON MARKET L. REV. 1519 (2004); Derek Ridyard, *Compulsory Access under EU Competition Law – A New Doctrine of 'Convenient Facilities' and the Case for Price Regulation,* 25 EUR. COMPETITION L. REV. 669 (2004); Brian Sher, *The Last of the Steam Powered Trains: Modernizing Article 82*, 25 EUR. COMPETITION L. REV. 243 (2004); John Kallaugher & Brian Sher, *Rebates Revisited: Anti-Competitive Effects and Exclusionary Abuse Under Article 82*, 25 EUR. COMPETITION L. REV. 263 (2004); John Temple Lang & Robert O'Donoghue, *The Concept of Exclusionary Abuse,* GCLC RESEARCH PAPERS ON ARTICLE 82 EC (JULY 2005), at: http://www.coleurop.be/content/gclc/documents/GCLC%20Research%20Papers%20on%20Article%2082%20EC.pdf.

[3] *See, e.g.*, Einer Elhauge, *Defining Better Monopolization Standards,* 56 STAN. L. REV. 253 (2003) and Robert Pitofsky, *Past, Present, and Future of Antitrust Enforcement at the Federal Trade Commission,* 72 U. CHI. L. REV. 209 (2005) (comparing with other fields of antitrust where there is more agreement as to the applicable standards).

[4] *Verizon Communications Inc. v. Law Offices of Curtis v. Trinko, LLP*, 540 U.S. 398 (2004).

[5] *For comment, see, e.g.*, Eleanor M. Fox, *Is There Life in Aspen After Trinko? The Silent Revolution of Section 2 of the Sherman Act*, 73 ANTITRUST L.J. 153 (2005); Herbert Hovenkamp, *Exclusion and the Sherman Act*, 72 U. CHI. L. REV. 147 (2005); John Thorne, A *Categorical Rule Limiting Section 2 of the Sherman Act:* Verizon v Trinko, 72 U. CHI. L. REV. 289 (2005); Thomas E. Kauper, *Section Two of the Sherman Act: The Search for Standards*, 93 GEO. L. J. 1623 (2005).

[6] Case T-201/04, *Microsoft Corp. v. Commission* (*Microsoft* judgment), 2007 E.C.R. II-3601.

[7] *Guidance on the Commission's Enforcement Priorities in Applying Article 82 EC Treaty to Abusive Exclusionary Conduct by Dominant Undertakings*, Communication from the Commission, COM (2008), available at: http://ec.europa.eu/competition/antitrust/art82/index.html.

Differences in the assessment of unilateral conduct in the EU and in the US are only a part of the story of antitrust and IP law intersection in the transatlantic context. The less discussed but equally important part is the relation between antitrust law and regulation that may disrupt competitive processes, the subject of Sections 3 and 4 of this chapter. In unregulated markets, competition enforcement is necessary to address specific market failures. In regulated markets, competition law may also be used to address externalities created by regulatory activity. Whereas Europeans see an important role for antitrust to address such distortions, Americans do not. Analogous patterns can be found in the approach to IP rights. US antitrust authorities avoid interfering with what is perceived to be the sphere of IP regulations. EU competition rules have been applied to correct national regulatory measures which disrupt competition, including IP laws, and have been used to shape substantive rules of IP protection. This has had a significant effect on the assessment of cases involving unilateral refusals to license. Further, the principles concerning the application of antitrust rules in cases where harm to competition results from a state action, or private parties' petitioning for a state action, were decisive for the European Commission's decision in the *AstraZeneca* case. This important precedent from the European Commission suggests that European antitrust enforcers may be moving towards subjecting the acquisition and enforcement of IP rights to greater antitrust scrutiny.

1. MONOPOLIZATION AND ABUSE OF DOMINANCE: BASIC ELEMENTS

Both §2 of the Sherman Act and Article 82 of the EC Treaty prohibit anticompetitive conduct by companies possessing market power. Yet, there are fundamental differences relating to the required degree of market power, the assessment of what constitutes anticompetitive conduct, and the requirement of a causal link between maintenance of monopoly power and anticompetitive conduct. The differences relating to the philosophy of antitrust enforcement may be even more crucial. One US official suggested that whereas the US system supports 'cowboy capitalism', allowing a monopolist to compete aggressively on the merits even if it entails injuries to its rivals, the Europeans require dominant firms to 'compete like gentlemen'.[8] Less poetically, but

[8] J. Bruce McDonald, *Section 2 and Article 82: Cowboys and Gentlemen*, Speech at Article 82 Second Annual Conference, Brussels, Belgium (16–17 June 2005). *See also* Mario Monti, *Comments to the Speech of Hew Pate, Antitrust in a Transatlantic Context,* Brussels, Belgium (7 June 2004) at Article 82 Second Annual Conference, Brussels, Belgium (16–17 June 2005); *see also* R. Hewitt Pate, *Antitrust*

more accurately, Advocate General Jacobs noted that §2 of the Sherman Act is designed to protect competition by prohibiting the acquisition or maintenance of 'monopoly power', whereas Article 82 is used to regulate the actions of companies in 'dominant positions'.[9] These differences and the discussion of how they affect the treatment of the refusals to deal and essential facilities in the US and in the EU are the subject of the next two sections of this chapter.

1.1 Monopoly Power

In principle, unilateral conduct gives rise to competitive concerns only if it is undertaken by a company with a significant degree of market power. The theory goes that if there are substitutes on the market, no company can raise prices substantially above a competitive level without losing market shares to its rivals. For the purpose of applying §2 of the Sherman Act, a monopolist is defined as a company which has power over prices and can engage in exclusionary conduct.[10] Along the same lines, the European Court of Justice (ECJ)'s definition of dominance refers to possession of economic power in a relevant market 'which enables [a company] to prevent effective competition being maintained in the relevant market by affording it the power to behave to an appreciable extent independently of its competitors, customers and ultimately of its consumers'.[11] Seemingly, these concepts are akin to the US definition of monopoly power as excessive power over prices or the ability to exclude competition.[12] The power to prevent effective competition can be equated with the power to engage in exclusionary conduct. The ability to act independently

---

in a Transatlantic Context – From the Cicada's Perspective, Address at Article 82 Second Annual Conference, Brussels, Belgium (16–17 June 2005).

[9] Opinion of AG Jacobs in *Oscar Bronner GmbH & Co. KG v. Mediaprint Zeitungs- und Zeitschriftenverlag GmbH & Co. KG, Mediaprint Zeitungsvertriebsgesellschaft mbH & Co. KG and Mediaprint Anzeigengesellschaft mbH & Co. KG*, 1998 E.C.R. I-7791, ¶46.

[10] *See Eastman Kodak Co. v. Image Technical Services, Inc.*, 504 U.S. 451, 481 (1992); *Rebel Oil Co. v. Atl. Richfield Co.*, 51 F.3d 1421, 1434 (9th Cir. 1995); *United States v. Microsoft Corporation*, 253 F.3d 34, 51 (D.C. Cir. 2001) (demonstrating that a firm which has taken such actions indicates that it has monopoly power); William E. Landes & Richard A. Posner, *Market Power in Antitrust Cases*, 94 HARV. L. REV. 937, 956–7 (1981); *see also* Elhauge, *supra* note 3, at 257–9.

[11] *United Brands v. Commission*, 1978 E.C.R. 207, ¶65; see *also Hoffmann–La Roche v. Commission*, 1979 E.C.R. 461, ¶¶38–9.

[12] *See, e.g.*, *United States v. E.I. Du Pont de Nemours & Co.*, 351 U.S. 377, 391 (1956); *United States v. Grinnell Corp.*, 384 U.S. 563, 571 (1966); *Eastman Kodak Co. v. Image Technical Services, Inc.*, 504 U.S. 451, 481 (1992).

on the market has been defined as the ability to restrict output and raise prices significantly above the competitive level.[13]

The conventional proxy for market power is the defendant's share of the relevant market and this is where significant differences between the US and the EU arise. In the US, market shares in the range of 70–90 percent are sufficient to establish a prima facie case of monopoly power, provided that they are held over a significant period of time.[14] A company that does not possess significant market power at the time of anticompetitive conduct may still violate §2 if it obtains monopoly power as a result of that conduct. If the conduct does not result in monopoly power, the company may be guilty of attempted monopolization.[15] The classic formulation of attempted monopolization requires that three elements are present: (1) a predatory or anticompetitive conduct, (2) an intent to monopolize, and (3) a dangerously high probability of achieving monopoly power.[16] In *Spectrum Sports*, the Supreme Court stressed that the dangerous probability of success could not be inferred from conduct alone[17] and that inquiry into the relevant product and geographic market and the defendant's economic power in that market is always required.[18] In particular, the defendant's position on the market must be so close to monopoly that its conduct threatens to bring about monopolization.[19] If the defendant does not have a significant market share, there is a presumption that the attempt does not occur. Though there are no precise market share boundaries, US courts rarely find market shares below 50 percent to be sufficient.[20]

---

13 *See Article 82 Discussion Paper*, ¶24 (referring to the influence over prices and other 'parameters of competition' such as output, innovation, and the variety of goods and services. Higher than 'normal' profits may be the evidence of dominance); *see also id.*, at 26; *United Brands*, 1978 E.C.R. 207, ¶126, and Case 322/81, *NV Nederlandsche Banden Industrie Michelin v. Commission* (*Michelin I*), 1983 E.C.R. 3461, ¶59; *see also* RICHARD WHISH, COMPETITION LAW 179–80 (2005).

14 *United States v. Aluminum Co. of America*, 148 F.2d 416, 424 (2d. Cir. 1945) (holding that a market share of 90 percent was 'enough to constitute a monopoly', and that it was 'doubtful whether 60 or 64 percent would be enough and certainly 33 percent is not.') *See also, e.g., Microsoft*, 253 F.3d at 54–5; *United States v. Dentsply International, Inc.*, 399 F.3d 181, 188 (3d Cir. 2005).

15 *See* PHILIP AREEDA & HERBERT HOVENKAMP, ANTITRUST LAW 802 (2002).

16 *See, e.g., Swift and Co. v. United States*, 196 U.S. 375, 396 (1905); *Lorain Journal Co. v. United States*, 342 U.S. 143, 153–5 (1951); *United States v. Aluminum Co.*, 148 F.2d 416, 431–2 (2d Cir. 1945); *Spectrum Sports v. McQuillan*, 506 U.S. 447, 455–6 (1993).

17 *Spectrum Sports*, 506 U.S. at 459.

18 *Id.*

19 *See* AREEDA & HOVENKAMP, *supra* note 15, at 807a.

20 *Id.* (discussing the trend in recent decisions to impose significant minimum market share requirements on the attempted offense); *see also H.L. Hayden Co. of N.Y. v. Siemens Medical Sys.*, 879 F.2d 1005 (2d. Cir. 1989) (20 percent market share

Unlike §2 of the Sherman Act, Article 82 does not distinguish between monopolization and an attempt to monopolize. Only companies which dominate a particular market at the time when the alleged abuse started may be charged with an Article 82 violation. Yet, it appears that companies can be charged with an abuse of dominance when they have less market power than would be required for monopolization under §2 of the Sherman Act. In *United Brands*, a market share between 40 and 45 percent was sufficient to establish dominance. Though it is uncommon, even a company holding less than 40 percent of the relevant market can be found dominant.[21] What is more, in the EU dominance is more likely to be found on the basis of market share alone than in the US: in *AKZO*, the ECJ held that a market share of 50 percent could be considered very large, so that in the absence of exceptional circumstances a company with such a market share would be presumed dominant.[22] The *Article 82 Guidance* advocates a more flexible approach. The Commission states that although high market shares held over a long time period constitute 'an important preliminary indication of the existence of a dominant position', it will not, as a general rule, make the determination on that matter without examining all the factors that may be sufficient to constrain the power.[23] The dynamics of the market, product differentiation, barriers to expansion and entry, and countervailing buyer power are among the factors which the Commission would ordinarily consider.[24] This position brings the EU position on using market shares as a proxy for market power closer to the mainstream economic literature.

Notably, the *Article 82 Discussion Paper* suggested that there may be different degrees of dominance. Some case law supports the proposition that companies having extremely high market shares leading to a 'super-dominant' position may be subject to stricter liability for exclusionary behavior.[25]

---

insufficient to support attempted monopolization claim under §2 of the Sherman Act) and *U.S. Anchor Mfg. v. Rule Indus.*, 7 F.3d 986, 1000–1 (11th Cir. 1993) (no dangerous probability of success if less than 50 percent of the market).

[21] *See* C-250/92, *Gøttrup-Klim and others v. Dansk Landbrugs Grovvareselskab*, 1994 E.C.R. I-5641.

[22] *See* Case C-62/86, *AKZO v. Commission*, 1991 E.C.R. I-3359.

[23] *See Article 82 Guidance,* ¶15.

[24] *Id.* ¶¶13–18.

[25] *See, e.g.*, Opinion of AG Fennelly in Cases C-395 & 396/96 P, *Compagnie Maritime Belge Transports SA and others v. Commission*, 2000 E.C.R. I-1365, ¶119 (declaring that the position of 'overwhelming dominance verging on monopoly' would give rise to 'particularly onerous special obligations' not to interfere with competitive process). The Commission referred to this line of case law in *Clearstream* (Commission Decision in case COMP/38.096 – Clearstream, 300) and in *Microsoft* (Commission Decision in case COMP/37.792 – Microsoft, 435); *see also* IVO VAN BAEL & JEAN-FRANCOIS BELLIS, COMPETITION LAW OF THE EUROPEAN COMMUNITY 119

According to Article 82 Discussion Paper, 'the degree of dominance may be relevant for finding abuse.'[26] The position of super-dominance is likely to be found when a company has market shares in excess of 75 percent and there is almost no competition from other actual competitors in the market.[27] The issue of 'super-dominance' also played a role in the *Microsoft* case, which is discussed in more detail below. In particular, the Commission's theory on Microsoft's obligation to share interoperability information with its rivals strongly relied on 'Microsoft's quasi-monopoly on the client PC operating systems market'.[28] The CFI embraced the Commission's arguments on 'quasi-monopoly',[29] suggesting that a company with very high market shares, whose market position is based on control over access to the technology, for example through the ownership of IP rights or trade secrets, would be typically subjected to onerous obligations to share interoperability information with its competitors in a vertically integrated market. These issues are discussed in more detail in Chapter 2 below. Though the *Article 82 Guidance* does not mention the concept of 'super-dominance', it makes clear that conduct of companies with very high market shares will be measured against a different standard. It states that 'the stronger the dominant position, the higher the likelihood that conduct protecting that position leads to anticompetitive foreclosure'[30] and suggests that efficiency justifications may not be available for companies holding very high market shares.[31]

1.2 Monopoly Power and IP

Antitrust agencies in Europe and in the United States concur that IP does not

---

(2005); ALISON JONES & BRENDA SUFRIN, EC COMPETITION LAW 235 (2002); DAMIEN GERADIN et al., THE CONCEPT OF DOMINANCE, GCLC RESEARCH PAPERS ON ARTICLE 82 EC*;* *supra* note 2*;* Whish, *supra* note 13, at 189–90.

[26] *See Article 82 Discussion Paper*, ¶59. The relevant section provides 'In general, the higher the capability of conduct to foreclose and the wider its application and the stronger the dominant position, the higher the likelihood that an anticompetitive foreclosure results. In view of these sliding scales, where in the following sections various factors are used to indicate circumstances under which a likely foreclosure effect is considered to occur with high(er) or low(er) likelihood, it needs to be kept in mind that these descriptions can not be applied mechanically.'

[27] *Id.* at ¶92.

[28] Case T-201/04, *Microsoft Corp. v. Commission* (*Microsoft* judgment), 2007 E.C.R. II-3601, ¶353.

[29] *Id.* at ¶392.

[30] *Article 82 Guidance,* ¶20.

[31] *Id.* ¶29.

confer market power,[32] and that the relevant market to be taken into account in the antitrust enquiry is that of alternative technologies and artistic offerings that are available or likely to be created, that is, the range of available substitutes.[33] The exclusive rights granted by IP laws are distinguished from the monopoly power that is the concern of antitrust law. Even if patented, it is likely that the product will have many substitutes in the market, some of which may be subject to IP rights. Further, the fact that the owner of an IP right may be able to charge a price higher than the marginal cost does not mean that she enjoys monopoly power, as there is usually a high sunk cost involved in the development of a new product.

To be sure, if the relevant market is defined narrowly so that it includes solely the product covered by an IP right, the IP holder will always be dominant. This was the case for example in *Magill*,[34] where the ECJ rejected the possibility that dominance could be inferred from possession of copyright, but accepted a very narrow definition of the market, basically coinciding with the copyrighted subject matter. Similarly, the US Supreme Court found that a single brand of product or service can be a relevant market under the Sherman Act prohibition against monopolization.[35] Further, under certain circumstances, IP rights may enhance market power and create barriers to entry. Barriers to entry are generally defined as factors that allow incumbent compa-

---

[32] *See* US Department of Justice & Federal Trade Commission, *Antitrust Guidelines for the Licensing of Intellectual Property* (6 April 1995), *at* http://www.usdoj.gov/atr/public/guidelines/ipguide.pdf, ¶2.2 [hereinafter *IP Licensing Guidelines*]; Commission Notice – Guidelines on the application of Article 81 of the EC Treaty to technology transfer agreements, 2004 O.J. (C 101) 2, ¶¶16–17 (discussing the need to assess the degree of market power in the relevant market) [hereinafter *Technology Transfer Guidelines*]; *Article 82 Discussion Paper*, ¶40; Joined Cases C-241/91 and C-242/91, *RTE and others v. Commission* (*Magill*), 1995 E.C.R. I-743, ¶¶46–7 and *Illinois Tool Works Inc. v. Independent Ink, Inc.*, 126 St. Ct. 1281 (2006); 3 AREEDA & HOVENKAMP, *supra* note 15, at 703; 1 HERBERT HOVENKAMP ET AL., IP AND ANTITRUST: AN ANALYSIS OF ANTITRUST PRINCIPLES APPLIED TO INTELLECTUAL PROPERTY LAW 4.1–4.2. (2002); Edmund W. Kitch, *Elementary and Persistent Errors in the Economic Analysis of IP*, 53 VAND. L. REV. 1727, 1729–30 (2000).

[33] *See IP Licensing Guidelines*, ¶3.2; *Technology Transfer Guidelines*, ¶¶19–25. The American and European antitrust agencies identify three markets that need to be taken into account in the application of antitrust law to IPRs: the market for products or services covered by the technology subject to IP protection, the market for the technology and the market for R&D (innovation markets).

[34] Case T-69/89, *RTE v. Commission,* 1991 E.C.R. II-485 (upheld on appeal by the E.C.J. in joined cases C-241/91 P and C-242/91 P, *RTE and ITP v. Commission*, 1995 E.C.R. I-743).

[35] *Eastman Kodak Co. v. Image Technical Services, Inc.*, 504 U.S. 451, 481–2 (1992).

nies to earn supra-competitive returns without attracting entry.[36] A patent, for example, may be a barrier to entry if it controls the only available technology.[37] In a differentiated product market, one company might enjoy a price–cost advantage that rivals cannot eliminate because patents or trademarks prevent its rivals from copying the product.

1.3 Abusive Conduct

The differences in the assessment of monopoly power shed some light on the 'two systems of belief about monopoly', but the definition of anticompetitive conduct is more telling. Neither in the United States nor in Europe is the mere possession of significant market power *ipso facto* sufficient for finding violation of antitrust laws. Both jurisdictions also demand anticompetitive conduct on the part of the dominant company.

US antitrust law prohibits exclusionary conduct: conduct which makes it more difficult for rivals to enter the monopolist's market or to increase their output.[38] Proving monopolization also requires showing that the improper practices made or were likely to have made a contribution to the defendant's monopoly power. Only those unreasonably exclusionary practices that also reduce social welfare merit antitrust intervention. The classic definition of monopolization distinguishes between 'the willful acquisition and maintenance of monopoly power' and 'growth or development as a consequence of a superior product [or] business acumen'.[39] This has been interpreted to mean a conduct which is reasonably capable of creating, enlarging or prolonging monopoly power by impairing the opportunities of rivals and which is not reasonably necessary to achieve any consumer gains that the conduct

---

36 *See* 2A AREEDA & HOVENKAMP, *supra* note 15, at 420a. The European Commission defines barriers to entry as 'factors that make entry impossible or unprofitable while permitting established undertakings to charge prices above competitive level'. *Article 82 Discussion Paper*, ¶38; *see also* Harold Demsetz, *Barriers to Entry*, 72 AM. ECON. REV. 47 (1982); David Harbord & Tom Hoehn, *Barriers to Entry and Exit in European Competition Policy,* 14 INT'L REV. L. AND ECON. 411 (1994); GEORGE J. STIGLER, THE ORGANIZATION OF INDUSTRY 67 (1968); Richard A. Posner, *The Chicago School of Antitrust Analysis*, 127 U. PA. L. REV. 925, 929–31 (1979) (advocating a narrower definition of the barriers to entry).

37 *Article 82 Discussion Paper*, ¶40. The European Commission also considers absolute cost advantages, including access to innovation, R&D and intellectual property, as barriers to entry.

38 *See* Herbert Hovenkamp, *The Monopolization Offence,* 61 OHIO ST. L.J. 1035–7 (2000).

39 *Grinnell*, 384 U.S. at 570–71.

promises.[40] The focus is on efficiency and the effect of the conduct on competition is weighed against efficiency considerations.[41]

This is the legacy of the Chicago School of Law and Economics, which revolutionized antitrust by applying price theory to the analysis of practices considered illegal under antitrust rules and by shielding antitrust law from industrial policies. The Chicago scholars showed that many unilateral practices condemned as anticompetitive, such as leveraging or vertical integration, may in fact enhance consumer welfare.[42] They also stressed the risk of error, the cost of condemning practices that are in fact beneficial for consumers,[43] and the difficulties in designing antitrust remedies that are both feasible to administer and enhance consumer welfare in a way that is superior to market mechanisms.[44] Highly skeptical of antitrust intervention, they believed that market mechanisms can protect themselves better than could be achieved by means of government intervention.[45] The pro-market and largely anti-government Chicago School approach has had significant and lasting consequences for the US antitrust analysis.[46]

Like the US Supreme Court, the ECJ distinguishes between 'normal competition' and abusive conduct, which is:

---

[40] *See* 3 AREEDA & HOVENKAMP, *supra* note 15, at 651A; *see also United States v. Microsoft Corp.* 253 F.3d 34, 58–9 (2001) (ruling that it was appropriate to balance harmful conduct against its efficiency-enhancing effects).

[41] *See e.g. Brooke Group Ltd. v. Brown & Williamson Tobacco Corp.*, 509 U.S. 209 (1991) (monopolization occurs when a company foregoes its short-term profits in expectation of reaping benefits by exercising monopoly power in the long term. Such conduct is deemed anticompetitive if it is capable of excluding from the defendant's market an equally or more efficient competitor); *see also* RICHARD A. POSNER, ANTITRUST LAW 194–96 (2ND edn 2001).

[42] *See generally* ROBERT BORK, THE ANTITRUST PARADOX: A POLICY AT WAR WITH ITSELF (1978); RICHARD A. POSNER, ANTITRUST LAW: AN ECONOMIC PERSPECTIVE (1976).

[43] *See, e.g.,* BORK, *supra* note 42; Frank Easterbrook, *The Limits of Antitrust,* 63 TEX. L. REV. 1 (1984).

[44] *See, e.g.*, William M. Landes, *Optimal Sanctions for Antitrust Violations,* 50 U. CHI. L. REV. 652 (1983); Abbott B. Lipsky & J. Gregory Sidak, *Essential Facilities,* 51 STAN. L. REV. 1187, 1188 (1999).

[45] *See, e.g.*, Eleanor M. Fox & Lawrence A. Sullivan, *Retrospective and Perspective: Where Are We Coming From? Where Are We Going?*, *in* HARRY FIRST ET AL., REVITALIZING ANTITRUST IN ITS SECOND CENTURY 2 (1991); Herbert Hovenkamp, *Antitrust Policy after Chicago*, 84 MICH. L. REV. 213 (1985).

[46] *See, e.g.*, Herbert Hovenkamp, *Post-Chicago Antitrust: A Review and Critique 2001*, COLUM. BUS. L. REV. 257 (2001); Robert Pitofsky, *Past, Present, and Future of Antitrust Enforcement at the Federal Trade Commission*', 72 U. CHI. L. REV. 209 (2005).

> an objective concept relating to the behavior of an undertaking in a dominant position which is such as to influence the structure of a market where, as a result of the very presence of the undertaking in question, the degree of competition is weakened and which, through recourse to methods different from those which condition normal competition in products or services on the basis of the transactions of commercial operators, has the effect of hindering the maintenance of the degree of competition still existing in the market or the growth of that competition.[47]

A dominant company may compete,[48] but it 'has a special responsibility not to allow its conduct to impair genuine undistorted competition on the Common Market.'[49] The concept of 'special responsibility' has been traced to Ordoliberal school of thought and is interpreted to mean that a dominant company cannot use its market power to exclude its rivals unfairly.[50] It justifies subjecting to antitrust liability dominant companies adopting a course of conduct which is not in itself abusive and would be unobjectionable if adopted by a smaller competitor.[51] The proposition that monopolists and firms in the process of acquiring market power are subject to greater scrutiny of their behavior than other firms is widely accepted not only in Europe, but also in the United States.[52] Aside from that, the concept of special responsibility is not helpful as a framework for identifying anticompetitive conduct, though it could be understood as a means of shifting the burden of proof on dominant companies. Indeed in the *Microsoft* judgment, the Court of First Instance found that condemning a refusal to deal under Article 82 did not require establishing that the refusal is likely to eliminate all competition; it was sufficient

---

47 *Hoffmann–La Roche*, ¶91.

48 *See, e.g.*, Case T-65/98, *Van den Bergh Foods Ltd v. Commission*, 2003 E.C.R. II-4653, 157; Case T-65/89, *BPB Industries PLC & British Gypsum Ltd. v. Commission*, 1993 E.C.R. II-389, 94.

49 *Michelin I*, 1983 E.C.R. 3461, at 57; *see also* Joined Cases T-191/98, T-212/98 to T-214/98, *Atlantic Container Line AB et al. v. Commission*, 2003 E.C.R. II-3275, 1460 [hereinafter *TACA*].

50 *See generally* DAVID J. GERBER, LAW AND COMPETITION IN TWENTIETH CENTURY EUROPE. PROTECTING PROMETHEUS, Chapter VII (1998).

51 *See, e.g.*, Commission Decision in Case COMP/A/37.507/F3 – *AstraZeneca* (*AZ* Decision), not yet published in the OJ, ¶325.

52 See, e.g., *Kodak Co. v. Image Tech. Servs.*, 504 U.S. 451, 488 (1992) ('[w]here a defendant maintains substantial market power, his activities are examined through a special lens: Behavior that might otherwise not be of concern to the antitrust laws – or that might even be viewed as procompetitive – can take on exclusionary connotations when practiced by a monopolist'); *United States v. Dentsply Int'l, Inc.*, 399 F.3d 181, 187 (3d Cir. 2005) ('behavior that otherwise may comply with antitrust law may be impermissibly exclusionary when practiced by a monopolist'); *LePage's Inc. v. 3M*, 324 F.3d 141, 151–2 (3d Cir. 2003) ('a monopolist is not free to take certain actions that a company in a competitive (or even oligopolistic) market may take, because there is no market constraint on a monopolist's behavior').

to show that there was a risk of elimination of effective competition.[53] The Court further found that it was not necessary to prove that the refusal to deal 'directly' caused prejudice to consumers, if the refusal impaired 'an effective competitive structure' by allowing the dominant company to acquire 'a significant market share' in a secondary market.[54] The burden of proof was thus shifted on Microsoft which had to prove that its conduct was 'objectively justified'.[55]

EU Courts have acknowledged that a dominant company may engage in exclusionary practices if it offers an objective justification for its conduct,[56] but the status of this defense is unclear. Efficiency considerations are not an absolute defense to an exclusionary conduct. In principle, abusive practices are prohibited regardless of the advantages which may accrue to the perpetrators of such practices or third parties.[57] Still, economic efficiency plays a role in assessing specific practices. For example, refusals to deal may be abusive only if the requested product or service is indispensable, which involves proving that an equally efficient competitor, operating on a comparable scale could not duplicate the input.[58]

In the *Article 82 Guidance*, the Commission states that 'what really matters is to protect an effective competition process and not simply protecting competitors.' Thus, 'competitors who deliver less to consumers in terms of price, choice, quality and innovation' may be eliminated from the market.[59] The Commission would 'normally intervene' only when the abusive conduct 'is likely to lead to anticompetitive foreclosure'.[60] In the Article 82 Discussion Paper, it took the view that 'in general only conduct which would exclude a hypothetical "as efficient" competitor is abusive.'[61] But the Commission stops short of stating the efficiency considerations should be the only focus of

---

[53] *Microsoft* judgment, ¶¶560–64.

[54] *Microsoft* judgment, ¶¶660–65.

[55] *Microsoft* judgment, ¶688.

[56] *United Brands*, ¶¶182–4; Case 311/84, *Centre belge d'études de marché – Télémarketing (CBEM) v. SA Compagnie luxembourgeoise de télédiffusion (CLT) and Information publicité Benelux (IPB),* 1985 E.C.R. 3261, ¶27; Case C-163/99, *Portugal v. Commission,* 2001 E.C.R. 2613, ¶53.

[57] *TACA*, 2003 E.C.R. II-3275, ¶1112.

[58] *Bronner,* 1998 E.C.R. I-7791, ¶¶42–44.

[59] *See Article 82 Guidance,* ¶6. In the *Article 82 Discussion Paper*, the Commission stated this point even more forcefully: 'the purpose of Article 82 is not to protect competitors from dominant firms' genuine competition based on factors such as higher quality, novel products, opportune innovation or otherwise better performance, but to ensure that these competitors are also able to expand in or enter the market and compete therein on the merits, without facing competition conditions which are distorted or impaired by the dominant firm.' *Article 82 Discussion Paper*, ¶54.

[60] *Article 82 Guidance,* ¶29.

[61] *Article 82 Discussion Paper,* ¶63.

antitrust enforcement. It reasons that 'in certain circumstances a less efficient competitor may also exert a constraint', and this must be taken into account when considering whether a particular conduct leads to anticompetitive foreclosure.[62] Efficiency defense is not available when the abusive conduct eliminates 'effective competition, by removing all or most existing sources of actual or potential competition'.[63] The Commission takes the view that if 'there is no residual competition and no foreseeable threat of entry, the protection of rivalry and the competitive process outweighs possible efficiency gains'. Consequently, 'exclusionary conduct which maintains, creates or strengthens a market position approaching that of a monopoly can normally not be justified on the grounds that it also creates efficiency gains.'[64] *Article 82 Guidance* brings the European position closer to the American views on exclusionary conduct, albeit with the important reservation about the protection of competitive process. This difference appears to be particularly important when it comes to the assessment of refusals to deal and essential facilities.

2. ESSENTIAL FACILITIES AND REFUSALS TO DEAL

The instances where Article 82 or §2 of the Sherman Act were applied to condemn unilateral refusals to deal are among the most controversial antitrust cases. They provide an excellent example of how the differences between the general concepts of an abuse of dominance and monopolization affect the assessment of unilateral conduct in the United States and in the EU.

Both in Europe and in the United States, the basic premise is that a monopolist does not have an obligation to deal with its competitors.[65] Yet, in a

---

62 *Article 82 Guidance,* ¶23.

63 *Id.* ¶29.

64 *Id.*

65 *Verizon Communications, Inc. v. Law Offices of Curtis v. Trinko, LLP*, 540 U.S. 398, 408 (2004). The ECJ held that refusals to deal give rise to liability under Article 82 of the EC Treaty only in limited circumstances. *See Bronner*, 1998 E.C.R. I-7791, ¶¶38–47. Advocate General Jacobs in his Opinion in this case said that 'the right to choose one's trading partners and freely dispose of one's property are generally recognized principles in the laws of the Member States, in some cases with constitutional status.' *Id.* ¶56; *see also* Case C-418/01, *IMS Heath GmbH & Co. OHG v. NDC Health GmbH & Co. KG* (IMS), 2004 E.C.R. I-5039, ¶34 (holding that refusal to license cannot in itself constitute an abuse of a dominant position) and the Opinion of AG Jacobs in Case C-53/03, *Synetairismos Farmakopoion Aitolias & Akarnanias (Syfait) and Others v. GlaxoSmithKline AEVE,* 2005 E.C.R. I-4609, ¶53. The Commission in the *Article 82 Guidance* confirms that a dominant company 'should have the right to choose its trading partners and to dispose freely of its property'. *Article 82 Guidance*, ¶74.

number of cases refusals to deal were condemned as anticompetitive in the two jurisdictions. This has been particularly the case where a refusal to supply concerned an 'essential' or 'bottleneck' facility: a product that is so superior that it is essential for the rivals to compete and that cannot practically be duplicated.[66] The essential facilities doctrine can be traced back to the 1915 Supreme Court decision in *United States v. Terminal Railroad Association*.[67] The Terminal Railroad Association acquired all railroad facilities necessary to load or unload freight traffic or passengers anywhere within the area of St Louis. The government brought an antitrust suit seeking to dissolve the Association. The Court found that consolidation of terminal facilities created important benefits, so instead of splitting the Association, it requested that competing railroad lines be given access to the facilities under fair and impartial terms.

Another case often discussed in the context of essential facilities theory is *Otter Tail Power Co. v. United States*.[68] Otter Tail, an electric power company, refused to sell energy at wholesale prices and to wheel power from other suppliers of wholesale energy to municipalities. The Supreme Court found that the company violated §2 of the Sherman Act because it preserved its monopolistic position by preventing the municipalities it served from establishing their own power supply systems when its retail franchises expired. In *Aspen*,[69] another refusal to deal case, the Supreme Court ruled that the monopolist, owner of the three flagship ski mountains in Aspen, violated §2 of the Sherman Act by refusing to cooperate with its smaller rival in providing a four-mountain ticket. Under *Aspen*, a monopolist's refusal is illegal when it significantly excludes rivals, unless the defendant proves an efficiency justification.[70]

All these refusal to deal cases involved a bottleneck facility, but the Supreme Court invoked the essential facilities theory in none of them. Thus, the most comprehensive pronouncement on the doctrine comes from the Seventh Circuit's *MCI v. AT&T*[71] decision. The Seventh Circuit identified the following four elements as necessary for establishing antitrust liability under

---

[66] *See, e.g.*, Philip Areeda, *Essential Facilities: An Epithet in Need of Limiting Principles*, 58 ANTITRUST L. J. 841 (1989); Elhauge, *supra* note 3, at 261–2; Abbott B. Lipsky, Jr. & J. Gregory Sidak, *Essential Facilities*, 51 STAN. L. REV. 1187 (1999).

[67] 236 U.S. 194 (1915).

[68] 410 U.S. 366 (1973).

[69] *Aspen Skiing Co. v. Aspen Highlands Skiing Corp.*, 472 U.S. 585 (1985).

[70] *Id.* at 605, 608. *See also* Eleanor M. Fox, *A Tale of Two Jurisdictions and an Orphan Case: Antitrust, Intellectual Property, and Refusals to Deal*, 28 FORDHAM INT'L L. J. 952, 957–8 (2005).

[71] *MCI Communications Corp. v. American Tel. & Tel. Co.*, 708 F.2d 1081 (7th Cir. 1983); s*ee also Twin Labs., Inc. v. Weider Health & Fitness*, 900 F.2d 566 (2d Cir. 1990).

the essential facility theory: (1) control of the facility by a monopolist; (2) a competitor's inability practically or reasonably to duplicate the facility; (3) refusal to provide the facility to a competitor; and (4) the feasibility of providing the facility.[72] If these conditions are satisfied, access to the facility may be ordered on reasonable and non-discriminatory terms.

The essential facilities doctrine has been the subject of severe criticism in the United States.[73] The Supreme Court joined this criticism in *Trinko*, where it held that unilateral refusals to deal are rarely, if ever, anticompetitive. The case challenged anticompetitive practices of Verizon, an incumbent local telephone service exchange carrier for New York. Verizon controls a local loop, access to which is necessary to provide local telephone services. Under the Telecommunications Act of 1996, incumbent local exchange carriers are obliged to share their networks with competitors and to give them access to individual network elements to the same extent and quality as they make it available to themselves. In particular, Verizon was obliged to provide access to operations support systems (OSS) used to provide services to customers and to ensure quality of service. The rivals complained to telecom regulators that many of their orders were going unfulfilled, in violation of Verizon's obligation to provide access to OSS functions. This impeded the rivals' ability to compete in the market for local telephone service. The investigation that ensued resulted in a consent decree subjecting Verizon to remediation measures and additional reporting requirements.

Following the publication of the consent decree, Trinko, a customer of one of Verizon's rivals, filed a class action alleging, *inter alia*, that Verizon's behavior with respect to providing access to its network was a §2 violation. The question before the Supreme Court was whether monopolists controlling a necessary input were obliged under the Sherman Act to provide its rivals with access to that input. The Court began its reasoning by stressing that firms which 'acquire monopoly power by establishing an infrastructure that renders them uniquely suited to serve their customers' should not be compelled 'to share the source of their advantage' with their competitors.[74] It warned of the cost of false condemnations and difficulties in administering remedies in refusal-to-deal cases.[75] Although the Court did not exclude the possibility that

---

[72] *Id.* at 1132–3.

[73] *See, e.g.*, 3A AREEDA & HOVENKAMP, *supra* note 15, 770E, 771b–c, 773a; Areeda, *supra* note 66; Lipsky & Sidak, *supra* note 66.

[74] *Verizon Communications Inc. v. Law Offices of Curtis v. Trinko, LLP*, 540 U.S. 398, 408 (2004).

[75] *Id.* The Court said that the doctrine 'requires antitrust courts to act as central planners, identifying the proper price, quantity, and other terms of dealing' and that it may chill the incentives to invest in infrastructure development, or even facilitate collusion.

a refusal to deal may violate §2 of the Sherman Act, it stressed that it has never recognized the essential facilities doctrine.[76] Without acknowledging the doctrine's validity, the Court gave it a very narrow reading. It held that it could not be applied in a situation like the one before it, where an inferior access to the facility is given, or if compelled sharing can be ordered under state or federal laws.[77]

The Court also recognized the *Aspen* exception to the freedom to deal principle. This exception could only be applied to a unilateral termination of a voluntary and profitable course of dealings suggesting that the defendant was willing to 'forsake short-term profits to achieve an anticompetitive end'.[78] It was not available in this case because Verizon had never voluntarily shared its infrastructure with rivals, and probably would not have done so without statutory compulsion. Under *Trinko*, the *Aspen* exception is only applicable if a monopolist (1) terminates a voluntary and presumptively profitable agreement with a competitor and (2) sacrifices its short-term profits to create or strengthen its monopoly and reap greater profits in the long run. Trinko suggests that there are two narrowly tailored exceptions to a general principle that a refusal to deal does not violate antitrust law: (1) essential facility theory (assuming that it is valid) and (2) in case of termination, a modified version of the short-term profit sacrifice test.[79]

The *Trinko* decision clearly limits the scope for antitrust scrutiny over unilateral refusals to deal and questions the merits of forcing monopolists to share their assets with competitors. The consensus in the United States appears to be that antitrust intervention in unilateral, unconditional refusals to deal is undesirable. In the report on Section 2 enforcement issued by the DOJ in September 2008, the agency clearly states that 'antitrust liability for unilateral, unconditional refusals to deal with competitors should not play a meaningful part in section 2 enforcement.'[80] Relying on *Trinko*, the DOJ forcefully argues

---

[76] *Id.* at 411.

[77] *Id.* at 410–11. The Court ruled that Verizon's insufficient assistance in the provision of services to its competitors did not give rise to antitrust liability under the Court's refusal-to-deal precedents.

[78] *Id.* at 408–9.

[79] *See* Eleanor M. Fox, *A Tale of Two Jurisdictions and an Orphan Case: Antitrust, IP, and Refusals to Deal*, 28 FORDHAM INT'L L. J. 952, 958–9 (2005); *see also* John Thorne, *A Categorical Rule Limiting Section 2 of the Sherman Act: Verizon v. Trinko*, 72 U. CHI. L. REV. 289, 298–99 (arguing that refusals to deal may violate Section 2 of the Sherman Act only when there is an element of discrimination and a history of previous dealings. In such cases, it is easier for courts to define the terms of granting access).

[80] Department of Justice, *Competition and Monopoly: Single-Firm Conduct under Section 2 of the Sherman Act*, 127, available at: http://www.usdoj.gov/atr/public/reports/236681.pdf.

against imposing an obligation to deal, noting that that it can 'diminish or eliminate incentives for firms (both the monopolist and other firms) to innovate in the future' and that 'judges and juries are ill-equipped to act as industry regulators deciding the terms on which a firm should be required to sell its products or services.'[81] The report concludes that antitrust intervention in such cases creates 'significant risk of long-run harm to consumers' due to 'the effect of economywide disincentives and remedial difficulties'.[82] The DOJ also rejects the essential facilities doctrine as a way of determining whether an unconditional, unilateral refusal to deal leads to consumer harm, noting that it provides little guidance as to what constitutes a facility, what makes a facility essential, and what constitutes a denial of access. Further, in the DOJ view, the same concerns about innovation incentives and judicial capacity to devise a remedy that arise in refusal-to-deal cases apply in essential-facility cases.[83] The report stops short of pronouncing that all unconditional, unilateral refusals to deal are *per se* legal, but one can hardly imagine circumstances where a unilateral, unconditional refusal to deal could be a Section 2 violation.

Unlike the US antitrust enforcers, the European Commission and the EU Courts see a relatively wide scope for antitrust intervention in cases involving unilateral refusals to deal. Over the years, many cases have been brought where vertically integrated companies were forced to deal with their competitors. In *Commercial Solvents*, the first case where a refusal to deal was held to be an Article 82 violation, the Commission condemned a refusal to supply raw materials to a competitor in a downstream market without making an inquiry into the actual effects of the refusal in the downstream market. The ECJ confirmed the Commission's decision, reasoning that a company in a dominant position violated Article 82 by reserving raw materials for manufacturing its own derivatives, refusing to supply a competing manufacturer of these derivatives, and thus creating the risk of 'eliminating all competition on the part' of the company.[84]

In *United Brands*,[85] the Commission targeted exclusive dealing. United Brands terminated a customer after the latter had participated in an advertising campaign of one of United Brand's competitors. The Court reasoned that this was abusive because a dominant company 'which cashes on the reputation of a brand name known to and valued by consumers cannot stop supplying a long standing customer who abides by regular commercial practice, if the

---

81 *Id.* at 123.
82 *Id.* at 126.
83 *Id.* at 127–9.
84 Cases 6 and 7/73, *Commercial Solvents v. Commission,* 1974 E.C.R. 223, ¶25.
85 Case 27/76, *United Brands Company v. Commission*, 1978 E.C.R. 207.

orders placed by that customer are in no way out of the ordinary'.[86] This was so, even though the terminated distributor retained other sources of supply and there was no danger that competition from the downstream market would be eliminated. Again, there was no evidence that a refusal to supply would lead to higher prices in the downstream market.

In *Bronner*,[87] the ECJ's last pronouncement on refusals to deal, a more conservative approach to imposing an obligation to deal on dominant companies has been adopted. The Court followed the Advocate General Jacobs's advice and set higher standards under which a duty to deal may be imposed.[88] Under the *Bronner* test, a refusal to deal is abusive only if (1) it is likely to eliminate all competition in the downstream market on the part of the person requesting the service; (2) it is not objectively justified; and (3) the requested service is indispensable for the person requesting it to carry on that person's business, inasmuch as there is no actual or potential substitute for the requested facility.[89] The requirement of indispensability is not fulfilled if there are other means to obtain the input, even if such means are less advantageous. In assessing the ability to obtain actual or potential substitutes, courts should not consider the situation of the company requesting the input, but rather a company of a comparable size and efficiency to the dominant firm. Absent from the earlier case law, the requirement of indispensability limits application of Article 82 to cases involving essential inputs. Under *Bronner* a duty to deal may be imposed only with respect to an input that can be validly characterized as an essential facility, even if there was a history of previous dealings.[90] Still, even *Bronner*, the case where the ECJ adopted the narrowest reading of the essential facilities doctrine, goes further than the US Supreme Court in *Trinko*.

In the *Article 82 Guidance*, the Commission concedes that forced sharing may have adverse effects on investment incentives and encourage competitors to free ride on investments made by the dominant company, but unreservedly embraces the essential facilities theory and waters down the *Bronner* test.[91] A dominant company may be subjected to a duty to deal when it controls an essential input and the refusal to supply it is 'likely to lead to the elimination

---

[86] *Id.* ¶182.

[87] Case C-7/97, *Oscar Bronner GmbH & Co. KG v. Mediaprint Zeitungs- und Zeitschriftenverlag GmbH & Co. KG* and others (*Bronner*), 1998 ECR I-7791.

[88] *See* Eilmansberger, *supra* note 2, at 156–7; Geradin, *supra* note 2, at 1526; Petros Mavroidis, Damien Neven & Bronner Kebab, *Beyond Refusal To Deal And Duty To Cooperate*, *in* EUROPEAN COMPETITION LAW ANNUAL (Claus D. Ehlermann & Isabella Atanasiu (eds), 2003); James S. Venit, *Article 82: The Last Frontier – Fighting Fire with Fire*, 28 FORDHAM INT'L L.J. 1157, 1173–4 (2005).

[89] *Bronner*, ¶41.

[90] *See* VAN BAEL & BELLIS, *supra* note 25, at 946–7.

[91] *See Article 82 Guidance*, ¶¶74–5.

of effective competition'.[92] The requested input must be 'objectively necessary' for others to compete with the dominant company in the downstream market, which implies that there must be no real or potential substitutes available on the market and that competitors cannot 'effectively duplicate' the input.[93] The threshold needed to prove market foreclosure is low. The refusal to deal will be abusive if it gives rise to market foreclosure, but it is only required that the conduct in question is 'generally liable to eliminate, immediately or over time, effective competition in the downstream market'.[94] A large market share in the downstream market may be treated as an indication of market foreclosure.[95] Though the Commission states that it would normally pursue cases when 'the likely negative consequences of the refusal to supply in the relevant market outweigh over time the negative consequences of imposing an obligation to supply', the standard of evidence necessary to establish consumer harm is set at a low level.[96] For example, it may be sufficient to prove that the refusal results in a situation where 'follow-on innovation is likely to be stifled'.[97] Thus, speculative assertions on the effects that the refusal sharing may have on innovation could suffice. At the same time, a high burden of proof has been imposed on dominant companies claiming that a refusal to supply is necessary to allow them to realize an adequate return on the investments they made to develop their input business.[98] The Commission's approach is largely based on the recent CFI decision upholding its *Microsoft* decision. The *Microsoft* case, perhaps the most prominent example of how the essential facilities theory may be used to restrict the exercise of IP rights by dominant companies, is discussed in Chapter 2 below.

Aside from an outright refusal to supply, other practices such as delaying tactics in supplying or imposing 'unreasonable' trading conditions may be caught under Article 82.[99] Termination of an existing customer attracts an even greater degree of antitrust scrutiny. In such a case, the Commission may find that the input is indispensable because the terminated company made 'relationship-specific investments' to use the input. Further, history of previous dealings is treated as a proof that an obligation to deal would not adversely affect the dominant company's investment incentives.[100] Interestingly, unlike

---

[92] *Id.* ¶80.
[93] *Id.* ¶82.
[94] *Id.* ¶84.
[95] *Id.*
[96] *Id.* ¶85.
[97] *Id.* ¶86.
[98] *Id.* ¶¶88–9
[99] *Id.* ¶77. Margin squeeze is treated similarly to a refusal to deal. *Id.* ¶79.
[100] *Id.* ¶83; *see also* VAN BAEL & BELLIS, *supra* note 25, at 941–5; JONES & SUFRIN, *supra* note 25, 376–7.

the *Trinko* Court, which saw the fact that an obligation to supply was imposed by a federal regulation as a reason against an antitrust intervention, the Commission's position is that antitrust intervention in such circumstances is appropriate. The Commission reasons that the fact that an obligation to supply was imposed in a 'regulation compatible with Community law' indicates that the public authority imposing such an obligation already considered the fact that forced sharing may negatively impact the dominant company's investment incentives.[101] All this points to the conclusion that dominant companies controlling inputs that give them an advantage in the downstream market may be forced to share them with competitors in a large spectrum of circumstances. The European approach in this regard is strikingly different from the approach taken by the US antitrust authorities.

3. LIMITS OF ANTITRUST: MONOPOLIES CREATED BY THE STATE

The transatlantic differences in the assessment of dominance and dominant companies' market conduct only partly explain the differences in the assessment of unilateral conduct involving IP rights in the two jurisdictions. Equally important are the differences in the approach to market distortions created by state action and private parties' dealings with the state. IP rights are a creation of the state, which decides to confer exclusive entitlements to holders of certain intangible assets. IP rights are designed to address a perceived market failure; lack of effective IP protection would result in free riding and underinvestment in creative efforts. Still, the existence and the use of IP rights may sometimes adversely affect competition in the market and consumer welfare. General principles guiding the application of the antitrust rules to state-created market distortions are crucial in determining the role of antitrust rules in addressing distortions relating to the existence and use of IP rights. This section briefly examines how general principles differ between the EU and the US.

3.1 The US: Antitrust Immunity for State Action

One of the basic principles of the US antitrust law is that it applies to private, discretionary exercise of market power, not to government decision making. The state action doctrine excludes the application of the antitrust laws to actions taken by states in *bona fide* exercise of their regulatory powers. In

---

[101] *Article 82 Guidance*, ¶81.

Parker,[102] the case in which the doctrine was coined, the Supreme Court ruled that the federal antitrust laws did not preempt the Californian Agricultural Prorate Act, which authorized cartel-like arrangements amongst raisin producers. The Act allowed a state commission to introduce price restrictions on a petition by raisin producers. Raisin prices allegedly rose more than 20 percent following the introduction of the Act.[103] The Supreme Court acknowledged that the objective and mechanics of the Act's scheme were potentially anticompetitive, but reasoned that the Sherman Act was not intended as a mechanism for challenging state policies.[104] Such anticompetitive laws may be successfully challenged under the Commerce Clause or other legal theories, but not under the Sherman Act.[105]

States may not simply authorize private antitrust violations or declare them lawful.[106] The state policy to displace competition with regulation must be clearly articulated and the state must actively supervise the conduct of private parties, so that anticompetitive conduct of private parties is a product of deliberate state intervention.[107] For example, a price maintenance scheme authorized by the state enjoys immunity from antitrust laws only if the state decides on prices, reviews the reasonableness of price schedules, regulates the terms of contracts, monitors market conditions, and engages in a review of the program.[108] The scope of the state action defense depends on the nature of the antitrust defendant and the type of challenged conduct: actions taken by government bodies are virtually always exempt; more stringent standards apply to actions taken by private parties, who must demonstrate that their conduct was both clearly authorized by the state and subject to active state supervision.[109]

Just like state legislatures, Congress can authorize behavior that would otherwise violate the antitrust laws. There are a number of federal statutes that

---

102 *Parker v. Brown*, 317 U.S. 341, 351 (1943).

103 *Id.* at 349.

104 *Id.* at 351–2.

105 *See* Herbert Hovenkamp, *Federalism and Antitrust Reform*, 40 U.S. F. L. REV. 627, 644 (2006), giving examples of such cases: *Granholm v. Heald*, 544 U.S. 460 (2005) (ban on out-of-state wine shipment violated Commerce Clause), *South Central Bell Telephone Co. et al. v. Alabama*, 526 U.S. 160 (1999) (discriminatory franchise tax levied on out-of-state corporations violated Commerce Clause).

106 *Parker*, 317 U.S. at 351–2.

107 *FTC v. Ticor Title Ins. Co.*, 504 U.S. 621, 634–5 (1992).

108 *See California Retail Liquor Dealers Ass'n v. Midcal Aluminum*, 445 U.S. 97 (1980).

109 These conditions were established by the Supreme Court in *Midcal*, 445 U.S. at 105–6; see also *Hallie v. Eau Claire*, 471 U.S. 34 (1985) and *FTC v. Ticor Title Ins. Co.*, 504 U.S. 621 (1992).

expressly exempt certain industries or regulatory frameworks from antitrust laws or that permit regulated firms to apply for, and agencies to grant, approval of various anticompetitive activities.[110] If a valid statute compels a certain kind of conduct, that conduct enjoys antitrust immunity. If a federal statute does not expressly confer antitrust immunity, antitrust immunity can be inferred if it is necessary to avoid conflict between regulatory and antitrust requirements. This will be typically the case, if an antitrust suit could interfere with the operations of a regulatory agency or if the agency has reviewed the source of competitive concerns.[111] There are important limits to the state action doctrine.[112] If the statute conveys no express antitrust immunity and the anticompetitive conduct is merely permitted (but not required), antitrust laws define the limits of private conduct.[113] Further, the fact that an agency approved a particular conduct does not mean that such conduct is immunized from antitrust scrutiny, if that agency did not consider the impact on competition.[114]

Trinko,[115] already discussed above, reduces the scope for antitrust intervention in regulated industries where there is no express or implied antitrust immunity. One of the pivotal issues in this case was the relation between antitrust laws and the Telecommunications Act, which imposed a network sharing obligation on incumbent phone companies. The Act includes an

---

[110] For examples of such regulations *see* 1A AREEDA & HOVENKAMP, *supra* note 15, ¶243b.

[111] *See in general* 1A AREEDA & HOVENKAMP, *supra* note 15, ¶¶221–7. The determination of whether, and in what respects, a federal statute implicitly precludes application of the antitrust laws depends upon 'the relation between the antitrust laws and the regulatory program set forth in the particular statute, and the relation of the specific conduct at issue to both sets of laws'. *Credit Suisse Sec. (USA) LLC v. Billing* (*Billing*), 127 S. Ct. 2383 (2007).

[112] *Southern Motor Carriers Rate Conference, Inc. v. United States*, 471 U.S. 48, 48 (1985), *United States v. National Assn. of Securities Dealers, Inc.*, 422 U.S. 694, 719–20 (1975), *Group Life & Health Insurance Co. v. Royal Drug Co.*, 440 U.S. 205, 231 (1979), and *Abbott Laboratories v. Portland Retail Druggists Assn., Inc.*, 425 U.S. 1, 11 (1976).

[113] 1A AREEDA & HOVENKAMP, *supra* note 15, ¶243a2.

[114] *California v. Federal Power Commission*, 369 U.S. 482 (1962) (agency approval of merger did not bar antitrust challenge when agency had no power to adjudicate antitrust issues). In *Billing*, the Supreme Court decided that securities law implicitly precludes the antitrust laws' application, reasoning that since the SEC is itself required to take account of competitive considerations when it creates securities-related policy and embodies it in rules and regulations, it is 'somewhat less necessary to rely on antitrust actions to address anticompetitive behavior'. *Billing*, 127 S. Ct. at 2396.

[115] *Verizon Communications Inc. v. Law Offices of Curtis v. Trinko*, LLP, 540 U.S. 398 (2004).

antitrust savings clause, which precluded the Court from finding implied antitrust immunity. Still, the *Trinko* Court reasoned that the existence of a regulatory structure designed to deter and remedy anticompetitive harm called into question the benefit to competition provided by antitrust enforcement.[116] The Court added that if application of antitrust rules is prone to error, it is unlikely to improve a regulatory framework. In this case this was so, because the plaintiffs invoked the controversial doctrine of essential facilities.[117] If anticompetitive concerns can be addressed by industry-specific regulation, antitrust intervention is unnecessary, and possibly harmful.

The *Trinko* reasoning was echoed in the Court's 2007 *Billing* ruling.[118] In *Billing*, the investors who had purchased securities through initial public offerings during the dot.com boom alleged that investment banks conspired to require plaintiffs to commit to additional unfavorable terms as a condition of their purchases. Unlike in the *Trinko* case, in *Billing* the applicable federal regulations did not explicitly address their relation with the antitrust laws. The Court held that immunity could be implied when application of the antitrust laws might create a conflict with the competing federal regulatory regime. Relying on *Trinko,* the Court held that the need for antitrust enforcement was 'unusually small', given that there were other laws and regulatory structures specifically designed to deter and remedy the anticompetitive conduct in question.[119] The Court ruled the securities laws impliedly repealed federal and state antitrust laws with respect to the alleged conduct because: (1) the area of conduct was subject to securities regulation; (2) the SEC had clear and adequate authority to regulate the conduct; (3) the conduct was subject to active and ongoing agency regulation; and (4) a serious conflict existed between antitrust law and securities regulation.[120] This was so even though the plaintiffs showed that the conduct in question could never be authorized by the SEC. The Supreme Court reasoned that the application of securities regulations involves an unusually difficult legal line-drawing problem and that non-expert courts and juries deciding on antitrust claims are likely to have difficulties in applying securities law consistently.[121] Thus, applying the Sherman Act and the treble damages remedy to the allegedly illegal conduct may discourage underwriters from engaging in efficient conduct which the SEC would permit.[122]

---

116 *Trinko*, 540 U.S. at 411–12.
117 *Trinko*, 540 U.S. at 410–11.
118 *Credit Suisse Sec. (USA) LLC v. Billing*, 127 S. Ct. 2383 (2007).
119 *Id.* at 2396.
120 *Id.* at 2392.
121 *Id.* at 2394–6.
122 *Id.*

As will be discussed in more detail in Chapter 2, the reluctance to apply the antitrust rules if this may interfere with the operation of a regulatory regime has profoundly influenced the views on the application of the antitrust rules to IP rights. This is particularly apparent when it comes to the application of antitrust rules in a way that could interfere with the basic entitlements of an IP holder. These basic entitlements are the right to exclude others from using the protected technology or work and the right to unilaterally set the price or license fee.

3.2 The EU: Promoting a Competitive Agenda

Contrary to the position taken by the US antitrust enforcers, EU Courts found that 'federal' competition rules must be given priority over regulatory measures adopted by the Member States. The EC Treaty lists 'the institution of a system ensuring that competition is not distorted' as one of the objectives of the European Community.[123] Article 4 of the EC Treaty provides that the activities of the Member States and the Community shall be conducted 'in accordance with the principle of an open market economy with free competition'. Accordingly, the EU has given competition rules significance akin to constitutional principles.[124] The Treaty imposes a duty on Member States not to adopt or maintain in force any measure which could undermine the effectiveness of EC competition law by requiring or encouraging anticompetitive conduct, reinforcing the effects of such conduct, or delegating to private traders responsibility for taking key decisions affecting the economic sphere.[125]

Though laws of the Member States are subject to scrutiny under EU antitrust rules, private parties can still rely on a limited state action defense.

---

[123] Article 3(1)(g) of the EC Treaty.

[124] See Case C-126/97, *Eco Swiss China Time Ltd v. Benetton International NV*, 1999 E.C.R. I-3055, ¶36 and Case C-453/99, *Courage Ltd. v. Crehan*, 2001 E.C.R. I-6297, ¶20.

[125] *See, e.g.*, Joined Cases 209 to 213/84, *Criminal proceedings against Lucas Asjes and others*, 1986 E.C.R. 1425, ¶72, Case 136/86, *BNIC v. Aubert*, 1987 E.C.R. 4789, ¶24, Case 267/86, *Pascal Van Eycke v. ASPA NV*, 1988 E.C.R. 4769, ¶16, Case C-185/91, *Bundesanstalt für den Güterfernverkehr v. Gebrüder Reiff GmbH & Co. KG.*, 1993 E.C.R. I-5801, ¶14, and Case C-198/01, *CIF Consorzio Industrie Fiammiferi v. Autorità Garante della Concorrenza e del Mercato* (CIF), 2003 E.C.R. I-8055, ¶46. *See also* Richard Wainwright & André Bouguet, *State Intervention and Action in EC Competition Law*, 2003 FORDHAM CORP. L. INST. 539, 541–51 (BARRY HAWK, ED. 2004). With respect to the conditions under which Member States may delegate their regulatory powers to private decision-making bodies, *see* Judit Szoboszlai, *Delegation of State Regulatory Powers to Private Parties – Towards an Active Supervision Test*, 29 WORLD COMPETITION 73 (2006).

Articles 81 and 82 of the EC Treaty apply only to anticompetitive conduct in which companies engage on their own initiative.[126] Private parties are not liable for conduct that is required by existing national legislation or for their actions taken in the context of a legal framework which excludes competition.[127] Still, if government intervention merely encourages or facilitates anticompetitive conduct, private parties may be liable for violation of EU competition law.[128] The EU Courts have always been skeptical about state action defense and private parties have prevailed on it only in extraordinary circumstances.[129] It is not sufficient, as it would be in the US, that the state (1) has articulated a clear and affirmative policy to allow the allegedly anticompetitive conduct, and (2) provides active supervision of allegedly anticompetitive conduct undertaken by private actors. If the regulation in question leaves any scope for competition, the conduct of private parties is not immune from scrutiny under the EU competition rules.

In the *CIF* case,[130] the ECJ indicated that private parties are liable if the regulatory framework leaves some scope, however little, for competitive behavior. The case concerned an Italian regulation granting a fiscal and commercial monopoly for the production and sale of matches in Italy to the CIF, a consortium of match producers. Until 1993 when these rules were liberalized, the state fixed retail prices for matches and the CIF members agreed on the allocation of production quotas.[131] Anticompetitive practices of the CIF

---

[126] *See, e.g.*, Case C-18/88, *RTT v. GB-Inno-BM*, 1991 E.C.R. I-5941, ¶20 and Joined Cases C-359/95 P and C-379/95 P, *Commission and France v. Ladbroke Racing Ltd.*, 1997 E.C.R. I-6265 (*Ladbroke*), ¶33.

[127] *See, e.g.*, *Ladbroke*, ¶33; Joined Cases 209/78 to 215/78 & 218/78, *Van Landewyck v. Commission*, 1980 E.C.R. 3125 (*Van Landewyck*), ¶¶130–34, Case 41/83, *Italy v. Commission*, 1985 E.C.R. 873, ¶19, and Joined Cases 240/82 etc., *Stichting Sigarettenindustrie and Others v. Commission,* 1985 E.C.R. 3831, ¶¶27–9.

[128] *See, e.g.*, *Van Landewyck*, ¶126 and Case C-198/01, *CIF Consorzio Industrie Fiammiferi v. Autorità Garante della Concorrenza e del Mercato (CIF)*, 2003 E.C.R. I-8055, ¶56. Though state encouragement is not an exculpatory excuse, it might constitute an extenuating circumstance for the purpose of calculating the fine; *see* Fernando Castillo de la Torre, *State Action Defense in EC Competition Law*, 28 WORLD COMPETITION 407, 425 (2005).

[129] According to The Commission promoted an even narrower reading of the state action defense. In its opinion the defense should only be available if state measures do not require that private parties engage in any conduct contrary to EU competition law, but rather create a legal framework that restricts competition. For example, state action defense would be available to private parties only if the state itself set prices, but not when it requires private parties to agree on prices. The ECJ rejected that interpretation, *Ladbroke*, ¶33; see Castillo de la Torre, *supra* note 128, at 412–15.

[130] Case C-198/01, *CIF Consorzio Industrie Fiammiferi v. Autorità Garante della Concorrenza e del Mercato* (*CIF*), 2003 E.C.R. I-8055.

[131] In 1993 a regulation was passed which abolished the CIF's fiscal monopoly,

members were challenged by the Italian antitrust authority and, in the course of these proceedings, an Italian court referred to the ECJ questions concerning the effect of national anticompetitive legislation on liability of private parties under EU competition rules. The ECJ held that national authorities must disregard national legislation which legitimates or reinforces private anticompetitive conduct that violates Article 81 or 82 of the EC Treaty.[132] Determination by a national authority that national law is contrary to EU law exposes the defendant companies to antitrust liability from the date on which the determination becomes definitive. Before that date, companies may only be penalized for their autonomous conduct not demanded by national legislation.[133] In this case, fixing of the retail price for matches by the state did not, on its own, preclude other forms of competition. Insofar as competition was possible and the match companies did not compete, they could be liable for violation of EC and national competition rules.[134]

The competition provisions of the EC Treaty may also be used to scrutinize how private parties use their rights based on EC secondary regulations. This was so in the *AstraZeneca* (AZ) case, the first EU case relating to patent 'evergreening' and one of the few cases involving misuse of patent procedures and acquisition of an IP right. It rests on allegations that AZ illegally used patent and regulatory procedures to extend protection for omeprazole, its anti-ulcer drug marketed under the name Losec.[135] The Commission alleged, among other things, that AZ infringed competition laws through the withdrawal of marketing authorizations for the capsule form of Losec in various Member States. AZ replaced the original capsule formulation of Losec with a new, improved tablet formulation and asked the regulatory authorities in some Member States to withdraw the marketing authorizations for the original capsule form. It was not clear how AZ's actions would affect related market-

---

allowed new match producers to enter the market, and made membership in the CIF voluntary.

[132] *CIF*, ¶¶47–8.

[133] *CIF*, ¶¶53–5; for comment on CIF *see*, *e.g.*, Cesare Rizza, *The Duty of National Competition Authorities to Disapply Anti-Competitive Domestic Legislation and the Resulting Limitations on the Availability of the State Action Defence (Case C-198/01 CIF)*, 24 Eur. Competition L. Rev. 126 (2004), Wainwright & Bouguet, *supra* note 125, at 553–7, John Temple Lang, *National Measures Restricting Competition and National Authorities under Article 10 EC*, 29 Eur. L. Rev. 397 (2004), and Castillo de la Torre, *supra* note 128.

[134] *CIF*, ¶¶67–9. See also Case T-513/93, *Consiglio Nazionale Spedizionieri Doganali v. Commisson*, 2000 E.C.R. II-1807, ¶60.

[135] Losec is a pioneer drug for the treatment of gastrointestinal acid-related diseases, more effective than previously developed methods of treatment. It was the best-selling prescription medicine ever, with sales reaching $6.3 billion in 2000. *See AZ* Decision, ¶¶31–8.

ing authorizations granted to generic manufacturers and parallel importers, though AZ allegedly had the intention of making the marketing of imported and generic Losec more difficult. AZ's actions had such an effect in some EU Member States, where pharmaceutical authorities decided to revoke the related marketing authorizations granted to importers and generic manufacturers of Losec in the capsule form.

The Commission held that AZ's withdrawal of marketing authorizations violated Article 82, reasoning that the applicable pharmaceutical laws did not confer 'any right to prevent other parties from entering the market',[136] and that dominant companies are under the obligation to 'use their specific entitlements (such as market authorizations) in a reasonable way'.[137] The Commission also specifically rejected the argument that the incorrect balancing of interests in the EU pharmaceutical legislation should be addressed by a legislative action rather than by applying competition law.[138] The fact that 'other laws and remedies prohibit misleading representations or provide for remedies against them' did not preclude application of the EU competition rules if such conduct has anticompetitive effects.[139] As will be discussed in more detail in Chapter 2 below, this proactive application of the antitrust rules to distortions resulting from regulatory measures has had a profound influence on the intersection between IP and competition laws.

4. APPLICATION OF THE ANTITRUST RULES TO PRIVATE PARTIES' INTERACTIONS WITH PUBLIC AUTHORITIES

The application of antitrust rules to market distortions resulting from state action is decisive for the scope of antitrust interference with IP rights. In the same vein, the principles which antitrust enforcers apply to private parties' interactions with public authorities are crucial for the application of antitrust rules to the enforcement and acquisition of IP rights by private parties. These principles are much more developed in the US antitrust law than they are in the EU, where the issue has been scantily addressed. The few EU cases that address these issues suggest that there are fundamental differences between the two jurisdictions.

136 *AZ* Decision, ¶¶840–43.
137 *AZ* Decision, ¶837 and ¶¶325–6.
138 *AZ* Decision, ¶836.
139 *AZ* Decision, ¶¶744 and 748.

In the US, the *Noerr-Pennington* doctrine shields from antitrust liability the act of petitioning governmental agencies, even if such petitioning has anti-competitive objects or effects.[140] The doctrine has a long tradition and complements the principle that antitrust laws should not interfere with government decision-making. Some commentators link it to the First Amendment's guarantee of 'the right . . . to petition the government for redress of grievances' as a basis for the doctrine.[141] Interestingly, in the few cases in which the problem has been addressed, the EU antitrust enforcers relied on the relevant U.S. authorities. However, the US standards transplanted into the EU case law have acquired a new meaning and immunity for government petitioning is much narrower in the EU than it is in the US.

4.1 The US: *Noerr-Pennington* and its Progeny

In principle, private parties' actions before legislatures, administrative agencies, and courts are immune from antitrust scrutiny.[142] Even false statements presented to support such petitions are protected,[143] unless the 'petitioning' is a 'sham'; that is, it does not truly seek legislation and is intended only to burden a rival with the governmental decision-making process itself.[144] In *Noerr*,[145] the case which established antitrust immunity for government petitioning, a number of trucking companies sued the railroads which had organized a publicity campaign aimed at enacting or retaining legislation hostile to the trucking industry, as well as impairing relations between truckers and their

---

[140] *See, e.g., United Mine Workers v. Pennington*, 381 U.S. 657, 670 (1965), *Eastern R.R. Conference v. Noerr Motor Freight*, 365 U.S. 127, 135–8 (1961), *Sandy River Nursing Care v. Aetna Cas.*, 985 F.2d 1138, 1141 (1st Cir. 1993).

[141] Courts and commentators differ as to whether the Noerr doctrine derives from the First Amendment or is of statutory nature. *See, e.g., Cheminor Drugs, Ltd. v. Ethyl Corp.*, 168 F.3d 119 (3d Cir. 1999) (Noerr is based on the First Amendment), *Kottle v. Northwest Kidney Ctrs.*, 146 F.3d 1056, 1059 (9th Cir. 1998) (same) and Stephen Calkins, *Developments in Antitrust and the First Amendment: The Disintegration of Noerr*, 57 ANTITRUST L. J. 327, 328 (1988) and 1 HOVENKAMP ET AL., *supra* note 32, ¶11.3b5 (A), with *Cardtoons, L.C. v. Major League Baseball Players Assoc.*, 208 F.3d 885, 890 (10th Cir. 2000) (Noerr immunity is based upon both the Sherman Act and the right to petition), and *Coastal States Marketing, Inc. v. Hunt*, 694 F.2d 1358, 1364–5 (5th Cir. 1983) (Noerr derives from the construction of the Sherman Act) and Einer Elhauge, *Making Sense of Antitrust Petitioning Immunity*, 80 CAL. L. REV. 1177, 1193–5 (1992) (same).

[142] *Otter Tail Power Co. v. United States*, 410 U.S. 366, 379–80 (1973); *California Transp. Co. v. Trucking Unlimited*, 404 U.S. 508, 510 (1972).

[143] *Pennington*, 381 U.S. at 670.

[144] *City of Columbia v. Omni Outdoor Adver., Inc.*, 499 U.S. 365, 380 (1991).

[145] *Eastern R.R. Conference v. Noerr Motor Freight, Inc.*, 365 U.S. 127 (1961).

customers. The campaign, described as malicious and fraudulent,[146] involved public criticism of trucking companies by ostensibly independent organizations, which were in fact engaged and financed by the railroads to conceal their economic bias.[147] It persuaded the governor of Pennsylvania to veto legislation that would have permitted truckers to carry heavier loads on Pennsylvanian highways and thus to compete with railroads more effectively. Still, the Supreme Court held that 'attempts to influence the passage or enforcement of laws' could not give rise to antitrust liability.[148] No violation of the Sherman Act could be found in a situation 'where a restraint upon trade or monopolization is the result of valid government action, as opposed to private action'.[149] An anticompetitive motive does not itself deprive government petitioning of its lawful status.[150]

In *Pennington*,[151] which substantially reinforced *Noerr*, the Supreme Court held that lobbying the executive branch of government is covered by Noerr exception, even if it is a part of a larger conspiracy to violate antitrust law.[152] In *California Motor*,[153] the Court added that Noerr applied to efforts to influence a judicial action.[154] In *Allied Tube*, the Court ruled that even efforts to affect a private association vote could constitute government petitioning where the association enacted enforceable rules.[155]

There are important exceptions to the *Noerr-Pennington* immunity. First, it does not apply to anticompetitive conduct, even if the objective of the conduct is the enactment of favorable legislation, if the alleged restraint of trade is not the intended consequence of public action, but the means of obtaining such action.[156] Thus, conduct in restraint of trade is not saved by being seen as a method of communicating with government; the restraint must flow from the government action. Second, the doctrine does not apply if the petitioning is a mere 'sham', which takes the form 'of illegal and reprehensible practice which may corrupt the administrative or judicial process'.[157] For example, a pattern

146 *Noerr*, 365 U.S. at 133, referring to 155 F.Supp. at 814.

147 *Noerr*, 365 U.S. at 129–30.

148 *Noerr*, 365 U.S. at 135–6.

149 *Noerr*, 365 U.S. at 135–6.

150 *Noerr*, 365 U.S. at 139.

151 *United Mine Workers v. Pennington*, 381 U.S. 657 (1965).

152 *Pennington*, 381 U.S. at 670.

153 *California Motor Transport Co. v. Trucking Unlimited*, 404 U.S. 508 (1972).

154 *Id. at* 510; earlier, in *Walker Process Equipment v. Food Machinery & Chemical Corp.*, 382 U.S. 172, 175–7 (1965), the Supreme Court, without referring to Noerr, held that the wrongful filing of a civil suit could constitute an antitrust violation.

155 *Allied Tube & Conduit Corp. v. Indian Head*, 486 U.S. 492, 499 (1988).

156 *FTC v. Superior Court Trial Lawyers Ass'n*, 493 US 411, 424–5 (1990).

157 *California Motor Transp.*, 404 U.S. at 513.

of 'baseless, repetitive claims' made without regard to their merits constituted a sham.[158]

The sham exception is extremely narrow. In *Allied Tube*, the Supreme Court held that genuine efforts to influence government are not sham, no matter how improper the methods used.[159] In *Omni Outdoor Advertising*,[160] the Court confirmed that even unlawful conduct, such as bribery, is not a valid reason to deny antitrust immunity to a genuine effort to influence a public authority.[161] In *Professional Real Estate Investors* (*PREI*),[162] the Court ruled that an objectively reasonable legal action could not be a sham solely because a subjective expectation of success did not motivate the litigant. The good or bad faith of the plaintiff becomes relevant only if the lawsuit is objectively baseless.[163] The Court crafted the 'sham' exception in the litigation context very narrowly. First, the suit must be 'objectively baseless' in the sense that no reasonable litigant could realistically expect success on the merits. If an objective litigant could conclude that the suit is reasonably calculated to elicit a favorable outcome, the suit is immunized and the antitrust claim will fail. This prong of the *PREI* test is designed to eliminate the risk that application of antitrust law would chill legitimate litigation. Second, the suit must be brought to disrupt a rival's business through the use of the governmental process – as opposed to the outcome of that process – as an anticompetitive weapon.

Noerr-Pennington immunity, as it now stands, permits interest groups to request virtually any kind of anticompetitive regulation they wish. Their efforts would rarely, if ever, qualify as a sham because it is unlikely that one hopes to injure a competitor merely through the process of petitioning for favorable legislation rather than through the enactment or enforcement of the legislation itself. Intentional misrepresentations, bribery, and other unlawful conduct do not preclude antitrust immunity. Private parties are also free to file lawsuits in courts or complaints before regulatory agencies, even though their motives are anticompetitive and their actions may have little merit. To be sure, such actions may have adverse legal consequences and trigger liability under various statutes, but not under antitrust rules.[164]

---

158 *Id. at* 512–13. *See also Otter Tail Power Co. v. United States*, 410 U.S. 366, 380 (1973).

159 *Allied Tube & Conduit Corp. v. Indian Head*, 486 U.S. 492, 507 n. 10 (1988).

160 *City of Columbia v. Omni Outdoor Advertising*, 499 U.S. 365 (1991).

161 *Omni Outdoor Advertising*, 499 U.S. at 378–9.

162 *Professional Real Estate Investors v. Columbia Pictures Indus.* (*PREI*), 508 U.S. 49 (1993).

163 *PREI*, 508 U.S. at 60.

164 Noerr-Pennington has been criticized as too broad. *See, e.g.*, John T. Delacourt, *The FTC's Noerr-Pennington Task Force: Restoring Rationality to Petitioning Immunity*, 17 ANTITRUST 36 (2003); Timothy J. Murris, *Looking Forward:*

4.2 The EU: Considering *Noerr-Pennington* and PREI?

The question of whether private parties' efforts to persuade governmental entities to limit competition are exempt from the competition rules has not been comprehensively addressed in EU antitrust cases or literature.[165] In principle, inducement of government action is not in itself an infringement.[166] Private parties are entitled to submit jointly their requests to public authorities,[167] just as dominant companies may invoke their rights.[168] However, such acts do not benefit from immunity in the *Noerr-Pennington* sense and may potentially constitute an abusive act, if, for example, the companies seek the assistance of the government in enforcing anticompetitive agreements or strengthening their dominant position.

In *French-West African shipowners' committees*, after acknowledging that 'the fact that an association of undertakings approaches a public authority in the common interests of its members is not in itself an infringement of the competition rules', the Commission concluded that petitioning public authorities with 'the *sole purpose* of securing the adoption of measures aimed at strengthening their dominant position' could not be exempted from the application of EU competition rules 'since it is to say the least paradoxical that enterprises should ask the public authorities to cover their restrictive practices

---

The Federal Trade Commission and the Future Development of U.S. Competition Policy, 2003 COLUM. BUS. L. REV. 359, 368–75 (2003); Timothy J. Murris, *Clarifying the State Action and Noerr Exemptions*, 27 HARV. J. L. & PUB. POL'Y 443, 454–7 (2004); 1 AREEDA & HOVENKAMP, *supra* note 15, ¶205a.; *but see* Lisa Wood, *In Praise of the Noerr-Pennington Doctrine*, 18 ANTITRUST 72 (2003).

[165] Among the few authors who have addressed this issue is Adrian J. Vossestein, *Corporate Efforts to Influence Public Authorities, and the EC Rules on Competition*, 37 COMMON MARKET L. REV. 1383 (2000); *see also* JONES & SUFRIN, *supra* note 25, at 522–4, Wainwright & Bouguet, *supra* note 125, at 560–62, and William Cooney, *Competition and the Noerr-Pennington Doctrine: When Should Political Activity Be Barred Under European Community Competition Law?*, 34 GEO. WASH. INT'L L. REV. 871, 884–6 (2003).

[166] *See, e.g.*, Opinion of Advocate General Jacobs in Case C-67/96, *Albany International BV v. Stichting Bedrijfspensioenfonds Textielindustrie*, 1999 E.C.R. I-5751, ¶289 citing Commission Decision in Cases IV/33.126 and 33.322 – *Cement*, OJ (L 343) 1, point 53, ¶8; *see also* Commission Decision in Case IV/32.450: *French-West African shipowners' committees*, OJ (L 134) 1, ¶68, and Case T-111/96 *ITT Promedia NV v. Commission*, 1998 E.C.R. II-2937, ¶60 (*ITT Promedia*).

[167] *See, e.g.*, Commission Decision in Cases IV/33.126 and 33.322 – *Cement*, OJ (L 343) 1, 53, ¶8, and Commission Decision in Case IV/32.450: *French-West African shipowners' committees,* OJ (L 134) 1, ¶68.

[168] Commission Decision in *Industrie des Poudres Sphériques,* XXVIth Report on Competition Policy 1996, at 157–8 (The Commission found that invoking a legal instrument of EU law by a dominant company, in this case antidumping procedures, was not in itself abusive).

only to maintain subsequently that the practices are not caught by Article [81] as they were imposed by the same public authorities'.[169]

The case in which the issue of antitrust immunity for government petitioning has been discussed most comprehensively is *Compagnie Maritime Belge*.[170] The Commission found that Compagnie Maritime Belge and other members of the Cewal liner shipping conference had abused their joint dominant position *inter alia* by implementing a cooperation agreement with Ogefrem, the Zairian shipping authority. Cewal members operated liner services between Zaire (now the Democratic Republic of Congo), Angola, and various European ports in the North Sea. The agreement between Ogefrem and Cewal provided that all goods shipped between Cewal ports are to be carried by Cewal members. The agreement specified that a derogation from the exclusivity clause is possible with Cewal's consent, but Cewal did not grant such consent and enforced the clause when Ogefrem permitted Grimaldi & Cobelfret, a non-Cewal company, to compete with Cewal. The Commission found that Cewal's insistence on strict enforcement of the arrangement fell within the prohibition of Article 82 of the EC Treaty. In defense of the Commission's charges, Cewal, referring to the *Noerr-Pennington* doctrine, argued that 'the mere inducement of government action cannot constitute an abuse within the meaning of Article 82' and that 'transmitting information to government authorities with a view to influencing their conduct is not affected by anti-trust laws.'[171]

The CFI held that the *Noerr-Pennington* defense was inapplicable because the Commission did not challenge political activity as such.[172] The ECJ affirmed the CFI's judgment, reasoning that 'there is a difference between a request to a public authority to comply with a specific contractual obligation and the mere incitement or inducement of the authority to take action'.[173] It defined government petitioning narrowly, as an activity

169 Commission Decision in Case IV/32.450: *French-West African shipowners' committees*, OJ (L 134) 1, ¶68, emphasis added.

170 Commission Decision 93/82/EEC of 23 December 1992 (*Cewal, Cowac and Ukwal*), 1993 O.J. (L 34) 20, upheld by the CFI in Case T-24/93 etc., *Compagnie Maritime Belge Transports SA and others v. Commission,* 1996 E.C.R. II-1201; the ECJ in Joined Cases C-395/96 P and C-396/96 P, *Compagnie Maritime Belge Transports SA and others v. Commission*, 2000 E.C.R. I-1365, ¶¶84–6, upheld the substance of the Commission's original decision, but annulled most of the fines on a procedural technicality.

171 Joined Cases T-24/93, *Compagnie Maritime Belge Transports SA and others v. Commission*, 1996 E.C.R. II-1201, ¶88.

172 *Id*, ¶110.

173 Joined Cases C-395/96 P and C-396/96 P, *Compagnie Maritime Belge Transports SA and others v. Commission*, 2000 E.C.R. I-1365, ¶82. For a comment on the case *see, e.g.*, Pat Treacy & Trudy Feaster, *Compagnie Maritime Belge Transports*

designed to influence a public authority in the exercise of its discretion. A request that a governmental entity comply with a contract is not 'petitioning' because its purpose is to 'enforce legal rights which the authority concerned is, by definition, bound to observe'.[174] This being so, it was 'not necessary to consider whether, and in what circumstances, mere incitement of a government to take action may constitute abuse within the meaning of Article [82] of the Treaty'.[175]

In the *AZ* case discussed above, the Commission, relying on *Compagnie Maritime Belge*, asserted that the use of public procedures and regulations, including administrative and judicial process, may constitute an abuse of dominance.[176] This is particularly so when the dominant company acts 'with the clear purpose of excluding competitors' and 'the authorities or bodies . . . have no or little discretion' in applying such public procedures and regulations.[177] In the *AZ* case, 'the national authorities concerned considered, as expected by AZ, that they did not have discretion to maintain the marketing authorisation when its withdrawal was requested' and, consequently, the anticompetitive effect was not the result of 'an independent review of the merits of the petition as regards its anticompetitive effect, but rather the automatic (or almost automatic) effect of a private request'.[178] AZ was not directly petitioning the public authority concerned to take a certain action that would harm its rivals. Rather, it took a seemingly neutral step (deregistration of Losec capsules), which triggered the action of a public authority which had in turn adverse effects on competition (revocation of parallel imports licenses and refusal to grant permissions to generic producers). The Commission's definition of discretionary powers is extremely narrow. In this case, the exclusionary effect of AZ's conduct depended fully on the interpretation of the applicable regulatory framework adopted by national medicinal agencies and courts, some of which, including the ECJ, adopted an interpretation that created no anticompetitive effects.[179]

The US case law also played a role when the EU enforcers decided on the circumstances where the conduct of litigation could constitute an antitrust

---

SA v. Commission of the European Communities (T24/93) [1997] 4 C.M.L.R. 273 (CFI), 18 EUR. COMPETITION L. REV. 467 (1997) and Steven Preece, *Compagnie Maritime Belge: Missing the Boat*, 21 EUR. COMPETITION L. REV. 288 (2000).

[174] *Id.*

[175] *Id*, ¶83.

[176] *AZ* Decision, ¶743.

[177] *AZ* Decision, ¶818 (emphasis added).

[178] *AZ* Decision, ¶819 (emphasis added).

[179] *AZ* Decision, ¶¶849–9 discussing the anticompetitive effects of the deregistration abuse.

offense. In *ITT Promedia/Belgacom*,[180] the Commission stated that the bringing of a lawsuit by a dominant company could violate Article 82 of the EC Treaty, if the dominant company brings an action '(i) which cannot reasonably be considered as an attempt to establish its rights and can therefore only serve to harass the opposite party, and (ii) which is conceived in the framework of a plan whose goal is to eliminate competition'.[181] Bringing a lawsuit can be an antitrust violation only if these two cumulative criteria are fulfilled. Litigation that may be reasonably regarded as an attempt to assert rights vis-à-vis competitors is not abusive, irrespective of the fact that it may be part of a plan to eliminate competition.[182] The action must be objectively and manifestly unfounded. If it is intended to assert what the plaintiff could, at the moment of bringing it, reasonably consider its rights, it cannot be an antitrust violation.[183] The second criterion requires the showing of an anticompetitive object of the dominant company bringing a legal action.[184] The Commission's two-prong test bears striking resemblance to the US Supreme Court's *PREI* test identifying sham litigation. The lawsuit can amount to an antitrust violation only if it is both objectively baseless and improperly motivated. The interpretation and application of these criteria in *ITT Promedia* confirms that *PREI* must have been the source of inspiration for the EU antitrust enforcers. Still, the status of the *PREI* test in EU competition law is uncertain, as the validity of the test adopted by the Commission has not been confirmed by the EU courts.[185]

The cases discussed above clearly show that the use of public procedures and regulations by private parties is subjected to greater antitrust scrutiny in the EU than it is in the United States. The concept of 'government petitioning' has been construed very narrowly in the EU; the *Compagnie Maritime Belge* ruling suggests that it would apply strictly only to activities akin to lobbying. The key assumption is that dominant companies are under an obligation not to use their legal entitlements in a manner that could disadvantage the competitive process. Unfortunately, the case law discussed above provides little guid-

---

180 The Commission Decision in Case IV/35.268 *Promedia/Belgacom* of 21 May 1996 has not been published. The references to the Commission Decision are derived from the CFI judgment in Case 111/96, *ITT Promedia NV v. Commission* (*ITT Promedia*), 1998 E.C.R. II-2937, reviewing the Commission's Decision in *Promedia/Belgacom*.

181 *ITT Promedia*, ¶30 (citing point 11 of the Commission Decision in *Promedia/Belgacom*).

182 *Id*, ¶72.

183 *Id*, ¶73. It is not required to show that the cause of action actually existed or that the action was well-founded

184 *Id*, ¶55–6.

185 *Id*, ¶¶57–8. On appeal, the CFI affirmed the Commission's decision without ruling on the correctness of the test adopted by the Commission.

ance as to when the use of a legal entitlement by a dominant company could give rise to liability under Article 82. *Compagnie Maritime Belge* and the AZ Decision suggest that a dominant company may violate Article 82 merely by enforcing its exclusive rights with a view to harming its rivals. As will be discussed in more detail in Chapter 3 below, this has had tremendous consequences on the scope of scrutiny over the acquisition and enforcement of IP rights by dominant companies.

2. Striking the balance between antitrust and IP*

IP law and antitrust law are both designed to correct market failures. Antitrust policy targets anticompetitive conduct, which, in essence, is the type of conduct that limits the output or increases prices. The purpose of IP laws is to increase the incentives for private investment in the development of new products or more efficient production processes. To this end, IP laws create exclusive rights that limit the access of third parties to information, technologies, and other intangible goods. The product of R&D, information, is a public good, and as such can easily be appropriated by rivals, who did not bear the R&D cost. Assigning exclusive rights in the outcomes of creative and intellectual efforts allows the inventor to make a return on his investment by preventing free riding by his competitors.[1]

---

* Parts of this Chapter have previously been published as: Katarzyna Czapracka (2006), *Where Antitrust Ends and IP Begins*, 9 YALE J.L. & TECH. 44 (2007).

[1] *See, e.g.*, Kenneth Arrow, *Economic Welfare and the Allocation of Resources for Inventions*, *in* R.R. NELSON (ED.), THE RATE AND DIRECTION OF INVENTIVE ACTIVITY: ECONOMIC AND SOCIAL FACTORS 619 (1962); WILLIAM NORDHAUS, INVENTION, GROWTH, AND WELFARE: A THEORETICAL TREATMENT OF TECHNOLOGICAL CHANGE (1969); 1 HERBERT HOVENKAMP ET AL., IP AND ANTITRUST: AN ANALYSIS OF ANTITRUST PRINCIPLES APPLIED TO INTELLECTUAL PROPERTY LAW ¶1.1 (2002); William M. Landes & Richard A. Posner, *An Economic Analysis of Copyright Law*, 18 J. LEGAL STUD. 325 (1989); Richard A. Posner, *IP: The Law and Economics Approach*, 19 J. ECON. PERSP. 57 (2005). Other authors rely on the Lockean labor-deserves argument: people are entitled to hold as property whatever they produce by their own initiative, intelligence, and industry, for example, Justin Hughes, *The Philosophy of IP*, 77 GEO. L. J. 287, 299–330 (1988), or the theories based on privacy and sovereignty of individuals, for example, MARGARET JANE RADIN, REINTERPRETING PROPERTY (1993); JEREMY WALDRON, THE RIGHT TO PRIVATE PROPERTY (1988). For an overview see, for example, William Fisher, *Theories of IP*, *in* STEPHEN R. MUNZER, NEW ESSAYS IN THE LEGAL AND POLITICAL THEORY OF PROPERTY (2001); ROBERT L. OSTERGARD, DEVELOPMENT DILEMMA: THE POLITICAL ECONOMY OF IPRS IN THE INTERNATIONAL SYSTEM 11 (2002). IPRs also play a role in the dissemination of innovation and facilitate commercialization of inventions. *See, e.g.*, Edmund W. Kitch, *The Nature and Function of the Patent System*, 20 J. L. & ECON. 265 (1977); James Anton & Dennis Yao, *Expropriation and Inventions: Appropriable Rents in the Absence of Property Rights*, 84 AM. ECON. REV. 190 (1994).

Yet, the IP system comes at a price. Granting exclusive rights in IP denies society the benefit of using and possessing something that all people could use and enjoy concurrently. It interferes with diffusion of ideas, follow-on innovation, and limits the opportunities for putting these ideas to work. It prevents competition in the commercialization of artistic works and scientific inventions and usually gives IP holders some power over prices, which typically leads to higher prices and lower output.[2]

Hence the apparent conflict between the IP and antitrust regimes. That conflict, however, is only illusory, as it is generally agreed that, in the long run, securing some form of protection or reward for the inventor results in higher R&D spending, more innovation, and, in effect, better and cheaper products for consumers. Thus, the current mainstream view is that IP and competition policies do not have conflicting goals and that they should work in unison to maximize wealth by promoting innovation and economic progress.[3]

Still, tension remains with respect to the means that the two policies use to promote these goals.[4] Antitrust law seeks to foster competition by constraining the way monopoly power is created and maintained. IP may in some cases permit or even encourage monopoly to create incentives to innovate. IP rights may be used to obtain unwarranted market power and interfere with competition in various ways. Overly broad IP rights can have a negative effect on competition and inhibit innovation. These issues are of particular importance

---

[2] It also means monopoly loss, which the monopolist imposes on society by limiting his output below the level which consumers would be willing to purchase at a competitive price. In simple terms, fewer people will be able to buy the work than if it were sold at a competitive price. For discussion of economics of IP see, for example, WILLIAM M. LANDES & RICHARD A. POSNER, THE ECONOMIC STRUCTURE OF IP (2003); Stanley M. Bessen & Leo J. Raskind, *An Introduction to the Law and Economics of IP*, 5 J. ECON. PERSP. 3 (1991); Mark A. Lemley, *Ex Ante versus Ex Post Justifications for IP*, 71 U. CHI. L. R. 129 (2004); Suzanne Scotchmer, *The Political Economy of IP Treaties*, 20 J. L. ECON. & ORG. 415 (2004).

[3] The idea was first proposed in WARD BOWMAN, JR., PATENT AND ANTITRUST LAW: A LEGAL AND ECONOMIC APPRAISAL (1973), and has been embraced by academia, for example, Lewis Anton & Dennis Yao, *Some Reflections on the Antitrust Treatment of IP*, 63 ANTITRUST L. J. 603 (1995); 1 HOVENKAMP ET AL., *supra* note 7, ¶1.3; Luc Peeperkorn & Emil Paulis, *Competition and Innovation: Two Horses Pulling the Same Cart*, *in* PAUL LUGARD & LEIGH HANCHER, ON THE MERITS: CURRENT ISSUES IN COMPETITION LAW AND POLICY (2005); as well as by antitrust enforcers, for example, *Atari Games Corp. v. Nintendo of America, Inc.*, 897 F.2d 1572, 1576 (Fed. Cir. 1990); *Carl Schenck, A.G. v. Nortron Corp.* 713 F.2d 782, 786 (C.A. Fed., 1983); and *Technology Transfer Guidelines*, ¶7.

[4] *SCM Corp. v. Xerox Corp.*, 645 F.2d 1195, 1203 (2d Cir. 1981) ('The conflict between the antitrust and patent laws arises in the methods they embrace that were designed to achieve reciprocal goals'); *see also* 1 HOVENKAMP ET AL., *supra* note 1, ¶1.3b.

in the context of high-technology industries, where IP rights are key for market players. Specific features of some high-technology markets, such as network effects, may also aggravate the undesirable effects of IP rights on competition.

For many years courts and commentators have struggled to determine the best regulatory environment for innovation and to identify the types of conduct involving IP which should be subject to antitrust intervention.[5] The most daunting questions arise when the application of antitrust rules interferes with the basic entitlements of an IP holder, in particular: (1) the right to exclude others from using the protected technology or work; (2) the right to unilaterally set the license fee for the use of protected technology or work; and (3) the right to acquire an IP right and enforce it against unauthorized uses. The next chapter deals with antitrust scrutiny of acquisition and enforcement of IP rights. This chapter discusses in more detail the approach which antitrust enforcers take to the first two entitlements. It discusses in particular the issues relating to unilateral refusals to license and exploitative IP pricing. As will be seen, there is a link between the way antitrust enforcers approach market distortions that result from state action and the way they approach IP rights. EU antitrust enforcers see the role for competition policy as to correct what is considered faulty IP rights, whereas US antitrust enforcers avoid direct interference with the core of IP rights. It also appears that the EU antitrust authorities see a role for themselves in regulating the level of profits the IP holder may derive from his rights. These divergent approaches are particularly important in the context of high-technology industries, which are characterized by a high degree of R&D spending and a high level of dependence on IP protection. These issues are discussed at the end of this chapter.

1. COMPETITION, MONOPOLY, AND INNOVATION: THE ECONOMIC THEORY

The roots of the debate on the scope of antitrust intervention in the IP realm can be traced to the classic contributions of Joseph Schumpeter and Kenneth Arrow. This section briefly outlines the two perspectives and their impact on

---

[5] For an overview of the history of the interaction between antitrust and IP see 1 HOVENKAMP ET AL., *supra* note 1, ¶1.3b (in the US); Abbott B. Lipsky, *To the Edge: Maintaining Incentives for Innovation After Global Antitrust Explosions*, 35 GEO. J. INT'L LAW 521, 523–30 (2004) (in the US); Valentine Korah, *The Interface Between IP and Antitrust: The European Experience*, 69 ANTITRUST L. J. 801, 802–08 (2002); Ian S. Forrester, *European Competition Law and IP*, in proceedings of the Twelfth St Gallen International Competition Law Forum, University of St Gallen (28–29 April 2005).

the modern discussion of the proper balance between IP and antitrust. In essence, Schumpeter highlighted the role played by market concentration in promoting innovation. Arrow, by contrast, assuming the existence of IP rights, showed that a competitive environment may be better for that purpose.

Schumpeter challenged the assumption that market power, as such, allows the company to exploit consumers and that elimination of market power would assure efficient allocation of resources. He argued that market power contributes to the ability to innovate and long-run gains from innovation may dwarf the gains from regulatory intervention designed to make the economy more competitive in the short term.[6] Further research showed that economies of scale may indeed make innovation less costly for a large firm and that the latter may be better placed to fund research projects.[7] By pointing out the role of innovation in economic development, Schumpeter exposed the limitations associated with static efficiency analysis. Still his thesis linking innovation to market power remains controversial and statistical studies examining multiple industries have found inconclusive evidence to support it.[8]

Unlike Schumpeter, Arrow focused on the significance of competition for innovation. His model shows that a monopolist not exposed to actual or potential competition has less incentive to invest in developing new products than a firm in a competitive industry. Though a monopolist and a firm operating in a competitive environment have essentially the same abilities to realize profits from an innovation, the monopolist's net benefit is smaller. A firm that has no market power can only gain market share and increase its profits, whereas a monopolist typically replaces at least a portion of the profits from its old technology with the profits from the new technology. Thus, the monopolist gives up the opportunity to continue to earn monopoly profits without innovating.[9]

---

[6] JOSEPH A. SCHUMPETER, CAPITALISM, SOCIALISM AND DEMOCRACY 105 (1950) ('The introduction of new methods of production is hardly conceivable with perfect – and perfectly prompt – competition from the start. And this means that the bulk of what we call economic progress is incompatible with it'). For an analysis of Schumpeter's thought and its impact on modern antitrust enforcement *see* Thomas K. McCraw, *Joseph Schumpeter on Competition*, 4 COMPETITION POL'Y INT'L 310 (2008).

[7] *See, e.g.*, FREDERIC M. SCHERER, INDUSTRIAL MARKET STRUCTURE AND ECONOMIC PERFORMANCE 414 (2nd edn, 1980).

[8] For an overview of empirical research on competition and innovation *see* Jonathan B. Baker, *Beyond Schumpeter vs. Arrow: How Antitrust Fosters Innovation*, 74 ANTITRUST L. J. 575, 583–6 (2007).

[9] *See* Kenneth J. Arrow, *Economic Welfare and the Allocation of Resources to Invention*,' in R.R. NELSON (ED.), THE RATE AND DIRECTION OF INVENTIVE ACTIVITY (1962).

Arrow's model, however, is based on the assumption that there is no actual or potential competition to the monopolist, which implies that the monopolist does not fear that another firm (perhaps a new entrant) will soon implement a similar invention. A monopolist fearing market entry or expansion by a competitor will have no less incentive to innovate than a firm operating in a competitive market.[10] It may even have more incentives to invest in R&D than a company operating in a competitive environment, if doing so can discourage its potential rivals from innovating.[11] Further, Arrow's theory holds true only for core innovations resulting in a product making its existing alternatives obsolete. The economic literature shows that in certain circumstances a monopolist can benefit from a product innovation more than a company operating in a competitive environment. A good example of this phenomenon is a monopolist operating in vertically integrated markets.[12]

Arrow and Schumpeter's work spurred the line of research based on the analysis of dynamic and static competition and the effect of competition on innovation.[13] At first, commentators sought to balance IP and competition by trying to ascertain what the appropriate level of IP owners' profits should be. For example, Baxter suggested that patent owners should be allowed to extract monopoly profits only if their income is of the kind contemplated in the patent system. He believed that any exclusive rights should be strictly confined to the invention and defined as narrowly and specifically as possible.[14] Bowman, by contrast, argued that patent owners should be allowed to use any method of extracting monopoly profits, as long as the reward they obtain stems from the patented product's competitive superiority over substitutes. Thus, any

---

[10] *See* Shane Greenstein & Garey Ramey, *Market Structure, Innovation, and Vertical Product Differentiation*, 16 INT'L J. INDUS. ORG. 285 (1988).

[11] *See* Richard J. Gilbert & David M.G. Newbery, *Preemptive Patenting and the Persistence of Monopoly*, 72 AM. ECON. REV. 514 (1982). For a discussion of preemptive patenting and related literature *see e.g.*, Baker, *supra* note 8, at 581.

[12] *See* Nicholas Economides, *Quality Choice and Vertical Integration*, 17 INT'L J. INDUS. ORG. 903 (1999). There are a number of conflicting economic studies on the relation between the market structure and innovation. In general, whether a competitive environment is better than a monopolistic situation depends on particular industry features. *See in general*, Michael A. Carrier, *Two Puzzles Resolved: Of the Schumpeter–Arrow Stalemate and Pharmaceutical Innovation Markets*, 93 IOWA L. REV. 393, 405–10 (2008).

[13] *See, e.g.*, Janusz A. Ordover, *A Patent System for Both Diffusion and Exclusion*, 5 J. ECON. PERSPECTIVES 43 (1991); Richard Posner, *Antitrust and the New Economy,* 68 ANTITRUST L. J. 925 (2001); Michael A. Carrier, *Unraveling the Patent–Antitrust Paradox*, 150 U. PA . L. REV 761 (2002).

[14] William F. Baxter, *Legal Restrictions on Exploitation of the Patent Monopoly: An Economic Analysis*, 76 YALE L. J. 267, 313 (1966). Baxter takes a very restrictive view as to allowed restrictive practices in licensing agreements.

restraints on competition should be allowed as long as the patent owner does not monopolize more than the patent grants.[15] Both tests are based on implicit assumptions as to a specific level of aggregate reward that the patentee is entitled to obtain and the optimal level of antitrust enforcement. Each focuses only on one aspect of the problem: the patent owner's reward in Bowman's case and the monopoly loss in Baxter's case.

In his seminal article, Kaplow criticized Baxter's and Bowman's theories and pointed out that the role of antitrust is to regulate not only the total reward the patentee gets, but also the means by which that reward is realized.[16] To address this problem, Kaplow proposed to balance the monopoly loss resulting from the exercise of a patent against the increase in the patent owner's *ex ante* incentive to innovate due to the additional reward. Based on the assumption that social benefits from innovation exceed private returns, Kaplow argued that the exercise of IP rights should be allowed as long as its anticompetitive effects are outweighed by the additional prospect of innovation brought about by the conduct.[17]

Kaplow's contribution was to merge the analysis of the short-term and long-term effects of a competitive restraint involving IP, but there are important limitations to his model. He approached balancing IP and antitrust as a tradeoff between static and dynamic efficiency considerations and assumed that a greater reward for a patentee will always produce desirable effects on innovation. There is little controversy that overzealous antitrust enforcement may restrict pro-competitive use of a patent and that the exercise of IP rights resulting in higher prices in the short term is socially desirable if it creates innovation in the long run. Still, the practical implications of these principles are limited by the fact that it is virtually impossible to measure the impact that the additional investments in R&D will have on competition from an *ex ante* perspective. The relation between R&D spending and innovation is unclear. Even the largest R&D investment is not guaranteed to produce a commercially

---

[15] Ward S. Bowman, Patent and Antitrust Law: A Legal and Economic Appraisal (1973).

[16] Louis Kaplow, *The Patent–Antitrust Intersection: A Reappraisal*, 97 Harv. L. Rev. 1813 (1984).

[17] The three crucial factors in determining the ratio between static inefficiencies and the increase in ex ante incentives to innovate are as follows: (1) the proportion of the reward that is pure transfer (a transfer without additional distortions); (2) the proportion of the reward that accrues to the patentee (*e.g.* if price-restricted licenses are used to cartelize an industry, other firms in the industry get the share of the reward roughly in proportion to their market share); and (3) the degree to which the additional reward serves as an incentive to innovate. In his model, Kaplow actually assumed that all rewards have the same effect on incentives to innovate. Kaplow, *supra* note 16, at 1829–38.

viable product, but projects that succeed frequently provide enormous payoffs. It is also impossible to determine which R&D programs will be successful at the outset and thus whether a conduct that reduces output and increases prices in the short term will, in the long term, lead to the development of a revolutionary technology that will outweigh these losses.[18] Further, it is wrong to assume that strong IP rights coupled with lenient antitrust rules always promote dynamic efficiencies. IP rights, particularly those that are improvidently defined or granted, may forestall innovation.[19] Similarly, competition not only ensures lower prices in the short term, but also stimulates innovation in a variety of ways. Competition encourages firms developing similar new technologies to strengthen their efforts, so that they can profit from being the first entrant to the market. Competition among firms manufacturing products embodying an existing technology forces them to lower costs and improve quality.

The limitations of the model weighing the short-term static efficiency loss against the long-term dynamic efficiency gain shifted the focus of the debate from the application of antitrust rules to IP rights to the effects of competitive restraints on innovation.[20] Many anticompetitive practices that involve the exercise of IP rights actually restrain innovation and thus have an adverse effect on competition.[21] This is, for example, the case when a dominant company uses invalid IP rights to impede the entry of competing technologies or when competitors enter into a licensing agreement that limits their ability to develop competing technologies. Antitrust policy should discourage dominant firms from employing tactics that hurt both downstream users and innovative competitors. The challenge lies in identifying practices that reduce innovation

---

[18] *See in general* Herbert Hovenkamp, *Schumpetarian Competition and Antitrust*, 4 COMPETITION POL'Y INT'L 273 (2008); Jonathan B. Baker, *Beyond Schumpeter vs. Arrow: How Antitrust Fosters Innovation*, 74 ANTITRUST L. J. 575 (2007).

[19] *See, e.g.*, ROBERT P. MERGES & JOHN F. DUFFY, PATENT LAW AND POLICY: CASES AND MATERIALS 644–6 (3rd edn, 2002), discussing the effects of George Selden's patent on the car industry. The invention covered by the patent was obvious and the patent claims were so broad that the patent covered essentially all gasoline car engines. High licensing fees charged by Selden forestalled the development of the car industry until Henry Ford and others successfully challenged the patent and its scope was judicially narrowed. The Federal Trade Commission's Report, *To Promote Innovation: The Proper Balance of Competition Law and Patent Policy* (Oct. 2003), available at: http://www.ftc.gov/opa/2003/10/cpreport.htm, describes various examples of how poor-quality patents can hinder innovation and competition, including blocking paths of innovation, taxing research, and spurring defensive patenting.

[20] See Richard Gilbert and Willard K. Tom, *Is Innovation King at the Antitrust Agencies? The Intellectual Property Guidelines Five Years Later*, 69 ANTITRUST L. J. 43 (2001).

[21] *See* Hovenkamp, *supra* note 18 and Baker, *supra* note 18.

and competition in developing new technologies and devising remedies that appropriately address competitive harm resulting from such practices.

The following sections analyze how the theories described above have influenced the approaches to IP rights taken by the US and EU antitrust authorities and how the application of apparently similar economic theories has resulted in divergent outcomes. The *Microsoft* case discussed below is a particularly good example of this phenomenon. The focus on dynamic efficiency considerations is apparent both in the EU and in the US rulings. The effect of Microsoft's refusal to license its interoperability protocols on innovation played a prominent role in the European Commission's reasoning that Microsoft should be obliged to share those protocols.[22] In the same vein, effects on innovation were crucial for the assessment of the tying of the Internet Explorer web browser and the Windows operating system in the DC Circuit Court ruling in the *Microsoft* case.[23] Despite this common focus the antitrust enforcers reached strikingly different conclusions. The arguments on possible adverse effects on Microsoft's incentives to innovate persuaded the US circuit to apply the rule of reason to the tying offense, but did not prevent the Commission and the CFI from obliging Microsoft to share its interoperability information with its rivals.

2. REFUSALS TO LICENSE AND REMEDIES AFFECTING THE CORE OF IP RIGHTS

IP laws are designed to strike a balance between the divergent interests of IP owners and IP users by granting the owners exclusive rights and protecting the interests of users through a variety of exceptions and limitations. IP rights never give unlimited protection against copying. Their duration is limited and they protect only certain aspects of a work or an invention. Copyright covers the form alone, but not the underlying ideas. Trade secrets do not protect against independent creation or against reverse engineering. A patent extends only to commercial exploitation of the protected invention. The scope of a patent is defined by patent claims and the claims may cover only the elements that are new and non-obvious. There are also numerous specific exceptions embodied in IP laws. The exercise of patent rights is restricted by patent misuse doctrine. 'Fair use' of copyrighted works is allowed and copyright law

22 *See infra* Section 2 discussing the criteria the Commission applied in assessing whether Microsoft's refusal to provide interoperability information violated Article 82 of the EC Treaty.

23 *United States v. Microsoft Corp.*, 253 F.3d 34, 89–95 (D.C. Cir. 2001).

creates a number of compulsory licensing provisions applicable *inter alia* to cover versions of musical compositions[24] and retransmission of broadcast stations by cable systems.[25]

Fine tuning IP law is not an easy task.[26] Poor patent quality, patent thickets, and defensive patenting are a reality in some industries.[27] Moreover, the system of IP protection is prone to abuse. Questionable IP rights may give rise to significant competitive concerns and sham litigation can paralyze technological process for years. Valid IP rights may also restrict competition. They can be a significant barrier to entry and can be used by dominant companies to restrict innovation and prevent new products from coming into the market. Difficult questions often arise when standards that allow interoperability of products or services incorporate technologies covered by IP rights held by one person or entity. Licensing agreements, which are crucial for the dissemination of technologies, may also affect competition, for example by dividing the markets among firms that would have competed using different technologies. The key question is whether and how antitrust should intervene when IP rights give rise to such problems.

As explained above, the standards for condemning unilateral practices are different between Europe and the United States. There are also fundamental differences when it comes to the application of the antitrust laws in cases where the source of competitive concern is state action or regulation. This has had a significant impact on the way unilateral practices that involve the use of IP rights are assessed in these two jurisdictions. Antitrust law limits the freedom of IP owners in many different ways, but the focus here is on cases where the attack on IP is direct and deprives the rights holder of exclusivity, the essence of all IP rights. This essentially happens if enforcement of an IP right as such constitutes an antitrust violation, or if antitrust law mandates forced

---

[24] 17 U.S.C. §115. Such exception was also included in the UK Copyright Act of 1911 and in the 1956 Act, but it was not retained in the 1988 Act. A compulsory license in such cases is permitted under Article 13 of the Berne Convention. *See also* J.A.L. STERLING, WORLD COPYRIGHT LAW ¶2.106 (2nd edn, 2003).

[25] 17 U.S.C. §111. A compulsory license in regard to the broadcasting and cable retransmission rights of authors is allowed under Article 11*bis* (2) of the Berne Convention.

[26] This reflects the rationale for granting IP protection, the benefit society obtains in exchange for granting exclusivity. *See, e.g.*, Louis Kaplow, *The Patent–Antitrust Intersection: A Reappraisal*, 97 HARV. L. REV. 1815, 1825–9.

[27] *See, e.g.*, Bronwyn H. Hall & Rosemarie Ham Ziedonis, *The Patent Paradox Revisited: An Empirical Study of Patenting in the U.S. Semiconductor Industry (1979–1995)*, 32 RAND J. ECON. 101 (2001) (finding that large-scale manufacturers of semiconductors were involved in patent portfolio races).

sharing of IP. Can refusal to license violate antitrust law? Can IP be an essential facility? Should antitrust law be concerned with the poor quality of IP rights? Cases in which courts have tackled these questions involve a true conflict between IP law and trade regulation. They are also among the most controversial antitrust disputes.

A number of theories appear prominently in the cases where the antitrust remedy affects the core of an IP right: (1) the right is invalid; (2) the IP at stake has been improvidently defined or granted; (3) the IP owner attempts to extend its right beyond the scope warranted by IP laws; (4) the IP held by a dominant company constitutes an 'essential facility', access to which is indispensable for the existence of viable competition on the market; (5) special rules may apply when the refusal concerns interoperability information. Below the leading US and EU cases are analyzed to identify how these theories of competitive harm are approached in the two jurisdictions.

2.1 Europe: Correcting Intellectual Property Laws by Competition Law

The first Article 82 cases involving IP rights involved spare parts and independent repairers. The issue of whether spare parts should benefit from the IP protection has been controversial for years, with some EU Member States granting protection and other refusing to do so. The attempts to harmonize these provisions have so far been unsuccessful.[28] In *Volvo/Veng*[29] and *Renault*,[30] the ECJ faced the question as to whether a refusal to grant a license for the import and sale of car spare parts can constitute an abuse of a dominant position. In both cases, the original car manufacturer, relying on its IP rights, prevented repairers from producing or importing cheaper spare parts. The Court stressed that the right to exclude was the 'substance of the exclusive right, and that a refusal to grant such a license cannot in itself constitute an

[28] The attempted harmonization of spare parts protection in the Directive 98/71/EC of the European Parliament and of the Council of 13 October 1998 on the legal protection of designs, 1998 O.J. (L 289) p. 28) was so contentious that the issue was omitted from the final version of the Directive. Article 14 of the Directive stipulated that Member States shall maintain their existing laws and may change those provisions only in a way that liberalizes the spare parts market. In an attempt to finally harmonize design protection for spare parts, the Commission presented in 2004 the draft of a Directive amending the Design Directive so that the design right will not be extended to spare parts. The proposal has not been adopted.

[29] Case 238/87, *Volvo AB v. Erik Veng (U.K.) Ltd.*, 1988 E.C.R. 6211.

[30] Case 53/87, *Consorzio italiano della componentistica di ricambio per autoveicoli and Maxicar v. Régie nationale des usines Renault,* 1988 E.C.R. 6039.

abuse of a dominant position'.[31] Further, the fact that the original manufacturers charge a higher price for the parts than the independent producers did not 'necessarily constitute an abuse, since the proprietor of protective rights in respect of an ornamental design may lawfully call for a return on the amounts which he has invested in order to perfect the protected design'.[32] The Court noted, however, that a refusal to license may violate Article 82 if it involves an additional element of an abusive conduct, such as 'an arbitrary refusal to deliver spare parts to independent repairers, the fixing of prices for spare parts at an unfair level or a decision no longer to produce spare parts for a particular model even though many cars of that model remain in circulation'.[33]

In *Magill*,[34] the ECJ had an occasion to elaborate on the circumstances that could make a refusal to deal abusive. This case also involved a controversial IP right: copyright covering TV listings. Each of the major Irish TV stations published its own weekly TV guide, in addition to distributing TV listings, free of charge,[35] to newspapers and other media. There was no comprehensive, weekly TV guide covering the programs of all TV stations until Magill began publishing one. TV stations successfully sued Magill for copyright infringement. Magill, on its part, lodged a complaint to the European Commission alleging that the TV stations' refusal to license their listings violated Article 82 of the EC Treaty. The Commission agreed with the complainant and decided that, by preventing the publication of the comprehensive weekly TV guide, the TV stations abused their dominant position in the market for their individual advance weekly program listings.[36] It ordered the infringement to cease by imposing a compulsory license on the TV stations concerned. The Commission's Decision was upheld by the CFI and, on appeal, by the ECJ.

The ECJ stressed that mere ownership of an IP right does not confer a dominant position,[37] and a unilateral refusal to license could not in itself

---

31 *Volvo/Veng*, ¶8 and *Renault*, ¶¶15–16.

32 *Renault*, 1988 E.C.R. 6039, ¶17.

33 *Renault*, 1988 E.C.R. 6039, ¶16.

34 Case T-69/89, *RTE v. Commission*, 1991 E.C.R. II-485, upheld on appeal by the ECJ in Joined Cases C-241/91 P and C-242/91 P, *RTE and ITP v. Commission*, 1995 E.C.R. I-743.

35 The license was subject to the condition that there should only be reference to programs intended for broadcasting within the next 24 hours (or 48 hours on weekends).

36 Though the Court upheld the market definition and the finding of dominance on the relevant market, an interesting question is whether such a narrow market definition was correct. The question is particularly interesting given the fact that the Court explicitly rejected the possibility that a dominant position could be implied from the possession of an IP right (see below).

37 *See* Case C-242/91 P, *Magill*, ¶46.

constitute an abuse of a dominant position.[38] Yet, it rejected the argument that a refusal to license a copyright should be considered *per se* legal.[39] It found that the TV stations possessed a *de facto* monopoly over the information necessary to compile TV listings;[40] they were 'the only source of information on program scheduling which is the indispensable raw material for compiling a weekly television guide'.[41] The refusal to license was abusive because it: (1) prevented the appearance of a new product (a comprehensive weekly TV listings), which the TV stations did not offer and for which there was a potential consumer demand; (2) there was no justification for the refusal (the Court did not elaborate further on this point); and (3) by refusing to license Magill and other such companies, the TV stations reserved for themselves the secondary market of weekly television guides by excluding all competition from the market.[42] The Court upheld the remedy imposed on the TV stations by the Commission: a compulsory license with the right to charge reasonable and non-discriminatory royalties.

Some commentators understood *Magill* as a leveraging case and the ECJ judgment as prohibiting a refusal to license that has anticompetitive effects 'other than those that would be caused in the market primarily protected by the IPRs',[43] but for most *Magill* was a corrective measure applied to questionable national IP laws.[44] Indeed, *Magill* can be explained by reference to the idea/expression dichotomy, as the copyrighted subject-matter was ancillary to the real inputs: the TV program information needed by Magill.[45] The *Magill*

---

38 *Id.* ¶49.

39 *Id.* ¶48.

40 *Id.* ¶47.

41 *Id.* ¶53.

42 *Id.* ¶¶54–6.

43 John Temple-Lang, *European Community Antitrust Law: Innovation Markets and High Technology Industries*, 20 FORDHAM INT'L L. J. 717, 730 (1997).

44 TV listings are not protected by copyright in most EU Member States. *See e.g.*, ALISON JONES & BRENDA SUFRIN, EC COMPETITION LAW 404 and 407 (2002); Maurits Dolmans, *Restrictions on Innovation: An EU Antitrust Approach*, 88 ANTITRUST L. J. 455, 470 (1998); Valentine Korah, *The Interface between IP and Antitrust: The European Experience*, 69 ANTITRUST L. J. 801, 810–13 (2002); Christopher Stothers, *The End of Exclusivity? Abuse of IPRs in the EU*, 24 EUR. INTELL. PROP. REV. 86, 92–3 (2002).

45 The idea/expression dichotomy prevents copyright from monopolizing information and ideas, and leaves these essential resources in the public domain. *See*, *e.g.*, P. Bernt Hugenholtz, *Abuse of Database Right: Sole-Source Information Banks under the EU Database Directive*, *in* FRANÇOIS LÉVÊQUE & HOWARD SHELANSKI, ANTITRUST, PATENT AND COPYRIGHT: EU AND US PERSPECTIVES 203 (2005); Burton Ong, *Anticompetitive Refusals to Grant Copyright Licenses: Reflections on the IMS Saga*, 26 EUR. INTELL. PROP. REV. 505, 506–7 (2004). Notably, the US Supreme Court has held

Court did not comment on the value of the IP rights at stake, but the condition relating to the lack of justification could be understood as referring to the fact that the broadcasters made little investment in the development of the listings, and a compulsory license would not be a real disincentive to continue their publishing activities.[46] Another factor not discussed by the ECJ, but noted by the CFI,[47] which may have had a bearing on the lack of objective justification was that the same TV listings were given free of charge to newspapers who published TV listings on a daily basis.[48] *Magill* effectively invalidated a national IP right, which was considered unreasonable in terms of providing an incentive to creative efforts.

An analogy may be drawn to *Höfner*,[49] where the ECJ effectively outlawed national legislation giving exclusivity over job brokerage services to a state employment agency. The Court held that granting an exclusive right is not incompatible with Article 82 as such, but it may violate EU competition law if the company in that position cannot avoid abusing its dominant position merely by exercising the exclusive rights granted to it. In *Höfner*, this condition was met because the state employment agency was not capable of meeting the demand for executive recruitment. In *Magill*, the exclusivity granted to the TV stations was not only unjustified by the quality of the protected intellectual property, but effectively allowed them to prevent the emergence of a new, useful product. By granting a compulsory license, the ECJ eliminated the competitive concern posed by the national copyright laws and modified national copyright laws by determining the scope of protection to which TV stations were entitled. Notably, the core competitive concern in *Magill*,

that that bits of information that are not selected, coordinated, or arranged in an original way do not meet constitutional or statutory requirements for copyright protection. *Feist Publications, Inc. v. Rural Telephone Service Co., Inc.*, 499 U.S. 340, 361–4 (1991).

[46] Opinion of AG Jacobs in *Bronner*, 1998 ECR I-7791, ¶63; Dolmans, *supra* note 44; Korah, *supra* note 44, 811. It is worth noting that the US Supreme Court held that that bits of information that were not selected, coordinated, or arranged in an original way did not meet constitutional or statutory requirements for copyright protection. *Feist Publications, Inc. v. Rural Telephone Service Co., Inc.*, 499 U.S. 340, 361–4 (1991).

[47] Case T-69/89, *Magill*, 1991 E.C.R. II-485, 46–7, ¶73. See also the CFI judgment in 504/93 *Tiercé Ladbroke SA v. Commission*, 1997 E.C.R. II-923, ¶¶124–30 (finding that there was no discrimination in a situation where a refusal to license concerned a separate geographic market where the owner of IPRs did not exploit these rights on its own account by granting access to a third party).

[48] Case T-69/89, *Magill*, 1991 E.C.R. II-485, ¶73. *See also* Nicholas Green, *IP and the Abuse of Dominant Position under European Union Law: Existence, Exercise and the Evaporation of Rights*, 20 Brook. J. Int'l L. 141, 146 (1993).

[49] Case C-41/90, *Klaus Höfner and Fritz Elser v. Macrotron GmbH*, 1991 E.C.R. I-1979, ¶¶28–31.

national copyright law that granted overly broad protection, was eventually remedied by the adoption of the Broadcasting Act in Britain, which provided for compulsory licensing of program listings.[50]

Twelve years after *Magill*, the ECJ had the opportunity to revisit unilateral refusals to license in the *IMS* case.[51] As in *Magill*, at stake was the scope of a questionable copyright and the copyrighted work was distributed free of charge. IMS Health, a company engaged in tracking sales of pharmaceutical products, worked together with its clients to devise a 'brick structure', a geographical division of Germany based largely on post code zones. The brick structure was available free of charge to pharmacies, doctors and associations of health insurance schemes. It had become a *de facto* industry standard and IMS's rivals found it impossible to market the pharmaceutical data other than by using structures similar to that created by IMS. To prevent them from doing so, IMS brought proceedings before a German court alleging a copyright infringement.

The national courts found that the brick structure was protected as a database under German copyright law and issued an interim order restraining IMS's rivals from using any form of the brick structure derived from the one designed by IMS. The competitors' request for a license for the duration of the proceedings was denied and they filed a complaint with the Commission alleging that IMS abused its dominant position. The Commission, relying on the essential facilities theory, issued an interim measures decision finding that IMS's refusal to license violated Article 82.[52] The refusal was unjustified, likely to eliminate all competition in the downstream market, and the license was indispensable because there was no actual or potential substitute in existence for the requested service.[53] The EU Courts suspended the decision, but did not review the substantive issues raised by it.[54] The case reached the ECJ again through a request for a preliminary reference in national proceedings before a German court.

The *IMS* judgment remains so far the most comprehensive pronouncement of the ECJ on unilateral refusals to license. The Court began its reasoning by

---

[50] *See* JONES & SUFRIN, *supra* note 44, 403, n.242.

[51] Case C-418/01, *IMS Health GmbH & Co. OHG v. NDC Health GmbH & Co. KG* (*IMS*), 2004 E.C.R. I-5039.

[52] Commission Decision 2002/165/EC of 3 July 2001 (*NDC Health/IMS Health: Interim Measures*), 2002 O.J. (L 59) 18.

[53] *Id.* ¶¶70–74.

[54] Case T-184/01 R, *IMS Health v. Commission*, 2001 E.C.R. II-3193, *upheld*, Case C-481/01 P(R) *NDC Health Corporation and NDC Health GmbH & Co. KG v. IMS Health Inc. and Commission,* 2002 E.C.R. I-3401. The original decision was withdrawn by Commission Decision 2003/741/EC of 13 August 2003 (*NDC Health/IMS Health: Interim Measures*), 2003 O.J. (L 268) 69.

confirming the presumption that a refusal to license is legal, even if it is the act of a dominant company. Only exceptional circumstances can make it abusive.[55] Combining *Magill* and *Bronner*, the Court held that a refusal to license by a dominant company is abusive if four cumulative conditions are met: (1) the protected product or service is indispensable to compete in a particular market; (2) the refusal to provide it is 'such as to exclude any competition on a secondary market'; (3) the company which requested the license intends to offer new products or services not offered by the right holder and for which there is potential consumer demand; and (4) the refusal is not justified by any 'objective considerations'.[56] The Court left open the question of whether these conditions are necessary or merely sufficient for finding that a refusal to license violates Article 82, but its interpretation of the new product criteria suggests that they may be both sufficient and necessary.[57]

It reiterated the *Bronner* definition of indispensability: the requested service or product would be deemed indispensable only if an equally efficient competitor of the company that controls the existing product or service could not produce it.[58] The participation of the pharmaceutical industry and its dependency on the brick structure was relevant for the assessment of indispensability.[59]

The condition relating to the likelihood of excluding all competition on the secondary market implies that the upstream market for the requested product or service and the secondary market, where the product or service in question is used as an input, must be identified.[60] The Court agreed with the Advocate General that this condition is fulfilled if a potential or hypothetical secondary market could be identified.[61]

The requirements of indispensability and exclusion of all competition in the downstream market are closely related one to another. One can hardly imagine a situation where a refusal to provide a product or service that is indispensable to compete in the downstream market would not lead to elimination of competition in that market. Perhaps the best way of interpreting the two requirements together is that the facility must be critical both to the competi-

---

55 *IMS*, 2001 E.C.R. II-3193, ¶¶34–5.

56 *Id.* ¶¶37–8.

57 AG Tizzano clearly treated the new product requirement as indispensable in his opinion. Opinion of AG Tizzano in *IMS*, 2001 E.C.R. II-3193, ¶62. *See also* Christian Ahlborn, David S. Evans, & Jorge Padilla, *The Logic and Limits of the 'Exceptional Circumstances Test' in* Magill *and* IMS Health, 28 FORDHAM INT'L L. J. 1109, 1127–8 (2005).

58 *IMS*, 2001 E.C.R. II-3193, ¶28.

59 *Id.* ¶29.

60 *Id.* ¶42.

61 *Id.* ¶44; Opinion of AG Tizzano in *IMS*, 2001 E.C.R. II-3193, ¶¶56–9.

tive viability of the company requesting the license and to enhancing competition in general.[62] It can also be seen as an attempt to limit compulsory licensing to situations where IP constitutes an 'essential facility', that is, where its existence effectively precludes any competition in the downstream market.

The *IMS* Court also confirmed the *Magill* condition that a refusal to license is abusive when it prevents a company requesting the license from offering a new product or service not offered by the right holder. In *Magill*, the CFI and the ECJ held that this requirement was satisfied because the new product (a comprehensive TV guide) and the product offered by right holders (separate TV listings) 'were only to a limited extent substitutable'.[63] Advocate General Tizzano suggested that it is sufficient that the new product is of a 'different nature' from the product available on the market and that it does not exclude the possibility that the new product is in competition with the products offered by the IP holder.[64] The ECJ held that the new product condition is satisfied when the company which requested the license 'does not intend to limit itself essentially to duplicating the goods or services already offered on the secondary market by the owner of the IP right, but intends to produce new goods or services not offered by the owner of the right and for which there is a potential consumer demand'.[65] The Court reasoned that the refusal to grant the license must prevent 'the development of the secondary market to the detriment of consumers',[66] but it did not comment on the degree to which the new product must be different from the product offered by the IP holder and whether the two products could be substitutable.

Finally, the Court confirmed that the refusal to license must not justified by 'objective considerations', but did not specify what circumstances may be sufficient to constitute such an objective justification or the party that bears the burden of proving the existence of an objective justification or lack of it.

Like *Magill*, *IMS* involved a right that protected a controversial subject-matter, arguably something that did not merit protection. The EU Database Directive,[67] the source of the German copyright provisions applicable to the IMS brick structure, specifically instructs the Commission to examine whether the right granted in a database has led to an abuse of a dominant position or

---

[62] This is the interpretation taken by the US courts in essential facility cases. *See, e.g.*, *Fishman v. Estate of Wirtz*, 807 F.2d 520, 539 (7th Cir. 1986); *TCA Bldg. Co. v. Northwestern Resources Co.*, 873 F.Supp. 29, 39 (S.D.Tex. 1995). *See also* 3A PHILIP AREEDA & HERBERT HOVENKAMP, ANTITRUST LAW, ¶¶773a, 773b, and ¶773b3 (2002).

[63] *Magill*, 1995 E.C.R. I-743, ¶46.

[64] Opinion of AG Tizzano in *IMS*, 2001 E.C.R. II-3193, ¶62.

[65] *IMS*, 2001 E.C.R. II-3193, ¶49.

[66] *IMS*, 2001 E.C.R. II-3193, ¶48.

[67] Council Directive 96/9/EC of 11 March 1996, 1996 O.J. (L 77) 20 [hereinafter Database Directive].

other interference with free competition that would justify the introduction of compulsory licensing provisions. Moreover, the original draft directive contained a compulsory licensing provision,[68] which was eventually replaced with a provision allowing Member States to introduce limited exceptions to the database right.[69] Ultimately, the source of competitive concern in *IMS*, just as in *Magill*, was not really the refusal to license, but rather the scope of copyright over the brick structure. The latter was contestable and in the course of litigation the German courts found a solution based in copyright law to address the competitive concerns arising from IMS's refusal to license.[70] Such a solution to the problem caused by an overly broad IP right may be more suitable than the *ad hoc* relief provided by antitrust laws.

The most recent and perhaps the most controversial case involving compulsory licensing in the EU is *Microsoft*.[71] Microsoft was accused of abusing its dominant position in the market for PC operating systems by refusing to

---

[68] Art. 8(1) of the draft Directive provided that '[n]otwithstanding the right provided for in Article 2(5) to prevent the unauthorized extraction and re-utilization of the contents of a database, if the works or materials contained in a database which is made publicly available cannot be independently created, collected or obtained from any other source, the right to extract and re-utilize, in whole or substantial part, works or materials from that database for commercial purposes, shall be licensed on fair and non-discriminatory terms.' Council Communication, 1992 O.J. (C. 156) 9.

[69] *See* Database Directive, art. 9. For a discussion of the legislative history of the Database Directive see Mark Powell, *The European Union's Database Directive: An International Antidote to the Side Effects of Feist?*, 20 FORDHAM INT'L L. J. 1215 (1997).

[70] Although the Frankfurt Higher Regional Court on appeal upheld the finding that IMS's brick structure was protected under German copyright law and that direct reproduction of IMS's structure was illegal, it found that IMS's competitors 'could not simply be prohibited from developing freely and independently a brick structure that is similarly [to the IMS structure] based on a breakdown by district, urban district and post-code district and for that reason comprises more or less the same number of bricks . . . In particular, the defendant or third parties could not be expected to produce a data structure that does not sufficiently satisfy the practical requirements simply in order to keep as much distance as possible from the plaintiff's product. Instead, variations cannot be demanded where the overlaps are based on material technical requirements and, in the light of taking into account "the need of availability" for competitors, the appropriate performance of the technical task depends on these features.' Commission Decision 2003/741/EC of 13 August 2003 (*NDC Health/IMS Health: Interim Measures*), 2003 O.J. (L 268) 69, ¶10. The Commission found that as a result of this ruling IMS's competitors were able to devise a structure that allowed them to compete with IMS and that the ruling coincided with the improvement of their market position.

[71] Commission Decision in Case COMP/C-3/37.792 – *Microsoft* [hereinafter *Microsoft Decision*]; on appeal Case T-201/04, *Microsoft v. Commission*, 2007 E.C.R. II-3601 [hereinafter *Microsoft* judgment].

supply interoperability information[72] allegedly necessary for Microsoft's rivals to compete effectively in the workgroup server operating market.[73] According to the Commission, Microsoft's strategy was to preserve privileged connections between its Windows PC operating system and its work group server operating system to the detriment of its competitors in the work group server operating market. This, in the Commission's view, allowed Microsoft to leverage its dominant position in the market for client PC operating systems into the market for workgroup server operating systems, and ultimately to preserve its monopoly in the market for PC operating systems.[74] As a remedy, Microsoft was ordered to license proprietary information concerning the communications protocols[75] by which Microsoft's server operating systems communicate with one another.

The EU Decision was preceded by a settlement of the US case against Microsoft. Although there were a number of important differences, the EU and the US cases against Microsoft both focused on exclusionary practices, such as bundling middleware, with immediate effects on neighbouring markets. The allegations in the US case concerned Microsoft's strategies aimed at Netscape and Sun's Java programming language.[76] The government's theory was that both Netscape and Java could potentially serve as a platform on which applications could run largely without reliance on the operating systems. Microsoft developed Internet Explorer (IE), its own internet browser, and included it in the Windows operating system. The government asserted that IE was integrated

---

[72] The Commission defined 'interoperability information' as 'the complete and accurate specifications for all the Protocols implemented in Windows Work Group Server Operating Systems and . . . used by Windows Work Group Servers to deliver file and print services and group user administration services, including Windows Domain Controller services, Active Directory services and Group Policy services, to Windows Work Group Networks'. *Microsoft Decision*, art. 1. The interoperability information concerned both server-to-server and server-to-client communication.

[73] Microsoft was also accused of the tying of media functionality (Windows Media Player) and the Windows PC operating system. According to the Commission, this practice affected competition on the media player market. *Microsoft Decision*, ¶¶792–813.

[74] *Microsoft Decision*, ¶¶185–279.

[75] A protocol is defined as 'a set of rules of interconnection and interaction between various instances of Windows Group Server Operating Systems and Windows Client PC Operating Systems running on different computers in a Windows Work Group Network'. *Microsoft Decision*, *supra* note 71, art. 1(2).

[76] For a comment on the US Microsoft case, *see*, *e.g.*, Herbert Hovenkamp, *The Monopolization Offense*, 61 OHIO STATE L. J. 1035, 1047–9 (2000); David S. Evans et al., *United States v. Microsoft: Did Consumers Win?*, 1 J. COMPETITION L. & ECON. 497 (2005); William H. Page & Seldon J. Childers, *Software Development as an Antitrust Remedy: Lessons from the Enforcement of the Microsoft Communications Protocol Licensing Requirement,* 14 MICH. TELECOMM. TECH. REV. 77 (2007).

into Windows in a way that prevented PC manufacturers from removing Microsoft's browser and limited the user's ability to choose Netscape as a default browser. It also alleged that Microsoft imposed various licensing restrictions, preventing PC manufacturers from displaying other browsers more prominently than IE or using the computer startup sequence to promote competing web browsers. According to the government, this had the effect of discouraging PC manufacturers from marketing competing Internet browsers and coerced them into favoring Microsoft's product, thus foreclosing vital distribution channels from Netscape.

Microsoft's agreements with software developers and Internet access providers had a similar foreclosing effect. Microsoft also obtained a license to include Java in the Windows operating system. Microsoft's version allowed Java applications to run faster on Windows than the original Sun's Java, but it was also made incompatible with the original Sun's Java and other non-Windows platforms. The government asserted that Microsoft took actions that impeded the distribution of Sun's Java and tricked software developers into writing programs in its version of Java, thus preventing adoption of Sun's cross-platform Java. It alleged that by engaging in these practices Microsoft had maintained a monopoly in the market for PC operating systems in violation of Section 2 of the Sherman Act and had attempted to gain a monopoly in the market for Internet browsers in violation of Section 2 of the Sherman Act. In addition, Microsoft was accused of violating Section 1 of the Sherman Act by illegal tying of its Internet browser and Windows operating system.

The District Court found that Microsoft was dominant in the market for PC operating systems and that its market position was protected by strong networks effects.[77] It also found that Microsoft adopted contractual and design measures described above to exclude Netscape's browser from the most efficient distribution channels and to prevent Netscape from gaining a sufficient usage share to succeed as an alternative platform. The District Court also confirmed the government allegations relating to Microsoft's treatment of Java.[78] Following failed settlement negotiations, the District Court found Microsoft guilty of monopolizing the operating systems market, attempting to monopolize the browser market, and illegal tying of Windows and Internet Explorer.[79] As a remedy, it ordered that Microsoft be broken into two separate

[77] The theory advanced by the court was that the large number of users of the Windows platform was an incentive for software developers to write programs that would run on Windows. This, in turn, encouraged more users to use Windows and fostered Microsoft's monopoly. *See U.S. v. Microsoft Corp.*, 84 F. Supp. 2d 9, 15–24 (D.D.C. 1999).

[78] *Id.* at 46–112.

[79] *U.S. v. Microsoft Corp.*, 87 F. Supp. 2d 30, 35–46 (D.D.C. 2000).

units, one to produce the operating system, and one to produce other software components (applications).[80]

On appeal, the DC Circuit Court confirmed the District Court finding that Microsoft monopolized the PC operating system market, but reversed the finding that Microsoft violated Section 2 by illegally attempting to monopolize the Internet browser market. The Court applied a balancing test, assessing the anticompetitive effects of Microsoft's conduct against pro-competitive justifications offered by Microsoft.[81] It ruled that Microsoft violated Section 2 by imposing restrictive licensing provisions on PC manufacturers and concluding exclusive agreements with Internet access providers and software developers, which prevented the effective distribution and use of products that threatened Microsoft's monopoly. It also condemned deceiving developers into using a Windows-specific version of Java rather than the cross-platform version offered by Sun.[82] Still, the Court firmly rejected the finding that Microsoft violated antitrust laws by developing software incompatible with the products of its rivals, such as the Windows-specific version of Java. [83] It also reversed the finding that Microsoft was guilty of tying of Internet Explorer and Windows, reasoning that technological tying in computer industry should be assessed under the rule of reason, considering the efficiencies that such conduct may create.[84] The case was remanded for consideration of a proper remedy.

The case settled when the government announced that it was no longer seeking to break up Microsoft. Instead, the government proposed conduct remedies aimed at preserving the contractual and economic freedom of computer manufacturers to distribute and support non-Microsoft middleware products. Most remedies proscribed specific conduct that was found to violate antitrust rules on appeal. In particular, Microsoft was obliged to provide utilities in Windows that give original equipment manufacturers (OEMs) the flexibility to enable or delete various means of access to Microsoft middleware products and to designate non-Microsoft middleware to launch instead of the Microsoft applications. Microsoft also agreed to permit OEMs to install icons and other means of launching non-Microsoft middleware and that it would not pay software developers for not distributing competing software or for using exclusively Microsoft's software.

In addition, the settlement imposed certain licensing obligations on Microsoft. It obliged Microsoft to disclose all interfaces used by its middleware (including IE and the media player) to operate with other parts of Microsoft operating systems. That obligation was not directly linked to any of

---

80 *Id.* at 64.
81 *U.S. v. Microsoft Corp.* 253 F.3d 34, 59 (D.C. Cir. 2001).
82 *Id.* at 64–78.
83 *Id.* at 75.
84 *Id.* at 89–95.

the liability findings, but related to the allegations that Microsoft corrupted applications programming interfaces (APIs) to unfairly eliminate rivals' applications.[85] It was meant to place middleware suppliers in a position to compete with Microsoft. Although related offenses had not been raised at the trial, Microsoft was also required to license the communications protocols necessary for software located on a computer server to interoperate with the Windows PC operating system.[86] That provision was in turn linked to the assumption that at some point middleware running on servers might pose a threat to Microsoft's position in the operating systems market. Allegations that Microsoft intended to leverage its monopoly in the market for desktop operating systems to gain control over the market for server operating systems appeared in the Netscape complaint. The government did not rely on these allegations in its case against Microsoft and did not base the theory of liability on Microsoft's failure to disclose interoperability information to rivals. Still the court and the government felt that it was necessary to address the server issue in the settlement to ensure that the remedies do not become obsolete when the applications move to servers or are run remotely over the Internet.[87]

The liability theories relating to the interoperability of Microsoft's software with competing software products, which were a side issue in the United States, became the crux of the European case against Microsoft. The European Commission was not satisfied with the disclosures made by Microsoft under the US settlement.[88] It concluded that Microsoft's refusal to provide interoperability information was abusive. The Commission asserted that Microsoft was under the obligation to share interoperability information with its competitor in the work group server operating market because: (1) interoperability information was necessary for competing providers of work group server operating systems to 'viably stay on the market';[89] (2) Microsoft's

---

[85] *U.S. v. Microsoft Corp.*, 231 F. Supp. 2d 144 (D.D.C. 2002). For an extensive discussion and an assessment of the remedies imposed by the US settlement *see in general* Page & Childers, *supra* note 76.

[86] Under Section III.E of the US settlement 'Microsoft shall make available for use by third parties, for the sole purpose of interoperating or communicating with a Windows Operating System Product, on reasonable and non-discriminatory terms . . . any Communications Protocol that is . . . (i) implemented in a Windows Operating System Product installed on a client computer, and (ii) used to interoperate, or communicate, natively (i.e., without the addition of software code to the client operating system product) with a Microsoft server operating system product.' *New York v. Microsoft*, 224 F. Supp.2d 76, 269 (D.D.C. 2002).

[87] *U.S. v. Microsoft Corp.*, 253 F.3d 34, 89–95 (D.C. Cir. 2001). *See* Page & Childers, *supra* note 76, at 95–100.

[88] *Microsoft Decision*, ¶¶273–9, 703–8.

[89] *Microsoft Decision*, ¶779.

conduct involved a disruption of previous levels of supply;[90] (3) there was 'a risk of eliminating all competition in the work group server operating system market';[91] (4) the refusal to supply had the consequence of 'preventing innovation in the work group server market and of diminishing consumers' choice by locking them into a homogenous Microsoft's solution';[92] and (5) the refusal was not objectively justified because on balance the 'negative impact of an order to supply on Microsoft's incentives to innovate is outweighed by its positive impact on the level of innovation of the whole industry (including Microsoft)'.[93]

The Microsoft Decision was announced a few weeks before the ECJ ruling in the *IMS* case was published, so the Commission could not take it into consideration. Notably, the new product condition used as a limiting principle in *Magill* and in *IMS* was largely omitted in the Commission's reasoning. Instead, the Commission argued that a refusal to license may be abusive also if it concerns technology protected by IP rights, which is indispensable as a basis for follow-on innovation by competitors. It also specifically rejected the proposition that there is an 'exhaustive checklist of exceptional circumstances' which make a refusal to license abusive,[94] and asserted that the standards that apply to compulsory licensing of IP rights should not apply to interoperability information that is protected under trade secret laws.

The CFI upheld the Commission's *Microsoft* Decision,[95] but did not decide on many controversial legal questions posed by the case. It did not decide how the various circumstances listed by the Commission, such as the history of prior dealings, leveraging, and super-dominance, influenced the assessment of Microsoft's refusal to supply the interoperability information.[96] Nor did it rule whether trade secrets deserve the same level of protection as IP rights[97] and

---

90 *Id.* ¶¶780, 578–84.

91 *Id.* ¶¶781, 585–692.

92 *Id.* ¶¶782, 693–708.

93 *Id.* ¶¶783, 709–78. The Commission also found that Microsoft violated Article 82 by illegal tying of its Windows operating system and media player, by not providing consumers with the opportunity to buy Windows without Windows Media Player.

94 *Microsoft Decision*, ¶555. In the *Microsoft* case, the Commission argued against the position that a refusal to license may be abusive only if the *Magill/IMS* test is met. The *Article 82 Guidance* adopts a similar approach. *See Article 82 Guidance*, ¶74–89.

95 Case T-201/04, *Microsoft v. Commission* ('*Microsoft* judgment'), 2007 E.C.R. II-3601.

96 The Court held that there would only be a need to assess the criteria listed by the Commission if it found that Microsoft's refusal to license was not abusive under the IMS criteria. *Microsoft* judgment, ¶336 and ¶711.

97 *Microsoft* judgment, ¶336.

instead it applied the rules applicable to compulsory licensing of IP rights, reasoning the Commission conceded that the interoperability information in question might be protected by IP rights.[98] The Court confirmed that a refusal to license is anticompetitive 'only in exceptional circumstances',[99] which occur 'in particular' when the conditions coined by the *IMS* Court are satisfied, namely that: (1) the refusal relates to a product that is indispensable to the exercise of a particular activity in a neighboring market; (2) the refusal 'is of such kind as to exclude any effective competition on that neighboring market'; (3) the refusal prevents the appearance of a new product for which there is potential consumer demand.[100] If these conditions are met, the refusal by the holder to grant a license may infringe Article 82, unless it is objectively justified.[101] Unlike the *IMS* Court, the CFI clearly indicated that it is for the dominant company to prove that its refusal to license was objectively justified.

The CFI relaxed the interpretation of the 'exceptional circumstances' which make a refusal to license abusive. Under *Bronner* and *IMS*, the requested product or service is indispensable if there is no actual or potential substitute for that product, which implies that 'it is not economically viable' to create alternative products or services on a scale comparable to that of the company which controls the existing product or service.[102] The *Bronner* Court specifically stressed that the requirement of indispensability is not satisfied when such alterative products or services are 'less advantageous' than those controlled by the dominant company.[103] In *Microsoft*, there were alternative means to achieve interoperability and those methods were used by Microsoft's competitors, who continued to compete on the work group server operating market following the refusal and throughout the dispute.[104] Still, according to the CFI the interoperability information was indispensable because competing products had to interoperate with Windows domain architecture on an equal footing with Microsoft's systems in order to *compete viably* on the market.[105]

The Court also held that it is not required to show that the refusal eliminates all competition in the secondary market. The issue here was of the degree and the evidence necessary to show that all competition on the secondary market is elim-

---

[98] *Microsoft* judgment, ¶¶283–90.
[99] *Microsoft* judgment, ¶331.
[100] *Microsoft* judgment, ¶332.
[101] *Microsoft* judgment, ¶333.
[102] *Bronner*, ¶¶43–6; *IMS*, ¶28. The *Bronner* Court clarified that this would be typically the case if there are 'technical, legal or even economic obstacles capable of making it impossible, or. . . unreasonably difficult' to replicate the product or service. *Bronner*, ¶44; *see also IMS*, ¶28.
[103] *Bronner*, ¶41.
[104] *Microsoft*, ¶¶342–50.
[105] *Microsoft* judgment, ¶¶230, 248–50.

inated. Microsoft argued that a refusal is abusive only if it is 'likely to eliminate all competition'[106] and that the prospect of eliminating competition must be 'immediate and strong'.[107] The CFI rejected this argument and agreed with the Commission that it is sufficient that the refusal creates a risk of elimination of all *effective* competition and that the fact that the competitors retain 'a marginal presence in certain niches on the market cannot suffice to substantiate the existence of such competition'.[108] The evidence of the rapid growth of Microsoft's shares in the market for work group server operating systems coinciding with declining shares and interoperability problems experienced by Microsoft's rivals supported the Commission's findings that the refusal to license created the risk of eliminating all effective competition in the relevant market.[109]

CFI's interpretation of the indispensability and the elimination of competition criteria suggests that dominant companies controlling successful technologies may be under an obligation to share interoperability information with their competitors in adjacent markets. Control over a widely prevalent technology would nearly always create an advantage for a dominant company and its special responsibility not to allow its conduct to impair competition would dictate providing its competitors with information necessary to achieve seamless interoperability.[110] Once it is established that seamless interoperability is indispensable, it is highly unlikely that the dominant company could raise any viable defenses.

The new product criterion, as interpreted by the CFI, is unlikely to serve as a viable limiting principle. The CFI affirmed the Commission's position that a refusal to license may be abusive not only if it prevents the marketing of a new product, but also when it limits 'technical development'.[111] In *IMS* and *Magill*, a refusal to license prevented the emergence of an identifiable, new product that was different from the product offered by the IP holder, and for which there was consumer demand. The CFI held that it was not necessary to identify any particular product that the refusal prevented from coming into being.[112] The Court agreed with the Commission that Microsoft's refusal to license limited technical development because it created an 'artificial interoperability advantage' which together with Microsoft's market position discouraged the development of competing server operating systems.[113] The new

---

106 *Microsoft* judgment, ¶439.
107 *Microsoft* judgment, ¶440.
108 *Microsoft* judgment, ¶¶563–4.
109 *Microsoft* judgment, ¶¶567–71 and 580.
110 *Microsoft* judgment, ¶229.
111 *Microsoft* judgment, ¶¶647–9.
112 *Microsoft* judgment, ¶647.
113 *Microsoft* judgment, ¶653.

product test as spelled out by the *IMS* Court can arguably serve as a reasonable limiting principle, granting some level of legal certainty for dominant companies holding IP rights in valuable technologies.[114] If the new product and the product offered by the IP holder are not close substitutes, the IP holder can still exploit its own technology. The use of antitrust to define the scope of IP rights *ex post* is limited to cases where it is very clear that the refusal to license paralyzes follow-on innovation. The new product test limits the risk of over-enforcement, is feasible to administer, and leads to more predictable results than the new CFI test focusing on future technical progress. By contrast, the test applied by the *Microsoft* Court broadens the scope of antitrust intervention and provides little guidance as to when exactly a refusal to license is anticompetitive. This may significantly undermine the effectiveness of the IP protection system and, consequently, discourage dominant companies from investing in new technologies.

The possibility of offering an objective justification for a refusal to license does not appear to be a viable defense for dominant companies. The CFI rejected the proposition that the existence of an IP right[115] or the innovative or original character of the protected subject-matter can be, in itself, a sufficient justification for a refusal to license.[116] It offered little guidance as to what is a sufficient 'objective justification'.[117] A dominant company can refuse to share its IP that is indispensable for its competitors to compete 'effectively' on a neighboring market only if it can prove that it would have 'a significant negative impact' on its incentives to innovate and that that impact outweighs the competitive harm resulting from the refusal.[118] Neither the fact that the technology concerned is secret and valuable nor the fact that it contains important

[114] *See, e.g.*, Ahlborn, Evans & Padilla, *supra* note 57, (arguing that the new product test is in line with economic theory); David S. Evans & A. Jorge Padilla, *Designing Antitrust Rules for Assessing Unilateral Practices: A Neo-Chicago Approach*, 72 U. CHI. L. REV. 73, 87–8 (2005); Ian S. Forrester, *Regulating Intellectual Property via Competition? Or Regulating Competition via Intellectual Property? Competition and Intellectual Property: Ten Years on, the Debate Still Flourishes*, proceedings of the Tenth Annual EU Competition Law and Policy Workshop, Robert Schuman Centre for Advanced Studies, European University Institute, Florence, Italy (3–4 June 2005) (suggesting that the new product test makes sense from 'an orthodox antitrust point of view'). *But see* Thomas Eilmansberger, *How to Distinguish Good from Bad Competition under Article 82 EC*, 42 COMMON MARKET L. REV. 158–9 (2005); Damien Geradin, *Limiting the Scope of Article 82 EC*, 41 COMMON MARKET L. REV. 1531–2 (2004); Derek Ridyard, *Compulsory Access under EU Competition Law*, 25 EUR. COMPETITION L. REV. 670 (2004).

[115] *Microsoft* judgment, ¶690.

[116] *Microsoft* judgment, ¶693.

[117] *Microsoft* judgment, ¶¶704–10.

[118] *Microsoft* judgment, ¶697.

innovations justifies a refusal to license.[119] A dominant company has to furnish specific evidence that a compulsory license would affect its incentives to innovate in relation to identified technologies or products.[120] The Court found that Microsoft did not provide such evidence and that compulsory licensing would not adversely affect Microsoft's incentives to innovate, reasoning that the compulsory license would not allow competitors to clone Microsoft's products, that sharing interoperability information is a standard practice in the software industry, and that the obligation to share interoperability information imposed on Microsoft in the US settlement did not adversely affect Microsoft's incentives to develop its operating systems.[121]

The high burden of proof placed on the dominant company is striking given that compulsory licensing could be presumed to have a negative effect on the dominant company's incentives to innovate, in particular if, as in this case, it can only charge reduced royalties.[122] It is even more striking considering that the Court essentially found that the Commission satisfied the burden of proof that a refusal to license thwarted technological progress by a general statement that the lack of perfect interoperability and Microsoft's growing share in the work group operating systems discouraged the development of competing work group server operating systems.

Overall, the Court's rulings relating to the burden of proof and the scope of its scrutiny over the Commission's findings of fact are troubling. The Commission's factual findings on the degree of interoperability necessary for a competitor to compete 'viably' on the market, the information that has to be disclosed to achieve this level of interoperability, and the effect which compulsory licensing would have on Microsoft's incentives to innovate were hotly disputed. The Commission acts both as the judge and the prosecutor and its decisions, particularly those imposing huge fines and compulsory licensing

---

119 *Microsoft* judgment, ¶¶692–5.

120 *Microsoft* judgment, ¶698.

121 *Microsoft* judgment, ¶¶699–703. The comparison with the US settlement is not fully justified, given that the obligations imposed on Microsoft in the US are much narrower (they were insufficient to address the Commission's concerns). Furthermore, unlike in the EU, where Microsoft's right to charge royalties and to preserve the secrecy of its interoperability information has been questioned by the Commission, the US settlement leaves no doubt that Microsoft is entitled to do so.

122 The issue of royalties has been the subject of dispute between Microsoft and the Commission. Initially, Microsoft had demanded a royalty rate of 3.87 percent of a licensee's product revenues for a patent license and of 2.98 percent for a license giving access to the secret interoperability information. The Commission considered that the pricing proposed by Microsoft was unreasonable. Eventually, Microsoft was forced to provide a license giving access to the interoperability information for a flat fee of 10 000 and an optional worldwide patent license for a reduced royalty of 0.4 percent of licensees' product revenues.

obligations, should be given more than just a cursory review. Yet, the CFI essentially accepted the Commission's factual findings, asserting that it has only limited power to review complex technical and economic appraisals.[123] The Court's review was limited to checking 'whether the relevant rules on procedure and on stating reasons have been complied with, whether the facts have been accurately stated and whether there has been any manifest error of assessment or a misuse of powers'.[124]

To be sure, the CFI's decision was strongly influenced by the specific circumstances of the case and, in particular, Microsoft's market position. The Court hinted that Microsoft's 'quasi-monopoly' was decisive for its assessment of the facts. The Court's statement that Microsoft impeded technological progress by 'impairing an effective competitive market structure' on the work group server operating systems market 'by acquiring a significant market share' can hardly be applied to other companies.[125] Still, there is nothing in the ruling that excludes the possibility of applying the *Microsoft* test to a refusal to license of an IP right by a start-up company with market shares in the range of 40–50 percent in a narrowly defined market. The test used by the CFI to determine whether Microsoft's refusal to license was abusive is difficult to administer and the ruling left many important questions open. All in all, *Microsoft* gives rise to legal uncertainty that may inhibit competitive and welfare-enhancing conduct and creates a serious risk that antitrust enforcement undermines IP protection measures.

Microsoft is perhaps the most prominent example of how competition rules are used to shape substantive standards for IP protection in the EU. As will be discussed in more detail below, the Commission decision and the Court's ruling had a significant impact on the scope of software and trade secret protection. Neither the Commission nor the Court had any doubt that antitrust principles trump over conflicting EU directives and national IP protection measures.

2.2 America: Searching for Solutions in IP Laws

The application of antitrust law to unilateral conduct involving IP rights has a longer history in the United States than in Europe. Unlike in Europe, however, a refusal to license or the enforcement of a valid IP right can hardly give rise to antitrust liability in the United States. The US Courts have been most recep-

---

123 *Microsoft* judgment, ¶¶87–8.
124 *Id.*
125 *Microsoft* judgment, ¶664.

tive to claims involving allegations that an IP right has been improperly acquired or enforced.[126] Some commentators argue that the existence of IP rights by themselves is sufficient justification for a refusal to license,[127] while others see the scope for antitrust intervention in only very limited circumstances.[128]

American courts have been highly reluctant to condemn unconditional unilateral refusals to license IP rights.[129] The DC Circuit took the most extreme position on unilateral refusals to license in *In re Independent Service Organizations Antitrust Litigation.*[130] The case involved similar facts and legal issues to the European *Volvo/Veng* case, namely the use of IP rights to protect the original manufacturer's position in the aftermarket. Xerox had the policy of not selling spare parts to independent service organizations (ISOs) and cut off ISOs' purchase of imported parts. A group of ISOs sued Xerox, claiming that its refusal to sell or license patented parts, manuals, and copyrighted software violated antitrust laws. Xerox counterclaimed that the ISOs infringed patents covering Xerox's machines' parts and copyrights in Xerox's service drawings. The district court dismissed the ISOs' claims, holding that there is no prohibition from lawfully using a patent to acquire a monopoly in more than one relevant antitrust market and that the IP right holder's intent in refusing to deal is irrelevant to antitrust laws.[131] The DC Circuit reasoned that though IP rights are not immune from antitrust scrutiny, they 'do not negate the patentee's right to exclude others from patented property'.[132] It affirmed the district court finding that Xerox's subjective motivation in refusing to

---

[126] 'By far the most common allegations relating to IP concern the allegedly improper acquisition or enforcement of an IP right, which act is commonly claimed to be in furtherance of monopolization or attempted monopolization.' 1 HOVENKAMP ET AL., *supra* note 1, ¶11.1.

[127] *See, e.g.*, See 1 HOVENKAMP ET AL., *supra* note 1, ¶¶13.3c2, 13.3d4; Abbott Lipsky & J. Gregory Sidak, *Esssential Facilities*, 51 STAN L. REV. 1187, 1218–19 (1999); Paul D. Marquard & Mark Leddy, *The Essential Facilities Doctrine and Intellectual Property Rights: A Response to Pitofsky, Patterson and Hooks*, 70 ANTITRUST L. J. 847, 859–63 (2003); Einer Elhauge, *Defining Better Monopolization Standards*, 56 STAN L. REV. 253, 300–5 (2003).

[128] *See, e.g.*, Ian Ayres & Paul Klemperer, *Limiting Patentee's Market Power Without Reducing Innovation Incentives: The Perverse Benefits of Uncertainty and Non-Injunctive Remedies*, 97 MICH. L. REV. 985 (1999); Robert Pitofsky, Donna Patterson & Jonathan Hooks, *The Essential Facilities Doctrine Under U.S. Antitrust Law*, 70 ANTITRUST L. J. 443, 452–4 (2003).

[129] 1 HOVENKAMP ET AL., *supra* note 1, ¶12.3d1.

[130] *In re Independent Serv. Orgs. Antitrust Litig.*, 203 F.3d 1322 (Fed. Cir. 2000).

[131] *In re Independent Serv. Orgs. Antitrust Litig.*, *989* F. Supp. 1131 (D. Kan. 1997).

[132] *In re Independent Serv. Orgs. Antitrust Litig.*, 203 F.3d at 1325.

license its patented technologies was irrelevant for the purpose of assessing its conduct under Section 2, concluding that:

> [i]n the absence of any indication of illegal tying, fraud in the Patent and Trademark Office, or sham litigation, the patent holder may enforce the statutory right to exclude others from making, using, or selling the claimed invention free from liability under the antitrust laws.[133]

Unless tying is involved, *Xerox* essentially excludes the possibility that a unilateral refusal to license a valid IP right can be a Section 2 violation.

Other Circuit Courts which dealt with similar cases adopted a strong but rebuttable presumption that a refusal to license is legal. Just like *Xerox*, *Data Gen. Corp. v. Grumman Systems Support Corp.*[134] involved a refusal to provide ISOs with access to protected technologies necessary to do business in the aftermarket. In particular, Data General stopped supplying its copyrighted diagnostic software to ISOs repairing Data General's computer hardware with the aim to increase its sales in the aftermarket. ISOs used the software without permission and Data General sued for copyright infringement. The ISOs counterclaimed that cutting off the supply of software violated Section 2 of the Sherman Act. Unlike the DC Circuit, the First Circuit refused to immunize unconditional unilateral refusals to license from antitrust scrutiny.[135] The First Circuit reasoned that, though neither antitrust nor IP should be given primacy one over the other, 'an author's desire to exclude others from use of its copyrighted work is a presumptively valid business justification for any immediate harm to consumers.'[136] The plaintiffs relied on *Aspen*, contending that Data General's new licensing policies constituted an illegal termination of supply by a monopolist.[137] The Court held that *Aspen* did not apply because there was no competitive market prior to Data General's refusal to license its diagnostic software. Plaintiffs were also unsuccessful in rebutting the legality presumption with any other evidence, such as that the copyright protecting the requested technology was invalid.[138]

The Ninth Circuit took a somewhat different route in *Kodak*.[139] This case, like the other two cases discussed above, concerned a refusal to supply patented spare parts to ISOs. Kodak, however, claimed that its refusal to deal was justified by IP only towards the end of the litigation. The Ninth Circuit,

---

133 *Id.* at 1327.

134 *Data Gen. Corp. v. Grumman Sys. Support Corp.*, 36 F.3d 1147 (1st Cir. 1994).

135 *Id.* at 1184–7.

136 *Id.* at 1187.

137 *Id.* at 1188.

138 *Id.* at 1188–9.

139 *Image Tech. Serv. v. Eastman Kodak Co.*, 125 F.3d 1195 (9th Cir. 1997).

referring to *Data General*, held that 'while exclusionary conduct can include a monopolist's unilateral refusal to license a [patent or] copyright', or to sell its patented or copyrighted work, a monopolist's 'desire to exclude others from its [protected] work is a presumptively valid business justification for any immediate harm to consumers'.[140] Unlike the First Circuit, however, the Ninth Circuit reasoned that the evidence of a pretext could rebut the presumption. Ultimately, the Court found that the presumption did not apply and upheld the jury's finding that Kodak's refusal to supply ISOs violated §2 of the Sherman Act. Notably, the Ninth Circuit, just like the DC Circuit, drew parallels from cases where enforcement of an IP right was condemned as an antitrust violation. Indeed, the Ninth Circuit's discussion of a pretext can be explained in the context of 'sham' litigation to enforce IP rights, which, unlike a valid enforcement action, is not immune from antitrust scrutiny. This issue is discussed in more detail in Chapter 3 below.

Although the proposition that an IP right may constitute an essential facility has not been entirely ruled out,[141] US courts have been highly skeptical about applying the essential facilities doctrine to IP. The essential facilities theory failed, for example, in the *Intel v. Intergraph* case.[142] In this case, Intel cut off the supply of microprocessors and proprietary information to Intergraph, one of its customers, as the retaliatory measure for the latter's attempt to enforce its IP rights against Intel and its other customers. Intergraph claimed, among other things, that Intel's chips and technical knowledge were so vital for its interests that they constituted an essential facility and that they should be licensed on reasonable and non-discriminatory terms. The District Court agreed and granted a preliminary injunction that obliged Intel to supply Intergraph with the relevant Intel product information and microprocessors.[143]

The DC Circuit reversed the decision. In the Court's view the essential facilities doctrine can be applied only if there is a competitive relationship between the company controlling the facility and the company requesting the access.[144] Since Intel did not compete with Intergraph in the downstream market for workstations, the essential facilities doctrine did not apply. The

---

140 *Id.* at 1218.

141 *Bell South Adver. & Publ'g Corp. v. Donnelly Info Publ'g Inc*, 719 F. Supp. 1551, 1566 (S.D. Fla. 1988), *rev'd on other grounds*, 999 F.2d 1436 (11th Cir. 1993) is cited as a case suggesting that information and other intangibles could constitute essential facilities. *See* HOVENKAMP ET AL., *supra* note 1, ¶13.3c2; James B. Kobak, Jr., *Intellectual Property, Refusals to Deal and the U.S. Antitrust Laws*, 832 PLI/P at 385.

142 *Intergraph Corp. v. Intel. Corp.*, 195 F.3d 1346 (Fed. Cir. 1999).

143 *Intergraph Corp. v. Intel Corp.*, 3 F. Supp. 2d 1255 (N.D. Ala. 1998).

144 *Intergraph Corp. v. Intel. Corp.*, 195 F.3d 1346, 1357 (Fed. Cir. 1999). The Court's reasoning suggested, however, that the essential facilities doctrine could be applied to IPRs.

Court was also skeptical about the claim that the refusal to supply proprietary information was anticompetitive. Even though Intel's withholding proprietary information lacked business justification, it was unclear whether it contributed to creating, maintaining or enlarging Intel's dominance.[145] The Court squarely rejected the leveraging theory, again on the ground that no harm to competition in the downstream market was established.[146]

Interestingly, the government also challenged Intel's conduct, but on different grounds and with more success. The Federal Trade Commission (FTC) alleged that Intel maintained its monopoly power by denying or threatening to deny technical information about Intel microprocessors to Intel customers who have developed and patented innovations in microprocessor technology, as a means of coercing these customers into granting royalty-free licenses for their innovations to Intel.[147] The FTC alleged a pattern of conduct that helped Intel to maintain its monopoly by discouraging leapfrogging innovations.[148] The case ended with a consent decree obliging Intel not to cease dealing with companies merely because they enforced their IP rights. The essential facilities doctrine was not invoked. The FTC stressed that the remedy imposed was not compulsory licensing,[149] and that Intel was entitled to withhold its IP from rivals planning to compete directly with Intel's monopoly product.[150]

---

[145] *Id.* at 1358–9.

[146] *Id.* at 1359–60.

[147] *See* FTC Complaint, *In re Intel Corp.*, No 9288, ¶11 (filed 8 June 1998), *at* http://www.ftc.gov/os/1998/06/intelcmp.pdf. The FTC alleged in particular that when Digital Equipment Corporation, Intergraph Corporation and Compaq Computer Corporation, companies that hold important patents on microprocessor and related technologies, sought to enforce those patents against Intel or other computer companies who buy Intel products, Intel retaliated by cutting off the necessary technical information and threatening to cut off the supply of microprocessors. For a comment on Intel's case see 1 HOVENKAMP ET AL., *supra* note 1, ¶13.4d; Maureen A. O'Rourke, *Striking a Delicate Balance: Intellectual Property, Antitrust, Contract, and Standardization in the Computer Industry*, 12 HARV. J. L. & TECH. 1, 11–23 (1998).

[148] *See* 1 HOVENKAMP ET AL., *supra* note 1, ¶13.4d.

[149] The FTC stated that '[t]he Proposed Order does not impose any kind of broad "compulsory licensing" regime upon Intel. So long as it is otherwise lawful, Intel is free to decide in the first instance whether it chooses to provide or not provide information to customers, and whether to provide more information or earlier information to specific customers in furtherance of a joint venture or other legitimate activity. Moreover, the Order is limited to the types of information that Intel routinely gives to customers to enable them to use Intel microprocessors, not information that would be used to design or manufacture microprocessors in competition with Intel.' *See* FTC, *Analysis of Proposed Consent Order to Aid Public Comment*, http://www.ftc.gov/os/1999/03/d09288intelanalysis.htm.

[150] In an earlier case, the FTC explicitly recognized that a refusal to license IPRs providing a competitive advantage to direct competitors could not, as such, violate

An attempt to apply the essential facilities doctrine to IP was also rebuffed in *Aldridge*.[151] Aldridge was a seller of a disk cache computer program. Microsoft effectively preempted its market by including such a program in its new version of Windows (Windows 95). In addition, when Microsoft's operating system detected Aldridge's software, it displayed a series of message alerts, warning that Aldridge's software decreased system performance and advising that it should be removed. Aldridge argued that Windows was an essential facility and that Microsoft's behavior excluded it from the market. The court refused to apply essential facility doctrine, reasoning that the disk cache program relied upon an imperfection in Microsoft's software design and its sole purpose was to overcome these imperfections and improve system performance. Windows was essential to Aldridge only to the extent that it operated less efficiently. Microsoft should not be punished for improving its own product since 'antitrust laws do not require a competitor to maintain archaic or outdated technology; even monopolists may improve their products'.[152]

The scope for antitrust intervention in cases involving unconditional, unilateral refusals to license has been further limited by the Supreme Court's *Trinko* decision discussed in Chapter 1 above. For example, in *NYMEX*,[153] a case decided after *Trinko*, the trial court followed the Supreme Court's narrow reading of the exceptions to the principle that a refusal to deal is legal. The case involved a dispute between New York Mercantile Exchange (NYMEX), the world's largest exchange for the trading of physical commodity futures contracts and options, and a small competitor, the Intercontinental Exchange (ICE), which developed an Internet-based exchange. NYMEX acts as a clearinghouse for all the commodity futures contracts and options traded over its exchange and its settlement prices serve as the market prices for the underlying commodities. NYMEX is statutorily obliged to report its settlement prices, among other data, to the public. It makes them available on an almost instantaneous basis by reporting them on its website and by distributing them to subscribers. The real-time data was made available to subscribers subject to the condition that it could not be used in competition with NYMEX. ICE entered the market for executing the trades and was effectively forced to rely on NYMEX's settlement prices. NYMEX, allegedly to eliminate competition from ICE in the electronic trading market, sued ICE for violating NYMEX's

---

antitrust laws (*In the Matter of E.I. Du Pont de Nemours & Co.*, 96 F.T.C. 653, 206–7 (20 Oct. 1980)).

151 *David L. Aldridge Co. v. Microsoft Corp.*, 995 F. Supp. 728 (S.D. Tex. 1998).

152 *Id.* at 753.

153 *New York Mercantile Exch. v. Intercontinental Exch.*, 323 F. Supp. 2d 559 (S.D.N.Y. 2004).

copyright in the settlement prices. ICE counterclaimed that NYMEX's refusal to supply the data constituted a violation of §2 of the Sherman Act.

Relying on *Trinko*, the trial court found that the facts did not come within the *Aspen* exception or within the essential facilities doctrine. The essential facilities doctrine did not apply because ICE had some access to the data and because the scope of access was subject to sectoral regulation. The *Aspen* exception was unavailable because ICE and NYMEX had no history of previous dealings. Thus, there was no indication that NYMEX was foregoing short-term profits by refusing to cooperate with ICE. The Court held that NYMEX has a legitimate business interest in preventing ICE from free riding on its settlement prices.[154] Though competitive concerns posed by this case were not addressed by application of antitrust rules, the NYMEX court found the remedy in copyright law.[155] It dismissed NYMEX's claim for copyright infringement and related IP claims. The settlement prices were non-copyrightable words or short phrases. Moreover, the merger doctrine precluded copyright protection for the settlement prices, as NYMEX's idea of settlement price and fact of settlement price used by market participants could not be distinguished from its expression.[156]

The NYMEX case and the recent pronouncements of the US antitrust enforcers together make it clear that dominant companies are in principle free to rely on their valid IP rights to exclude rivals from neighboring markets. In the 2007 report on IP and antitrust intersection, the US antitrust enforcers state authoritatively:

> Antitrust liability for mere unilateral, unconditional refusals to license patents will not play a meaningful part in the interface between patent rights and antitrust protections. Antitrust liability for refusals to license competitors would compel firms to reach out, and affirmatively assist their rivals, a result that is in some tension with the underlying purpose of antitrust law. Moreover, liability would restrict the patent holder's ability to exercise a core part of the patent – the right to exclude.[157]

The last sentence encapsulates the basic principle that the US antitrust law is not applied in a manner that could interfere with other regulatory measures.

---

[154] For comment on the *NYMEX* case, see Eleanor M. Fox, *A Tale of Two Jurisdictions and an Orphan Case: Antitrust, Intellectual Property, and Refusals to Deal*, 28 FORDHAM INT'L L. J. 952, 959–61 (2005)

[155] *New York Mercantile Exch., Inc. v. Intercontinental Exch,, Inc.*, 389 F.Supp.2d 527 (S.D.N.Y. 2005).

[156] *Id.* at 541–3.

[157] U.S. Department of Justice & the Federal Trade Commission, *Antitrust Enforcement and Intellectual Property Rights: Promoting Innovation and Competition*, April 2007, available at: http://www.ftc.gov/opa/2007/04/ipreport.shtm.

US antitrust enforcers take the position that anticompetitive concerns resulting from patent policy are best remedied by changes in the patent laws. For example, the *NYMEX* decision addresses competitive concerns posed by NYMEX's refusal to provide pricing information by appropriate interpretation of copyright laws.

Along the same lines, in the Report 'To Promote Innovation: the Proper Balance of Competition and Patent Policy',[158] the FTC revealed its deep concerns relating to the quality of the patents issued by the PTO and the functioning of the patent system. The Report discusses the negative effects that questionable patents have on competition. They deter market entry by imposing additional costs[159] and may be difficult to eliminate because in many cases the cost of obtaining a license is much smaller than the cost of patent litigation. In industries with incremental innovation, such as the software industry, unwarranted patents contribute to defensive patenting and dramatic increases in transaction costs. The Report provides apt evidence of 'patent stacking' and 'patent thickets' in certain industries.[160] Uncertainty as to the validity of patents issued by the PTO and their scope aggravates the situation.[161]

Still, the FTC declared that antitrust policy is not an appropriate remedy for these concerns. It warned of overeager enforcement of antitrust laws, stressing that identifying anticompetitive conduct involving IP requires thorough understanding of the efficiencies that businesses might legitimately realize through particular types of patent-related conduct as well as the role of patents in innovation and competition in particular industries.[162] Instead of applying the

---

[158] Federal Trade Commission, *To Promote Innovation: The Proper Balance of Competition Law and Patent Policy* (Oct. 2003), Ch. 2, http://www.ftc.gov/opa/2003/10/cpreport.htm.

[159] *Id.* Chapter 5. Unwarranted patents create legal uncertainty which gives rise to difficulties in business planning and raising capital, increases investment risk and disrupts license negotiations.

[160] This is in particular an important issue in the computer hardware industry. Patent proliferation and defensive patenting gave rise to patent thickets that are harmful for innovation by diverting the R&D money to obtaining and maintaining defensive patent portfolios and negotiating licenses from numerous patent holders. Defensive patenting was also considered to accelerate in the software industry, and panelists explained that it was used to maintain détente with rivals, to obtain the necessary patent portfolio in order to enter into cross-licensing agreements, and as a shield in case of an infringement suit by a rival. *See* Federal Trade Commission (2003), *To Promote Innovation: The Proper Balance of Competition and Patent Law and Policy* (hereinafter 'FTC Report'), available at http://www.ftc.gov/os/2003/10/innovationrpt.pdf, Chapter 3; Hall & Ziedonis, *supra* note 27.

[161] FTC Report, *supra* note 160, Chapter 5.

[162] FTC Report, *supra* note 160, Chapter 1.

antitrust rules to solve the identified problems, the FTC made several recommendations for changes in the patent laws which could improve patent quality and minimize the anticompetitive costs of the patent system.

3. LICENSING AND THE APPROACH TO VERTICAL RESTRAINTS

A crucial element that determines the scope of an IP holder right is the ability to determine the terms under which the IP is licensed and the price at which the IP and products embodying the IP are sold. An IP holder enjoying some degree of market power can typically dictate prices and impose terms under which his IP is exploited or products embodying the IP are distributed. The ability to set the price and the conditions of sale are also important from the perspective of analyzing refusals to deal, as the latter may be a way to force the licensees to accept the conditions specified by the manufacturer.

Following the reform of antitrust enforcement in the EU and the publication of the Technology Transfer Block Exemption Regulation (TTBER)[163] and the Technology Transfer Guidelines[164] in 2004, the assessment of restraints in licensing agreements in the EU has been closer to the approach taken by the US antitrust enforcers. Still, over the past few years, the US position has been further liberalized and following the recent US Supreme Court decision in *Leegin*[165] essentially all vertical restraints, including resale price maintenance, are assessed in the US under the rule of reason. By contrast, the European Commission continues to view price restraints in licensing and distribution agreements with suspicion and there is no indication that its position is likely to change in the immediate future. Resale price maintenance in vertical licensing agreements and distribution agreements is nearly always an Article 81 violation. This approach may be linked with the Commission's reluctance to recognize the general principle that an IP holder should be free to unilaterally set the terms under which she licenses her IP rights or sells products embodying that IP.

---

163 Commission Regulation 772/2004 on the application of Article 81(3) of the Treaty to categories of technology transfer agreements, 2004 O.J. (L 123) 11.

164 Commission Notice – Guidelines on the application of Article 81 of the EC Treaty to technology transfer agreements, 2004 O.J. (C 101) 2.

165 *Bement v. National Harrow Co.*, 186 U.S. 70, 93 (1902) and *Leegin Creative Leather Prods. v. PSKS, Inc.*, 127 S. Ct. 2705 (2007).

3.1 The United States: the Rule of Reason for Vertical Restraints

Assessment of IP licensing agreements under US antitrust laws evolved over time. Back in the early 1970s, the US antitrust enforcers considered a number of licensing practices to be *per se* illegal without regard to economic effect. The list of prohibited licensing practices, known as the Nine No-No's,[166] comprised charging royalties not reasonably related to sales of the patented product, restraints on the licensee's commerce outside the scope of the patent (tie-outs), tying of unpatented supplies, mandatory package licensing, exclusive grant-backs, licensee's veto power over grants of further licenses, restraints on the sale of unpatented products made with a patented process, resale price maintenance and post-sale restraints on resale. These restrictions appear to have been largely based on the theory that an IP owner's reward should be strictly limited to what is contemplated by the patent system.

The Nine No-No's were abandoned in the late 1970s, when a more economics-based and flexible approach to IP licensing became prevalent. Since then the list of outright prohibited licensing practices has been shrinking. The current views of antitrust enforcers on IP licensing are summarized in the DOJ and FTC's Antitrust Guidelines for the Licensing of Intellectual Property (the 'IP Licensing Guidelines'). The Guidelines recognize IP licensing as generally welfare-enhancing and pro-competitive.[167] Most restrictions in IP licensing agreements are assessed under the rule of reason. They are allowed as long as they do not inhibit competition that would have been present but for the license. Application of the *per se* rule in the context of licensing restraints is limited to the types of restraints that are ordinarily accorded *per se* treatment that cannot be expected to 'contribute to an efficiency-enhancing integration of economic activity'.[168] With respect to tying,

---

[166] *Remarks by Bruce B. Wilson, Deputy Assistant Attorney General, Antitrust Division, before the Michigan State Bar Antitrust Law Section*, 21 September 1972, CCH Trade Reg. Rep. 50,146. For an economic assessment of the 'Nine No-No's' and the history of the IP and antitrust intersection *see, e.g.*, Richard Gilbert & Carl Shapiro, *Antitrust Issues in the Licensing of Intellectual Property: The Nine No-No's Meet the Nineties*, BROOKINGS PAPERS ON ECONOMIC ACTIVITY. MICROECONOMICS, Vol. 1997 (1997), 283–349, and ABA SECTION OF ANTITRUST LAW, THE FEDERAL ANTITRUST GUIDELINES FOR THE LICENSING OF INTELLECTUAL PROPERTY. ORIGINS AND APPLICATIONS 9 (2nd edn, 2002).

[167] *IP Licensing Guidelines*, ¶¶2.3 and 3.1; *see also Remarks by Mary L. Azcuenaga, Commissioner, Federal Trade Commission, before the American Law Institute–American Bar Association*, 26 January 1995, at: http://www.ftc.gov/speeches/azcuenaga/ali-aba.htm, and *Remarks by Makan Delrahim, Deputy Assistant Attorney General, Antitrust Division, The George Mason Law Review Symposium*, 6 October 2004, at: http://www.usdoj.gov/atr/public/speeches/205712.htm#N_13_ .

[168] *IP Licensing Guidelines*, ¶3.4.

the Guidelines note that in the context of licensing agreements such arrangements may 'result in significant efficiencies and procompetitive benefits' and that, '[i]n the exercise of their prosecutorial discretion, the Agencies will consider both the anticompetitive effects and the efficiencies attributable to a tie-in.'[169] Licensors are generally free to decide what royalties to charge, how to structure their royalties arrangements, and what limitations to impose on the field of use in which the licensee may apply the IP, the customers with which they can deal, and the territories in which they can sell. Territorial restrictions in trade secrets licenses are also considered valid,[170] as long as they do not amount to naked market division among competitors.[171] Grant-backs are assessed under the rule of reason;[172] non-exclusive grant-backs are deemed pro-competitive.[173]

Restrictions on price in licensing agreements are also assessed under the rule of reason. In *General Electric*, the Supreme Court held that a patentee should have the right to determine the price at which its licensee sells products manufactured using a patented process, because the patentee is entitled 'to acquire profit by the price at which the article is sold' and the licensee's pricing affects the patentee's profits.[174] The *General Electric* case involved a license agreement between direct horizontal competitors and was criticized as overly broad. The judgment has never been overruled, but it has been narrowed to exclude outright cartels.[175]

The Guidelines acknowledge antitrust concerns that may arise in the context of IP licensing. License restrictions that are a sham to cover a market allocation or price-fixing arrangement are *per se* unlawful.[176] Horizontal restraints are subject to a greater antitrust scrutiny, as there is a fear that they may lead to cartel-like arrangements.[177] In particular, patent pools and cross-

169 *IP Licensing Guidelines*, ¶5.3.

170 The Supreme Court confirmed the legality of territorial restrictions in *Dr. Miles*. *See also Shin Nippon Koki Co., Ltd. v. Irvin Industries, Inc.*, Not Reported in N.Y.S.2d, 1975 WL 15505 (territorial restrictions are valid as long as they reasonably related to licenses of know-how) and *IP Licensing Guidelines*, ¶¶2.3. and 5.1.

171 *See* 2 HOVENKAMP ET AL., *supra* note 1, ¶33.3.

172 *Transparent-Wrap Mach. Corp. v. Stokes & Smith Co.*, 329 U.S. 637, 645–6 (1947).

173 *See Shin Nippon Koki Co.* and *Santa Fe-Pomeroy, Inc. v. P & Z Co.*, 569 F.2d 1084, 1101–2 (9th Cir. 1978). *See also* 1 HOVENKAMP ET AL., *supra* note 1, ¶¶25.1–25.4 (2002) and 2 WILLIAM C. HOLMES, INTELLECTUAL PROPERTY AND ANTITRUST LAW, §29.3 (1983).

174 *United States v. General Elec. Co.*, 272 U.S. at 490.

175 *See, e.g., United States v. New Wrinkle, Inc.*, 342 U.S. 371 (1952).

176 *See, e.g., In re Cardizem CD Antitrust Litig.*, 105 F.Supp.2d 682, 707 (E.D. Mich. 2000).

177 In applying the rule of reason to horizontal license arrangements, the agencies consider whether the restraints increase the risk of price coordination, output restric-

licenses may give rise to serious competitive concerns, for example when two or more patentees-manufacturers use such arrangements to limit their output or fix prices.[178] Tying arrangements, package licensing, and exclusive dealing give rise to antitrust liability in limited circumstances.[179]

Though the patentee is allowed to fix prices at which the licensees can sell products manufactured under the license, until recently his right to decide on the pricing after the first sale of a patented product was limited. Provisions setting minimum resale prices were held to be unlawful in the 1911 Supreme Court decision in *Dr. Miles*.[180] Dr. Miles was a manufacturer of branded medicines prepared using secret methods and formulas. The company entered into consignment contracts with wholesalers and retailers for the distribution of its medicines. The consignees could only sell to retailers specified by the proprietor and retailers could only sell to consumers. Both consignees and retailers could only sell at a price specified by the proprietor. The company designed a system of tracking its products and sued discounters to ensure the minimum price maintenance.

In the case that ended before the Supreme Court, Dr. Miles sued John D. Park & Co., a drug wholesaler, which had refused to enter into a consignment agreement and instead procured Dr. Miles' medicines from Dr. Miles' distributors and sold them at discounted prices to department stores. According to Dr. Miles, this practice tarnished its brand image and discouraged its distributors from selling and promoting its medicines. Both the district court and the circuit court dismissed Dr. Miles' complaint, holding that the resale price maintenance contracts, the breach of which was allegedly induced, were illegal under the Sherman Act. The circuit court reasoned that the 'scheme is one to enhance or maintain prices by eliminating all possibility of competing rates between either jobbers or retailers'.[181] It also firmly rejected the argument that the 'secret process' by which Dr. Miles' medicine was manufactured gave it an additional interest entitling it to specify the resale price.[182]

---

tion, or the creation of market power. IP Licensing Guidelines, ¶¶3.3 and 5.1; *see also* 2 HOVENKAMP ET AL., *supra* note 1, ¶¶30.1.–30.5.

[178] *See, e.g., Hartford-Empire Co. v. United States,* 323 U.S. 386 (1945) and *American Equipment Co. v. Tuthill Bldg. Material Co.*, 69 F.2d 406 (7th Cir. 1934). *See also* 2 HOVENKAMP ET AL., *supra* note 1, ¶¶32.1–32.3 and 34.3–34.4 (discussing anti-competitive and pro-competitive effects of patent pools and cross-licensing).

[179] *IP Licensing Guidelines*, ¶¶5.3–5.4. Tying may be *per se* illegal if the party imposing the tie has market power to appreciably restrict competition in the market for the tied product and more than an insubstantial amount of trade in the tied product is affected by the tie. *See also* 1 HOVENKAMP ET AL., *supra* note 1, ¶¶24.3b2–24.4.

[180] *Dr. Miles Medical Co. v. John D. Park & Sons Co.*, 220 U.S. 373 (1911).

[181] *Dr. Miles Medical Co. v. John D. Park & Sons Co.*, 164 F. 803, 804 (6th Cir. 1908)

[182] *Id.* at 806–7.

The Supreme Court affirmed the circuit court decision. It recognized that 'a secret process may be the subject of confidential communication and of sale or license with restrictions as to territory and prices',[183] but rejected the suggestion that goods manufactured using a secret process should be exempted from rules against unlawful restraints of trade.[184] In addressing the interface between IP (the right to protect a secret medicine formula) and antitrust, the court focused on the scope of IP rights, reasoning that assuming that the owner of the secret formula had a 'monopoly of production', it does not entail 'the right to control the entire trade of the produced article and to prevent any competition that otherwise might arise between wholesale and retail dealers'.[185] Thus resale price maintenance is illegal when 'commodities have passed into the channels of trade and are owned by dealers'.[186]

Over the years, the *Dr. Miles* ruling evolved into a *per se* rule against minimum resale price maintenance or fixing retail prices, applicable whether or not a good was produced by a secret process, and whether or not it was patented, copyrighted, or trademarked.[187]

The *per se* prohibition against resale price maintenance has been subject to increased criticism in the United States since the 1960s, when Chicago School thinkers questioned its economic rationale.[188] More generally, the views on vertical restraints and vertical integration began to shift and by the end of the 1970s the consensus among economists was that vertical integration is highly efficient and beneficial to consumers.[189] Changes in the economic doctrine influenced the jurisprudence. In its ground-breaking *Sylvania* ruling,[190] the Supreme Court drew a distinction between vertical and horizontal restraints, noting that that '[t]he market impact of vertical restrictions is complex because of their potential for simultaneous reduction of intrabrand competition and stimulation of interbrand competition.'[191] The Court reasoned that vertical restraints might be an effective way to promote a particular brand and concluded that non-price vertical restraints should be assessed under the rule

---

[183] *Dr. Miles Medical Co. v. John D. Park & Sons Co.*, 220 U.S. at 402.

[184] *Id.* at 403.

[185] *Id.*

[186] *Id.* at 408.

[187] *See* HOVENKAMP ET AL., *supra* note 1, ¶24.2b.

[188] *See, e.g.*, Robert H. Bork, *The Rule of Reason and the Per Se Concept: Price Fixing and Market Division*, 75 YALE L. J. 373, 405–10 (1966). For an insightful overview of the debate on resale price maintenance see Barak Y. Orbach, *Antitrust Vertical Myopia*, 50 ARIZONA L. Rev. 261 (2008).

[189] *See, e.g.*, Benjamin Klein et al., *Vertical Integration, Appropriable Rents, and the Competitive Contracting process*, 21 J. L. & ECON. 326 (1978).

[190] *Continental TV, Inc. v. GTE Sylvania, Inc.*, 433 U.S. 36 (1977).

[191] *Id.* at 51–2 (footnotes omitted).

of reason. That decision largely brought an end to antitrust condemnation of non-price vertical restraints.

By contrast, the *per se* prohibition against resale price maintenance lasted far longer, even though the economic rationales for price and non-price vertical restraints are roughly similar. Resale price maintenance, like territorial protection, is chiefly used to guarantee dealer margins, and thus may encourage dealers to provide better service and to promote products. In-store services, delivery, repair, advertising, and other promotional activities enhance the value of certain goods, but are costly to the retailers. If discounters are free to offer the product cheaply and prices drop below a certain level, dealers may not be willing to provide the services the manufacturer desires or may drop the product altogether.[192] There are additional reasons that may justify resale price maintenance. For example, customers may prefer to pay full prices for luxury goods, because they ensure exclusivity which is an essential part of the products' appeal.[193] To be sure, resale price maintenance may also be anticompetitive and harmful for consumers. In particular, it has been pointed out that it may serve as a means to facilitate a retailers or manufacturers' cartel. For example, powerful retailers may force a manufacturer to restrain resale price. Further, it may eliminate manufacturers' incentives to cut prices to retailers or be used by manufacturers as a means to exclude competitors from the market.[194] In any case, most US commentators agree that is insufficient economic justification for the *per se* rule against minimum resale price maintenance and that all vertical price restraints should be assessed under the rule of reason.[195]

The scope of the *per se* rule against vertical price restraints was gradually reduced in a series of Supreme Court rulings in the 1980s and 1990s. In *State Oil v. Khan*,[196] the Court held that vertical agreements to fix maximum resale prices were not *per se* unlawful and courts have also consistently permitted manufacturers to provide suggested price lists to dealers and to print such prices on the product or price tags.[197] Another important limitation on the *per se* rule against vertical price fixing was the *Colgate* doctrine, which essentially

---

[192] *See id.* at 271–4 and AREEDA & HOVENKAMP, *supra* note 62, ¶1620.

[193] *See* Orbach, *supra* note 188, at 277–80.

[194] For a detailed description of these theories *see* Orbach, *supra* note 188, at 268–71.

[195] See *e.g.*, AREEDA & HOVENKAMP, *supra* note 62, ¶1620, Orbach, *supra* note 188.

[196] 522 U.S. 3 (1997).

[197] *See, e.g.*, *United States v. Parke, Davis & Co.*, 362 U.S. 29, 44 (1960), *Isaksen v. Vermont Castings*, 825 F.2d 1158, 1162–4 (7th Cir. 1987), *In re Nissan Antitrust Ligation*, 577 F.2d 910, 916 (5th Cir. 1978); *Mesirow v. Pepperidge Farm*, 703 F.2d 339, 344 (9th Cir. 1983).

allows manufacturers to announce a pricing policy unilaterally and refuse to do business with distributors that do not adhere to its pricing policy.[198] Further, in *Business Electronics v. Sharp Electronics*,[199] the Supreme Court held that an agreement between manufacturer and a distributor to terminate another distributor because of the latter's pricing practices was outside the scope of the *per se* rule against vertical price restraints, as long as it did not cover any understanding as to the price or price levels to be charged by the remaining distributors. Many manufacturers relied on *Colgate* and *Sharp* to engage in resale price maintenance; the difficulty was drawing a distinction between legal unilateral conduct and a *per se* illegal vertical price fixing agreement.[200]

The *per se* prohibition against vertical price maintenance came under increased criticism in the 1990s and 2000s. Finally, the Supreme Court overruled *Dr. Miles* in its 2007 *Leegin* decision.[201] Leegin, a manufacturer of high-end clothing, instituted a retail pricing and promotion policy and refused to sell to retailers that discounted its goods below suggested prices. This policy was challenged as an antitrust violation and when Leegin attempted to introduce expert testimony describing the pro-competitive effects of its pricing policy, the district court excluded the testimony, relying on the *per se* rule against vertical price fixing. Following an unsuccessful appeal by *Leegin*, the Supreme Court granted *certiorari* and held that vertical price restraints should be assessed under the rule of reason. The Court reasoned that such restrictions do not have 'manifestly anticompetitive' effects that justify the *per se* prohibition.[202] It embraced the view that vertical price restraints are often pro-competitive and that the primary purpose of the antitrust laws should be to protect inter-brand competition.[203] Though there is still some uncertainty about the consequences of the *Leegin* judgment and some state antitrust laws still treat vertical price maintenance as *per se* illegal, it is clear that the US federal courts and the enforcement agencies will generally apply the rule of reason to vertical price restraints. This creates another significant divergence between the US and EU antitrust laws. As explained below, though the EU antitrust enforcers significantly liberalized the rules relating to vertical restraints, there is still a firm presumption that both fixing resale prices and fixing prices of products manufactured under a license are anticompetitive.

---

[198] *See United States v. Colgate & Co.*, 250 U.S. 300, 307 (1919) and *Monsanto Co. v. Spray-Rite Svc. Corp.*, 465 U.S. 752, 761 (1984).

[199] 485 U.S. 717 (1988).

[200] *See* Orbach, *supra* note 188, at 279.

[201] *Leegin Creative Leather Prods. v. PSKS, Inc.*, 127 S. Ct. 2705 (2007).

[202] *Leegin*, 127 S. Ct. at 2720.

[203] *Id.*

3.2 The EU: Curbing the No-No's

The assessment of IP licensing agreements under EU competition rules evolved over time, corresponding to the changes in the assessment of vertical restraints. Since the late 1990s, the Commission has striven to model EU competition policy on modern economic thought. This has led to a revolution in the assessment of vertical restraints, which, as an impediment to the creation of the single European market, were the focus of the Commission's enforcement efforts in the past.[204] To ensure greater flexibility, the Commission also relinquished its monopoly to apply Article 81(3), which allowed for greater flexibility in the application of competition rules.[205] These changes were of tremendous significance for the analysis of IP licenses. The Commission gradually recognized that they are generally pro-competitive and liberalized the competition rules applicable to such agreements.

The first block exemption related to IP licensing, the 1984 patent licensing block exemption,[206] was essentially limited to patent licenses and covered only agreements between two parties.[207] Other types of restrictive licensing arrangements had to be individually cleared with the European Commission or else were invalid. Like other block exemptions adopted by the Commission in the 1980s, the patent licensing block exemption concentrated on the form of the agreement rather than its effect on the market. It applied without regard to market shares or sales and contained a list of clauses that generally do not violate Article 81(1) but the legality of which is confirmed by the block exemption ('white clauses') and a list of clauses that do violate Article 81(1) and the inclusion of which would bring the entire agreement outside the scope of the block exemption ('black clauses'). The white clauses were essentially limited to territory allocation and limited export bans on licensor and

[204] *See* European Commission, *Green Paper on Vertical Restraints in EC Competition Policy*, COM (96) 721 final (1997) and *Follow-up to the Green Paper on Vertical Restraints*, COM (98) 544 final (1998).

[205] Until the entry into force of the Council Regulation 1/2003 on the implementation of the rules on competition laid down in Articles 81 and 82 of the Treaty, 2003 O.J. (C1) 1, to obtain the benefit of an Article 81(3) exemption, a company had to notify the relevant agreement to the Commission or fall within one of the block exemption regulations that specified terms on which agreements were treated as satisfying Article 81(3).

[206] Commission Regulation 2349/84 of 23 July 1984 on the application of Article 85 (3) of the Treaty to certain categories of patent licensing agreements, 1984 O.J. (L 219) 15.

[207] The exemption covered pure patent licenses, mixed patent and know-how licenses (it would not apply to such agreements after the patent's expiry), technology package licenses as long as other IP rights included in the package were 'ancillary' to the licensed patent. Cross-licenses and patent pools were not covered.

licensees, but not on purchasers from the licensor or licensees.[208] The list of black prohibited clauses mirrored the Nine No-No's.

The combined effect of the strictness of the regulation and the fact that the agreements that did not fall within the block exemption had to be notified to the Commission had a negative impact on the legal certainty of IP licensing. Recognizing the need to change these rules to facilitate technology transfers,[209] in 1996 the Commission adopted the Technology Transfer Block Exemption Regulation (TTBER).[210] The TTBER covered patent, know-how and mixed technology licenses. It was less restrictive than its predecessor, with a longer list of 'white clauses' and a shorter list of 'black clauses',[211] but remained formalistic, complex, and narrow in scope, condemning a number of practices without sufficient economic justification. Only five years after the TTBER adoption, the Commission itself conceded that the TTBER 'imposed on industry a straitjacket forcing companies unduly to enter into agreements limiting their effectiveness and possibly limiting the competitiveness of the European industry'.[212] The TTBER revision was also an important part of the reforms of EU competition rules mentioned above. Following extensive public consultations, the Commission adopted a new TTBER[213] and the accompanying Technology Transfer Guidelines[214] in 2004, shifting from the complex and

---

208 The EC competition law makes a distinction between active sales prohibition, which after Maize Seeds is not *per se* illegal, and restraints on passive sales, which are considered *per se* illegal. This is reflected by the texts of all the block exemptions relating to licensing.

209 *See* the Commission's 1993 White Paper *Growth, Competitiveness and Employment. The Challenges and the Ways Forward in the 21st Century*, Bulletin of the EC Supp 6/93, at 9 and Jean-François Pons, *Competition and Dissemination of Innovation. The New Block Exemption Regulation for Technology Transfer Agreements*, at: http://ec.europa.eu/comm/competition/speeches/text/sp1997_067_en. html.

210 Commission Regulation (EC) No. 240/96 of 31 January 1996 on the application of Article 85(3) of the Treaty to certain categories of technology transfer agreements, 1996 O.J. (L 31) 2.

211 Blacklisted restrictions included price-fixing (in horizontal and in vertical agreements), customer allocation (in horizontal agreements), quantity limits on licensees, certain types of grant-backs, and automatically prolonging the duration of the license agreement by the inclusion of new improvements.

212 *See* Commission evaluation report on the transfer of technology block exemption regulation No. 240/96 – Technology transfer agreements under Article 81, COM/2001/0786 final.

213 Commission Regulation (EC) No. 772/2004 of 27 April 2004 on the application of Article 81(3) of the Treaty to categories of technology transfer agreements ('2004 TTBER'), 2004 O.J. (L 123) 11.

214 Commission Notice – Guidelines on the application of Article 81 of the EC Treaty to technology transfer agreements, 2004 O.J. (C 101) 2.

formalistic approach of is predecessors to a more economics-based, flexible approach.

The 2004 TTBER and Guidelines closed some of the gap between EC competition law and the US rules on IP licensing. Like the US IP Licensing Guidelines, the TTBER is based on the general principle that licensing is pro-competitive and should be allowed if the agreement does not restrict actual competition or potential competition that would have existed had no license been granted.[215] Licensing clauses are not reviewed taking account of the market position of the companies involved. Market shares and the nature of the relationship between the parties (vertical or horizontal) are crucial for the assessment of the agreement.[216] By abandoning the list of white clauses and shortening the list of hardcore restraints, the new regulations allow for a more flexible assessment of individual licensing agreements. The list of restrictions presumed to be anticompetitive was also significantly shortened in the processes of the public consultations held by the Commission.[217]

Having said that, there are still important differences in the assessment of licensing agreements in the United States and in the EU. In particular, EU competition law still condemns more vertical restraints than does US antitrust law, irrespective of the market shares of the companies involved. Unlike the US antitrust authorities, the European Commission treats resale price fixing in licensing agreements as 'severely anticompetitive restraints' regardless of whether the relationship between the parties is vertical or horizontal in nature.[218] Resale price maintenance in the context of all vertical agreements is

---

[215] Technology Transfer Guidelines, ¶12 (a). The EU test for the 'intra-technology' restraints is stricter than the US test, as an arrangement may be declared anticompetitive if an alternative agreement could have been made to accomplish the same legitimate ends while leading to greater consumer surplus. Under the IP Licensing Guidelines, an agreement is allowed as long as it generates surplus for consumers and the US antitrust authorities do not engage in search for the theoretically less restrictive means to achieve the aims sought by the parties.

[216] Technology Transfer Guidelines, ¶26.

[217] For example, field-of-use restrictions in horizontal licensing were originally blacklisted, but the Commission accepted the argument that such restrictions often reflect the different technological focuses of the parties or are used because the licensee does not want to pay for the possibility to exploit technology in all possible fields of use. Accordingly, the new Regulation and Guidelines exempt field-of-use restrictions (Recitals 179 and 180 of the Guidelines). Similar concerns were raised with respect to including running royalty obligations in cross-licenses among hardcore restraints. In the new Guidelines (Recital 157) this was limited to the situations where the license is a sham.

[218] *See* TTBER, Recital 13 and Article 4 and Technology Transfer Guidelines, ¶97. Non-price vertical restraints are generally allowed and though restrictions on passive sales are blacklisted in Article 4(2) of the TTBER, that provision also contains

considered a hardcore restraint of competition.[219] A licensing agreement containing such restriction is presumed anticompetitive and benefits neither from the TTBER exemption nor from the general presumption that licensing is procompetitive.[220]

The differences between the EU and US approaches to vertical price restraints are to some extent limited due to the difference between the US *per se* approach and the EU hardcore approach. Though in both cases no appraisal of its economic effect on the market is necessary to condemn an agreement, in the case of a hardcore restraint the company accused of an infringement can still argue that the agreement is pro-competitive and merits an exemption under Article 81(3). Still, the burden of proof under Article 81(3) is very difficult to overcome for a company bringing forward such defense. The Technology Transfer Guidelines specifically state that fixing the prices at which the products produced under license are sold is unlikely to qualify for an exemption under Article 81(3) because it 'will generally lead to a lower output and a misallocation of resources and higher prices for consumers'.[221] Moreover, the EU prohibition on vertical price fixing is very broad. The Guidelines make clear that all restrictions that have a direct or indirect object of fixing sale prices or minimum sale prices are treated as hardcore restraints on competition.[222]

Thus, unlike in the United States, where a company may impose prices unilaterally under the *Colgate* doctrine, in the EU 'contract terminations in response to observance of a given price level' may be treated in the same way as an outright vertical price fixing.[223] This, combined with the fact that dominant companies are subjected to even more restrictive rules with regard to vertical restraints, creates a situation where over-enforcement is likely.[224]

---

a long list of circumstances where such restrictions are permissible. Still, the Commission remains hostile to restrictions of parallel trade, which are seen as an obstacle to the creation of the common market and for that reason are considered a very serious infringement of Article 81(1). *See, e.g.,* Case T-62/98, *Volkswagen v. Commission*, 2000 E.C.R. II-2707 and Commission Decision in Case COMP/35.587 *Nintendo*, 2003 O.J. (L 255) 33.

[219] *See* Commission Regulation 2790/1999 on the application of Article 81(3) of the Treaty to categories of vertical agreements and concerted practices, 1999 O.J. (L 336) 21, Recital 10 and Article 4. For a thorough analysis of the EU approach to vertical restraints *see, e.g.*, Vincent Verouden, *Vertical Agreements and Article 81(1) EC: The Evolving Role of Economic Analysis*, 71 ANTITRUST L. J. 525 (2003).

[220] *See* TTBER, Recital 13.

[221] Technology Transfer Guidelines, ¶18.

[222] *Id.* at ¶97.

[223] *Id.*

[224] *See* James C. Cooper et al., *A Comparative Study of United States and European Union Approaches to Vertical Policy*, 13 GEO. MASON L. REV. 289 (2005).

Since the IP owner may set the price at which products embodying his IP are sold by his wholly-owned subsidiaries, he should also be allowed to do so when he outsources production and distribution to a third party. The prohibition to do so effectively discourages loose cooperation and encourages unitary businesses. Unless the license is a mere sham to cover a cartel, competition is unlikely to be harmed when the parties to the license agreement are not competitors and when they have no market power. Sale price maintenance in a license agreement should not be deemed anticompetitive regardless of market structure, ease of entry, purpose, or the possibility of collusion. Though the TTBER and the Guidelines do not exclude the possibility that such agreements may be exempted under Article 81(3), it appears that they create a strong presumption that they are anticompetitive. This unnecessarily limits the IP owner's ability to set the terms under which non-competing licensees will exploit his IP, and may discourage licensing or force IP owners to exploit their IP themselves even if a license would be a more cost-effective solution. Even though the restrictions not exempted in the TTBER would not necessarily be condemned under Article 81, it appears desirable, particularly in light of the Guidelines language, that the Commission should announce that it will look at price restrictions in licensing agreements more favorably.

4. NEW TECHNOLOGIES, INTEROPERABILITY, AND ANTITRUST

An important issue in the context of application of the antitrust rules to IP rights is whether the so-called 'new economy' industries deserve special treatment. These industries are characterized by large fixed costs, negligible marginal costs,[225] pervasive network effects,[226] and the associated tendency

---

[225] This is a textbook example of a natural monopoly. See Hal R. Varian, *High-Technology Industries and Market Structure* 13 (4 Sep. 2001), at: http://people.ischool.berkeley.edu/~hal/Papers/structure.pdf.

[226] The concept has been defined by Katz & Shapiro as relating to products 'for which utility that a user derives from consumption of the good increases with the number of other agents consuming the good'. Michael L. Katz & Carl Shapiro, *Network Externalities, Competition, and Compatibility*, 75 AM. ECON. REV. 424, 424 (1985). For, example, the instant messaging system with the largest user base is more valuable than a system with fewer users. Similarly, most consumers are likely to choose an operating system with a dominant market share for compatibility and interchange with other users. Further, the more popular the operating system is, the more complementary applications are offered, making the operating system even more valuable to consumers (this is sometimes referred to as 'indirect' network effects).

towards standardization.[227] As a result, high-technology markets are often highly concentrated, with one firm dominating the market.[228] They can be extremely competitive at the same time, with numerous firms competing 'for the market' rather than 'within the market'.[229] Since the stakes are so high, potential competitors are likely to invest heavily in developing new products to replace the incumbent company. Indeed, the history of IT industries offers numerous examples of industry leaders which went bankrupt a few years after they dominated the market. This was, for example, the case of Commodore and Atari, vital players in the home computer and video game field in the 1980s. Other firms, such as Apple and IBM, had to significantly change their business models to survive.

Still, once a firm has established market dominance with a particular product, it may be extremely hard to unseat it. Market entry of a competing standard will be difficult, since the potential entrant will have to acquire a critical mass of users for the new product. If switching costs are large, the monopolist may have a cost advantage that exceeds the benefit of a new superior technology, locking consumers into outdated choices.[230] In addition, a dominant firm controlling an established network or a proprietary standard has incentives to reduce transparency and interoperability between other networks and its own.[231] In such case, IP is likely to constitute a major barrier to entry. The firm controlling the dominant network may also be able to expand its monopoly power through vertical integration. Is there a role for antitrust to solve these problems? Predictably, the US and EU antitrust enforcers have different views on this matter.

4.1 The United States: the Hands-off Approach

The common theme in the US literature dealing with the application of the antitrust rules to new economy industries is caution. The commentators warn that new economy antitrust cases present daunting technical and economic questions which lay judges and jurors are not qualified to answer, that speed

---

[227] Michael L. Katz & Carl Shapiro, *Systems Competition and Network Effects*, 8 J. ECON. PERSPECTIVES 93, 105–6 (1994) and Varian, *supra* note 225, at 18–19 (4 Sep. 2001).

[228] *See, e.g.*, Varian, *supra* note 225, at 27.

[229] Katz & Carl Shapiro, *supra* note 227, at 107.

[230] *See, e.g.*, Joseph Farrell & Garth Saloner, *Installed Base and Compatibility: Innovation, Product Preannouncements, and Predation*, 76 AM. ECON. REV. 940 (1986), *but see* S.J. Lebowitz and Stephen Margolis, *Network Externality: An Uncommon Tragedy*, 8 J. ECON. PERSPECTIVES 133 (1994) (arguing that there is little empirical evidence in support of this theory).

[231] Varian, *supra* note 225, at 19–22.

of technological change makes it more likely that the case becomes obsolete by passage of time, and, last but not least, that markets deal better with competitive issues than antitrust regulators.[232] Yet, the prevailing view is that antitrust laws should apply to these industries and that the economic principles on which antitrust is based are flexible enough to accommodate the specific features and market dynamics of the IT sector.[233]

A recent report issued by the Antitrust Modernization Commission confirms that 'there is no need to revise antitrust laws to apply different rules to industries in which innovation, intellectual property, and technological change are central features.'[234] The Commission stressed that some concentrated markets are highly competitive and the firms having the largest share of the market are often the most efficient.[235] It also noted that, since the *Berkey Photo*[236] decision of the Second Circuit, the prevailing view has been that firms' incentives to innovate rest on the prospect of market success.[237] In that case, the court ruled that Kodak was under no obligation to give its competitors an advance notice of its new film design so that they could develop their own cameras to handle Kodak's films, reasoning that 'a firm can keep its innovations secret as long as it wishes, forcing [its competitors] to catch up on the strength of their own efforts after the new product is introduced.'[238] Referring to the *Trinko* decision, the Commission reiterated that dominant companies have no duty to deal with rivals in the same market as fully applicable also in the context of new economy industries.[239] It stressed that imposing a duty to deal on a monopolist is likely to reduce both the incentives of the monopolist to develop its product and the incentives of its

---

[232] *See, e.g.*, Richard A. Posner, *Antitrust in the New Economy*, 68 ANTITRUST L. J. 925, 936–40 (2001).

[233] *See, e.g.*, Posner, *supra* note 232, Ronald A. Cass & Keith N. Hylton, *Preserving Competition: Economic Analysis, Legal Standards and Microsoft,* 8 GEO. MASON L. REV. 1, 36–9 (1999) and Robert Pitofsky, *Challenges of the New Economy: Issues at the Intersection of Antitrust and Intellectual Property*, 68 ANTITRUST L. J. 913 (2001) and Herbert Hovenkamp, *The Monopolization Offense*, 62 OHIO STATE L. J. 1035, 1047–9 (2000) (analyzing the US Microsoft case and noting that the government's case against Microsoft is based on 'rather orthodox' antitrust claims, such as exclusive dealing and tying).

[234] Antitrust Modernization Commission, *Report and Recommendations* 9 (Modernization Report), April 2007, available at: http://www.amc.gov/report_recommendation/amc_final_report.pdf. *See also id.* at 38–9.

[235] *Id.* at 33–5.

[236] *Berkey Photo, Inc. v. Eastman Kodak Co.*, 603 F.2d 263 (2nd Cir. 1979), *cert.* denied, 444 U.S. 1093 (1980).

[237] Modernization Report, at 85–96.

[238] Modernization Report, at 85, citing *Berkey Photo*, 603 F.2d at 281.

[239] Modernization Report, at 101.

competitors to develop alternative technologies.[240] The FTC and the DOJ concur that they will not focus their enforcement efforts on unilateral and unconditional refusals to provide proprietary information.[241]

Considering the principles set out above, it is unlikely that the antitrust rules could be successfully used to force a monopolist controlling an industry standard to share it with competitors in an adjacent market, even if the control over that standard gives the monopolist significant advantage over the competitors. Still, American antitrust enforcers have been vigilant about unilateral exclusionary conduct in new economy industries. There have been a number of cases in which liability under Section 2 of the Sherman Act was found. None of these cases, however, involved an unconditional refusal to provide proprietary information, even if it embodied an industry standard or was otherwise essential for other companies to compete with the dominant company in a downstream market. Moreover, there is a general agreement that charging monopoly prices for technology related to that standard cannot be, in and of itself, an antitrust violation.[242]

Instead, the focus of US antitrust enforcers seems to be on abusive use of IP rights particularly in the context of collaborative standard setting.[243] To be sure, collective standard setting is, in principle, viewed as advancing the goal of maximizing consumer welfare through promoting competition: the primary goal of antitrust law.[244] Standards that ensure interoperability facilitate the sharing of information among users of competing products, thereby enhancing the utility of all products and enlarging the overall consumer market.[245] Standards enhance competition in upstream markets by reducing the risk of investing in a technology that ultimately may not gain widespread acceptance, and moving the focus away from the development of potential standards

---

240 *Id.* at 102.

241 DOJ and FTC, *Antitrust Enforcement and Intellectual Property Rights: Promoting Innovation and Competition* (Antitrust and IP Report), April 2007, at 6; *see* also DOJ, *Competition and Monopoly: Single-Firm Conduct under Section 2 of the Sherman Act*, available at: http://www.usdoj.gov/atr/public/reports/236681.pdf.

242 By contrast, monopoly pricing has been challenged under Article 82 of the EC Treaty. *See in general*, Michal S. Gal, *Monopoly Pricing as an Antitrust Offense in the U.S. and the EC: Two Systems of Belief about Monopoly*, 49 ANTITRUST BULLETIN 343 (2004).

243 *See* the Modernization Report, at 119–121 and the Antitrust and IP Report, at 33–56; *see also* Anne Layne-Farrar, *Antitrust and Intellectual Property Rights: Assessing The Link Between Standards and Market Power*, 21 ANTITRUST 42 (Summer 2007).

244 *Broadcom Corp. v. Qualcomm Inc.*, 501 F.3d 297, 308 (3d Cir. 2007).

245 *Id.* at 308–9.

toward the development of means for implementing the chosen standard.[246] Yet, if the standard-setting process is manipulated, the adoption of an industry standard does not necessarily result in pro-competitive benefits.[247] The manipulation of the standard-setting process and subsequent use of the resulting standard to gain competitive advantage over rivals has been the primary target of antitrust interventions in the United States.

The FTC has brought a number of cases against patent holders alleging that they have manipulated standard-setting procedures. In the *Matter of Dell Computer Corp.*, the FTC challenged Dell's right to enforce its patents incorporated in the industry standard under Section 5 of the FTC Act.[248] The FTC alleged that the standard-determining organization (SDO) had adopted the standard relying in part on Dell's certification that it did not have any patents that covered the proposed standard. It reasoned that the SDO would have implemented a different non-proprietary design had it been informed of the patent conflict during the certification process. The case ended with a consent order prohibiting Dell from enforcing its patent against those using the proposed standard.

The *Unocal* case, in which the FTC found that Unocal had misrepresented to a state standards-determining board that certain gasoline research was non-proprietary and in the public domain, had the same outcome.[249] The FTC concluded that Unocal's misrepresentation led directly to its acquisition of monopoly power and harmed competition because refiners became locked in to regulations that required the use of Unocal's proprietary technology.[250]

Finally, the Third Circuit decision in *Broadcom Corp. v. Qualcomm Inc.*[251] extended this line of case law to a patent holder's intentional false promise to license essential proprietary technology on fair, reasonable, and non-discriminatory (FRAND) terms made in a private standard-setting environment. The Court held that making such commitment, coupled with an SDO's reliance on that commitment when including the technology in a standard and the patent holder's subsequent breach of that commitment, constitutes an actionable anti-competitive conduct.[252]

---

[246] *Id.* at 309.

[247] *Id.* at 310.

[248] *In the Matter of Dell Computer Corp.*, 121 F.T.C. 616 (20 May 1996). Section 5 of the FTC Act is broader than Section 2 of the Sherman Act and prohibits 'unfair methods of competition'.

[249] *In the Matter of Union Oil Co. of Cal.*, No. 9305 (F.T.C. 27 July 2005), 2005 WL 2003365.

[250] *Id.*

[251] 501 F.3d 297 (3d Cir. 2007).

[252] *Id.* at 314.

Manipulation of the standard-setting process as such is insufficient to hold a patent holder liable under the Sherman Act. In *Rambus*, the DC Circuit pointed out that the focus of the antitrust analysis is on the resulting harm rather than the deception itself.[253] In this case, the FTC alleged that Rambus violated antitrust laws by failing to disclose to the Joint Electron Device Engineering Council (JEDEC), an industry-wide standard-setting organization, certain patents that were later incorporated in a standard.[254] The FTC ordered Rambus to license the patents incorporated in the standard and set the maximum royalty rates that Rambus can charge.[255] It found that Rambus engaged in exclusionary conduct leading it to monopolize markets for computer memory technology, reasoning that had Rambus disclosed its patents, JEDEC would have excluded Rambus's patented technologies from the standard, *or* could have demanded reasonable and non-discriminatory (RAND) assurances *ex ante*.[256] The DC Circuit reversed the FTC opinion.[257] The Court noted that the FTC conceded in its remedial opinion that there was insufficient evidence that JEDEC would have standardized other technologies.[258] Thus, the case turned on the point of whether JEDEC's loss of opportunity to negotiate RAND terms harmed competition.[259] The Court firmly opposed treating JEDEC's loss of the ability to negotiate better terms as an antitrust violation, reiterating the principle that an otherwise lawful monopolist's use of deception simply to obtain higher prices, even when deceptive or fraudulent, does not alone present a harm to competition in the monopolized market.[260] Moreover, the Court concluded that had JEDEC limited Rambus to reasonable royalties and required it to provide licenses on a non-discriminatory basis, there would be *less* competition because high prices tend to attract competitors.[261] Though the Court did not mention the *Walker Process* line of case law, this requirement makes the *Rambus* type of claim similar to a *Walker*

---

253 *See Rambus Inc. v. FTC*, 522 F.3d 456 (Fed. Cir. 2008).

254 According to the FTC, Rambus participated in JEDEC's DRAM (dynamic random access memory) standard-setting activities for over four years without disclosing to JEDEC or its members that it was actively working to develop, and possessed, a patent and several pending patent applications that involved specific technologies ultimately adopted in the standards. Though JEDEC's disclosure policies were not a model of clarity, the FTC insisted that Rambus was under the obligation to disclose its plan to patent the technology which was likely to be incorporated into the standard.

255 These rates are quite low, ranging from 0.025 to 0.5 percent, and after three years the rates would drop to zero.

256 *Rambus,* 522 F.3d at 463.

257 *Id.* at 466.

258 *Id.* at 463–4.

259 *Id.* at 466.

260 *Id.* at 464.

261 *Id.* at 466.

Process claim. To prevail on a *Walker Process* claim, the plaintiff must show that the patent would not have been issued had it not been for the fraud on the patent office.[262] To prevail on a *Rambus* type of claim, an antitrust plaintiff must prove that a standard-setting organization (SSO) would not have adopted the standard in question but for the defendant's misrepresentation or omission.[263] In other words, there is no antitrust violation unless there is clear evidence of direct adverse effect of the conduct on the market.

4.2 The European Union: an Open Access Agenda

Unlike their American counterparts, EU antitrust enforcers see a wide scope for antitrust intervention in the new economy industries. In this context, it appears that the Commission focuses its attention on vertical integration of dominant companies whose market position is entrenched by network effects. The Commission's concern is that in such situation control over a *de facto* industry standard may give the dominant company an advantage that its competitors in the downstream market will find difficult to overcome.

The Commission's position on this issue, advanced in the course of the Microsoft litigation, is summarized in the *Article 82 Discussion Paper*. In this document, the Commission classified a '[r]efusal to supply information needed for interoperability' which allows a dominant company 'to extend its dominance from one market to another'[264] as a separate offense from a refusal to license an IP right. It reasoned that it 'may not be appropriate to apply to

---

[262] *See Walker Process Equip., Inc. v. Food Mach. & Chem. Corp.*, 382 U.S. 172 (1965); *C.R. Bard, Inc. v. M3 Sys., Inc.*, 157 F.3d 1340, 1365 (Fed. Cir. 1998) and *Nobelpharma Ab v. Implant Innovations*, 141 F.3d 1059, 1071 (Fed. Cir. 1998). The *Walker Process* line of case law is discussed in Chapter 3 below.

[263] *Rambus*, 522 F.3d at 466. Notably, reliance on the misrepresentation of the patent holder was alleged both in the *Dell* case and in the *Unocal* case discussed above. In *Dell* the enforcement action was premised on the fact that the SDO would have implemented a different non-proprietary design had it been informed of the patent conflict during the certification process. *In the Matter of Dell Computer Corp.*, 121 F.T.C. 616, 624 (20 May 1996). In *Unocal*, the FTC alleged that the SDO would have implemented a different non-proprietary design had it been informed of the patent conflict during the certification process. The *Rambus* decision is also reconcilable with the Third Circuit ruling in the *Broadcom* case: the *Rambus* Court itself noted that the *Broadcom* ruling rested on the argument that the patent holder's deceit 'lured the SSO away from non-proprietary technology'. *Rambus Inc. v. FTC*, 522 F.3d 456, 466 (D.C. Cir. 2008).

[264] *See Article 82 Discussion Paper*, ¶241. The Commission characterizes a refusal to supply interoperability information as a 'special case' among refusals to deal.

such refusals to supply information the same high standards for intervention as those [applicable to refusals to license an IP right]'.[265] The Commission conceded that dominant companies are not under a general obligation 'to ensure interoperability', but stated that a refusal to supply interoperability information would be abusive, if (1) the interoperability information is controlled by a dominant company; (2) it is necessary for interoperability between one market and other; and (3) the refusal is a means to leverage market power from one market to another.[266] Under this test, any dominant vertically integrated software company would essentially have to ensure interoperability, if it could be alleged that its control over the interoperability gave it an advantage in the downstream market where it also holds a substantive market share.

Eventually, the CFI did not address these theories in its judgment upholding the *Microsoft* Decision. Instead, as discussed above, the Court applied a modified *IMS* test, reasoning that since the Commission conceded that Microsoft's interoperability information could be protected by IP rights, rules applicable to IP should be applied. Though *Article 82 Guidance* does not include a reference to the 'interoperability offense', the CFI's reasoning boosted the Commission's enforcement efforts.

Shortly after the Commission agreed with Microsoft on the terms and the scope of its obligation to disclose interoperability information, it directed a new Statement of Objections to Microsoft alleging that the tying of the Windows operating system and Internet Explorer, which gave Microsoft's browser a distribution advantage over competing Internet browsers, constituted an Article 82 infringement.[267] The new case shows that simply having an interoperability advantage or a distribution advantage in such a situation may be sufficient to constitute an antitrust violation.

Arguably, there are reasons that support the proposition that the IT industry requires a higher degree of antitrust scrutiny. As explained above, the sector is characterized by extensive vertical integration and network effects, which can lead to a collective lock-in of an established technology.[268] The Commission,

---

[265] *Id.* ¶242.

[266] *Id.* ¶241.

[267] *See Antitrust: Commission confirms sending a Statement of Objections to Microsoft on the tying of Internet Explorer to Windows*, European Commission Press Release, 17 January 2009, at: http://europa.eu/rapid/pressReleasesAction.do?reference=MEMO/09/15&format=HTML&aged=0&language=EN&guiLanguage=en.

[268] On the economics of high-tech markets see, for example, Michael L. Katz & Carl Shapiro, *Antitrust in Software Markets*, *in* COMPETITION, INNOVATION AND THE MICROSOFT MONOPOLY: ANTITRUST IN THE DIGITAL MARKETPLACE 29 (EISENACH & LENARD, EDS, 1998); Robert Pitofsky, *Antitrust at the Millennium (Part II): Challenges of the New Economy: Issues at the Intersection of Antitrust and Intellectual Property*,

however, takes the radical view that the problems stemming from the existence of a monopolist that controls a *de facto* industry standard should be addressed by giving an extensive access to valuable bottlenecks. The Commission's approach is based on the theory that a monopolist may use its market power in one market to 'leverage' a monopoly into another. This is controversial from an economic perspective.[269] Though a monopolist may be able to use its market power to force consumers to buy products it offers in a related competitive market, any supra-competitive profit obtained in the second market would have to be offset by lower prices in the monopolized market. Though such a strategy may harm competitors in the secondary market, without predation, it is unlikely that it will harm consumers. On the contrary, vertical integration may be the source of efficiency gains, from which consumers also benefit. If a secondary market is not likely to be monopolized, leveraging should not be a concern of antitrust policy.[270]

To be sure, a dominant company's expansion into a related market may give rise to competitive concerns under certain circumstances. For example, a monopolist may want to take over a complementary market in an attempt to defend its existing monopoly against perceived competitive threats. This may raise barriers to entry, as the entrant would have to attack the monopolist in two markets at the same time.[271] Denying interoperability information to competitors in the neighboring market may also help raise the profits of the monopolist, by impairing rivals' ability to compete in this market.[272] A refusal

---

68 ANTITRUST L. J. 913 (2001); and Richard A. Posner, *Antitrust at the Millennium (Part II): Antitrust in the New Economy*, 68 ANTITRUST L. J. 925 (2001).

[269] *Cf.* AREEDA & HOVENKAMP, *supra* note 62, ¶652; BORK, *supra* note 188, at 373–4; Louis Kaplow, *Extension of Monopoly Power Through Leverage*, 85 COLUM. L. REV. 515 (1985); François Lévêque, *Innovation, Leveraging and Essential Facilities: Interoperability Licensing in the EU Microsoft Case*, 28 WORLD COMPETITION 71, 80–82 (2005).

[270] *See, e.g., Alaska Airlines v. United Airlines*, 948 F.2d 536, 549 (9th Cir. 1991) (pointing out that leverage activity may tend to undermine monopoly power, just like monopoly pricing); *Spectrum Sports v. McQuillan*, 506 U.S. 447, 459 (1993) (holding conduct of a single firm unlawful under §2 only when it actually monopolizes or dangerously threatens to do so; finding of an attempt to monopolize requires market inquiry and cannot be based solely on the existence of 'unfair' or 'predatory' tactics); 3 AREEDA & HOVENKAMP, *supra* note 62, ¶652. Both in *Bronner* and in *IMS*, the ECJ required the proof that a refusal to deal leads to elimination of competition in the downstream market.

[271] For an analysis of the dynamic two-level entry theory see, for example, Timothy J. Murris, *Is Heightened Antitrust Scrutiny Appropriate for Software Markets?*, *in* COMPETITION, INNOVATION AND THE MICROSOFT MONOPOLY: ANTITRUST IN THE DIGITAL MARKETPLACE 95–7 (JEFFREY A. EISENACH & THOMAS M. LENARD, EDS, 1998).

[272] Janusz A. Ordover & Robert D. Willig, *Access and Bundling in High-Technology Market*, *in* COMPETITION, INNOVATION AND THE MICROSOFT MONOPOLY:

to provide interoperability information warrants an antitrust intervention only if the dominant company is likely to succeed in eliminating competition in the downstream market.[273] The key issue is how much evidence is required to prove that the dominant company's conduct is likely to have such an effect and whether there are efficiencies that outweigh the competitive harm resulting from such conduct. The Microsoft case suggests that the European Commission stops short of presuming that a refusal to share interoperability information by a vertically integrated dominant company is an Article 82 violation. At the same time, the Commission imposes a high burden of proof on a dominant company to establish efficiencies and to prove that a company license should have adverse effects on its incentives to innovate. Such an approach lacks balance and is inconsistent with current economic learning.

The Commission's insistence on ensuring interoperability creates a serious risk of over-enforcement and may discourage investment in the development of new technologies. Forcing dominant companies to share their technologies raises daunting questions relating to the scope of the obligation to deal and setting the terms of access.[274] The timing, scope and conditions of access are crucial if it is to improve competitive conditions on the market. If antitrust enforcers err in answering these questions, there is a great risk that the enforcement action will thwart the development of a new technology. Moreover, open access favors intra-system competition over inter-system competition. Several commentators noted that, whereas it is not clear whether antitrust should be concerned with intra-system competition, protecting inter-system competition is crucial in the context of new technologies.[275] The focus

---

ANTITRUST IN THE DIGITAL MARKETPLACE 108 (JEFFREY A. EISENACH & THOMAS M. LENARD, EDS, 1998). Leveraging theory played a significant role in the US government case against Microsoft.

[273] The Commission itself suggests that a conduct of a dominant company may be abusive only if "a likely market distorting foreclosure effect may be established" and that a refusal to supply in general may be abusive when there is a vertical foreclosure. See Article 82 Discussion Paper, ¶¶58, 72.

[274] One difficulty is the precise definition of 'interface'. This gave rise to a dispute between Microsoft and the Commission on the implementation of the Microsoft Decision. European Commission, *Competition: Commission sends new letter to Microsoft on compliance with decision*, Press Release No. IP/06/298 of March 10, 2006, *available at* http://europa.eu.int/rapid/pressReleasesAction.do?reference=IP/06/298&format=HTML&aged=0&language=EN&guiLanguage=en; see generally JONATHAN BAND & MASANOBU KATOH, INTERFACES ON TRIAL: INTELLECTUAL PROPERTY AND INTEROPERABILITY IN THE GLOBAL SOFTWARE INDUSTRY 6–7 (1995).

[275] On this point, see David Balto & Robert Pitofsky, *Antitrust and High-Tech Industries: The New Challenge*, 606 PLI/P at 513; Roberto, Pardolesi and Andrea Renda, *The European Commission's Case against Microsoft: Kill Bill?*, 27 WORLD COMPETITION 513, 552 (2004) and Pamela Samuelson & Suzanne Scotchmer, *The Law and Economics of Reverse Engineering*, 111 YALE L. J. 1575, 1615–26 (2002).

on open access may leave the antitrust enforcers with insufficient resources to address these issues and, consequently, creates the risk of under-enforcement in this area. Last but not least, there is the looming question of the effectiveness of the compulsory licensing remedies. Neither in the US nor in the EU, has there so far been a lot of demand for the interoperability information Microsoft was obliged to disclose. There is little evidence that the remedies imposed by the Commission changed the circumstances of the marketplace or effectively addressed the competitive concerns identified by the Commission. It may simply be the case that antitrust enforcers are not best-suited to develop software that meets specific market needs.

3. (Mis)use of regulatory procedures and IP

The focus of this chapter is on how the approaches to state-created distortions have influenced the application of antitrust law to unilateral conduct involving the acquisition or enforcement of IP rights in Europe and in the United States. As explained above, enforcement of valid IP rights is largely immune from antitrust scrutiny in the US and the foremost means to challenge anticompetitive unilateral use of IP rights is to allege that they have been improperly acquired or enforced.[1] Yet, use of regulatory procedures to achieve exclusionary goals does not, as such, constitute a Sherman Act violation, with the narrow exception of obtaining a patent by fraud on the PTO.[2]

By contrast, EU antitrust enforcers challenge the use of regulatory procedures and legal enforcement of rights by dominant companies if it has an exclusionary objective. For example, in *Compagnie Maritime Belge*, the ECJ held that requesting a public authority to enforce an agreement giving exclusive rights to a private company was an Article 82 violation.

On a number of occasions, the ECJ intervened in the way dominant companies exercised their exclusive rights. In *General Motors*[3] and *British Leyland*,[4] the Court held that these car producers, which had a legal monopoly to confirm that a car of their own make conformed to a previously approved type vehicle, abused their dominant position by charging excessive prices for issuing the certificate of conformity. In *Télémarketing*, a state-owned company granted exclusive rights in a particular market was found to have violated Article 82 by reserving 'to itself an ancillary activity which might be carried out by another undertaking as a part of its activities on a neighboring but separate market, with the possibility of eliminating all competition from such undertaking'.[5]

---

1 1 HERBERT HOVENKAMP ET AL., IP AND ANTITRUST: AN ANALYSIS OF ANTITRUST PRINCIPLES APPLIED TO INTELLECTUAL PROPERTY LAW, ¶11.1 (2002).

2 See *infra* Section 3.1.

3 Case 26/75, *General Motors v. Commission*, 1975 E.C.R. 1367.

4 Case 226/84, *British Leyland v. Commission*, 1986 E.C.R. 3263.

5 Case 311/84, *Centre belge d'études de marché – Télémarketing v. SA Compagnie luxembourgeoise de télédiffusion and Information publicité Benelux*, 1985 E.C.R. 3261, ¶¶25–7.

In spite of these general principles, the EU Courts have been reluctant to apply Article 82 to address competitive concerns stemming from the acquisition and enforcement of IP. That reluctance arguably could have been rooted in the exercise/existence distinction made by the ECJ in its early jurisprudence to delimit the application of competition rules to IP.[6] In its *AZ* Decision,[7] the Commission rejects the exercise/existence theory and suggests that it will subject acquisition and enforcement of IP rights by dominant companies to heightened antitrust scrutiny.

This chapter discusses the *AZ* Decision and its consequences for IP holders in the EU against the background of the relevant US jurisprudence. It starts with some general remarks about the US and EU theories on antitrust immunity for IP rights. The second section addresses the antitrust assessment of the acquisition of IP rights in the US and in the EU and analogizes the *AZ* decision to the US *Walker Process* doctrine. The application of antitrust rules to IP enforcement and litigation is the focus of the third section.

1. SPECIAL IMMUNITY FOR IP RIGHTS?

1.1 The US: Towards Dialectic Unification of IP and Antitrust

In the US, antitrust and IP have traditionally been considered separate and conflicting spheres. The question as to which of the two regimes should prevail in case of a conflict has been controversial since the passage of the Sherman Act. In the early 1900s the courts uniformly favored patentees and refrained from subjecting patent-related conduct to antitrust rules. This led to immunizing from antitrust liability such restrictions as patent pools with outright price fixing[8] or tying.[9] Before long the Supreme Court resigned from immunizing IP rights from antitrust scrutiny and attempted to formulate a test that would allow identifying impermissible practices. In its 1917 judgment in *Motion Picture*[10] the Court noted that the 'scope of every patent is limited to the intention described in the claims contained in it'. Since the 1926 *General*

[6] According to that distinction, the competition provisions of the EC Treaty do not interfere with the existence of IP (as opposed to its exercise).

[7] Commission Decision in Case COMP/A/37.507/F3 – *AstraZeneca* (*AZ* Decision), not yet published in the OJ.

[8] *Bement v. National Harrow*, 186 U.S. 70 (1902).

[9] *Henry v. A.B. Dick Co.*, 224 U.S. 1, 32, 35 (1912).

[10] *Motion Picture Patents Co. v. Universal Film Manufacturing Co.*, 243 U.S. 502, 510, (1917).

Electric decision, the focus shifted towards 'the reward which the patentee by the grant of patent is entitled to secure'.[11] The 1969 *Zenith Radio* opinion provides that 'the patentee [may not] extend the monopoly of his patent to derive a benefit not attributable to use of the patent's teachings.'[12] All these tests are based on two assumptions: (1) that patents and antitrust are separate and conflicting fields; and (2) that there exists some notion of what constitutes a normal exercise of patent rights, and as long as the conduct in question could be qualified as such there is no antitrust violation.

The more recent trend in the US antitrust policy is to see antitrust and IP as complementary policies designed to reach the same economic goal: greater consumer welfare.[13] For the purpose of antitrust analysis, IP is viewed as being essentially comparable to any other form of property.[14] The US Courts have repeatedly refused to encroach upon IP rights and they see a very narrow scope for application of §2 of the Sherman Act to enforcement of valid IP rights.

1.2 The EU: in Search of the Core of IP Rights

Shortly after the Rome Treaty came into force, it became clear that national IP rights had the potential to jeopardize the free movement of goods and competition within the EU internal market. The ECJ developed a number of approaches to solve this problem. In *Consten & Grundig*,[15] the Court, faced for the first time with the question of how to reconcile the single market with the protection of nationally based IP rights, favoured the free trade. The case involved an agreement between Grundig and Consten, Grundig's distributor in France, which gave Consten an exclusive right to use Grundig's trademark in France. Consten registered Grundig's mark in France and used its right to prevent others from importing to France products marketed by Grundig in Germany. The European Commission found that these arrangements were anticompetitive and that they violated Article 81 of the EC Treaty. On appeal from the Commission's Decision, Consten and Grundig argued that their IP rights could not be compromised by Article 81 or any other provision of the EC Treaty. The ECJ dismissed these arguments. It reasoned that though the

---

11 *United States v. General Electric Co.*, 272 U.S. 476, 489 (1926)

12 *Zenith Radio Corp. v. Hazeltine Research*, 395 U.S. 100, 143 (1969).

13 See, e.g., *Atari Games Corp. v. Nintendo of America, Inc.*, 897 F.2d 1572, 1576 (Fed. Cir. 1990) and *IP Licensing Guidelines*, Section 1.0, and 1 HOVENKAMP ET AL., *supra* note 1, ¶1.3.

14 *IP Licensing Guidelines*, ¶¶2.0 and 2.1.

15 Cases 56/64 and 58/64, *Consten & Grundig v. Commission*, 1966 E.C.R. 299.

Treaty does not affect the grant of rights recognized by national IP legislation, the exercise of those rights may nevertheless fall within the prohibitions laid down by the Treaty. Thus the controversial existence/exercise distinction was created.[16]

Though the Court repeatedly stated that the 'normal exercise' of IP rights was shielded from antitrust scrutiny,[17] its main concern was to facilitate the creation of the single market, which meant curbing IP rights where need be.[18] For example, in *Sirena*,[19] the ECJ held a trademark holder could not use its national right to prevent imports of products bearing the same trademark put on the market in another Member State by an independent company. Advocate General Dutheillet de Lamothe advised the Court that trademarks did not merit special respect because they are 'nothing more than an aid to advertising'.[20] The Court endorsed the AG's reasoning with respect to the value of trademarks[21] and continued that, although the existence of a trademark itself does not violate the Treaty's competition rules, the exercise of a trademark right may fall within the ambit of prohibitions set out in the EC Treaty.[22]

The exercise/existence distinction has been nearly uniformly criticized as vague, artificial, and unhelpful.[23] Indeed, the value of an IP right depends on

---

[16] Though the existence/exercise dichotomy has been traced back to *Consten & Grundig*, the Court did not use the notion of existence/exercise in this judgment; it spoke instead of the grant of IP rights as opposed to their exercise. The ECJ first referred to existence/exercise in Case 24/67, *Parke Davis & Co. v. Probel*, 1968 E.C.R. 55.

[17] *See, e.g.*, Case 24/67, *Parke Davis & Co. v. Probel*, 1968 E.C.R. 55 and *Case 78/70, Deutsche Grammophon GmbH v. Metro SB-Grossmarkte GmbH & Co. KG*, 1974 E.C.R. 1147; *see also* STEVEN D. ANDERMAN, EC COMPETITION LAW AND INTELLECTUAL PROPERTY: THE REGULATION OF INNOVATION, 12–13 (1998).

[18] For an overview of the early case law *see, e.g.*, Ian S. Forrester & Christopher Norall, *The Laicization of Community Law: Self-Help and the Rule of Reason: How Competition Law Is and Could Be Applied*, 21 COMMON MARKET L. REV. 11 (1984) and Andreas Reindl, *Intellectual Property and Intra-Community Trade*, 1996 FORDHAM CORP. L. INST. 453 (BARRY HAWK, ED., 1997).

[19] Case 40/70, *Sirena S.r.l. v. Eda S.r.l.*, [1971] E.C.R. 69.

[20] Opinion of Advocate General in *Sirena*, ¶¶13–17.

[21] *Sirena*, ¶7.

[22] *Sirena* was promptly overruled by the Court in Case 86/75, *EMI Records Limited v. CBS Grammofon A/S*, 1976 E.C.R. 871 (an assignment of trademark rights did not fall within Article 81(1) unless there was evidence of a continued agreement between the parties aimed to divide the markets). See also Case 119/75, *Société Terrapin (Overseas) Ltd. v. Société Terranova Industrie CA Kapferer & Co.*, 1976 E.C.R. 1039.

[23] *See, e.g.*, DAVID T. KEELING, INTELLECTUAL PROPERTY RIGHTS IN EU LAW,

the ability to exercise it: if an IP right cannot be exercised, the fact that its existence is unaffected is of little consolation to the right holder. Though the Court has never explicitly renounced the distinction, it has gradually abolished it.[24] Since the Court's 1982 decision in *Coditel II*,[25] the existence/exercise dichotomy has never featured as an important element of the Court's reasoning in cases involving IP rights.[26]

With a view to clarifying how the Treaty provisions on free movement of goods and competition applied to national IP rights, the Court developed the concept of the 'specific subject-matter' of an IP right, the core package of rights that make up the IP right itself, which would not be affected by the Treaty rules.[27] In the famous *Café Hag I*[28] case, the question was whether the local trademark holder could object to the use of the Hag trademark by the other party, who independently had obtained the right to use the mark in another Member State. Relying exclusively on the EC Treaty provisions on free movement of goods, the Court held that the derogation for IP rights included in the Treaty rules on free movement of goods is applicable only 'to the extent that such derogations are justified for the purpose of safeguarding rights that constitute the specific subject-matter of this property'.[29] The core of the IP right, its 'specific subject-matter', could not be encroached on. With respect to the subject-matter of trademark rights the Court concluded that though 'the indication of origin of a product covered by a trade mark is useful, information to consumers on this point may be ensured by means other than such as would affect the free movement of goods'.[30] Thus, importation into a Member State of a product bearing a trademark legally attached to the product in another Member State must not be prevented if the two marks have a common origin. This condition was satisfied in this case even though the two

---

VOL. 1. FREE MOVEMENT AND COMPETITION LAW, 54–6 (2003), VALENTINE KORAH, AN INTRODUCTORY GUIDE TO EC COMPETITION LAW AND PRACTICE, 292 (2004), Guy Tritton, *Articles 30 and 36 and Intellectual Property: Is the Jurisprudence of the ECJ Now of an Ideal Standard?*, 16 EUR. INTELL. PROP. REV. 422, 423 (1994), Warwick A. Rothnie, *Hag II: Putting the Common Origin Doctrine to Sleep*, 13 EUR. INTELL. PROP. REV. 24, 29 (1991) and the Opinion of Advocate General Fennelly in Cases C-267 and 268/95, *Merck and Co. Inc. v. Primecrown Ltd.* (*Merck*), 1996 E.C.R. I-6285, ¶95.

[24] *See, e.g.*, the Opinion of Advocate General Fennelly in *Merck*, ¶93, Rothnie, *supra* note 23, at 29, and KEELING, *supra* note 23, at 55.

[25] Case 262/81, *Coditel SA v. Ciné Vog Films SA,* 1982 E.C.R. 3381.

[26] KEELING, *supra* note 23, at 55.

[27] Case 24/67, *Parke Davis & Co. v. Probel*, 1968 E.C.R. 55, and Case 78/70, *Deutsche Grammophon GmbH v. Metro SB-Grossmarkte GmbH & Co. KG*, 1974 E.C.R. 1147.

[28] Case 192/73, *Van Zuylen frères v. Hag AG*, 1974 E.C.R. 731.

[29] *Id*, ¶9.

[30] *Id*, ¶14.

producers owned trademark rights to exactly the same trademark 'Café Hag' in two different countries independently of each other as a result of historical events following World War II.

The Court's approach to IP rights has begun to change since the mid-1980s. It overruled some of its earlier case law that undermined national IP rights. In *Café Hag II*,[31] a dispute between the same parties and under very similar circumstances to *Café Hag I*, the ECJ rehabilitated trademarks as 'an essential element in the system of undistorted competition which the Treaty seeks to establish and maintain'[32] and reversed *Café Hag I* by holding that the role of a trademark is to guarantee that 'all goods bearing it have been produced under the control of a single undertaking which is accountable for their quality'.[33] This condition would not be satisfied if the trademark holder has never consented to the marketing of the goods bearing the trademark to which he has exclusive rights. The Commission, reflecting on the concept of the specific subject matter of an IP right in the context of the application of Article 81 to technology transfer agreement, summed up the debate on this issue as follows:

> according to some the normal use of an IPR, to ensure for the right holder the benefit of the specific subject matter of that right, is regarded as preserving the existence of the right and can not be overruled by the competition provisions of the Treaty. Specific subject matter and existence are thus overlapping concepts, although it is not always clear how the notions of 'normal use' and benefit are to be applied in concrete cases. Others claim that the existence only covers the authority of Member States to determine the conditions for granting IPRs. According to this view the use of the IPR to ensure the benefit of the specific subject matter of that right can in principle be scrutinised under the competition provisions, however it may fall outside the competition provisions for other reasons such as objective justification.[34]

---

[31] Case C-10/89, *SA CNL-Sucal NV v. HAG GFAG*, 1990 E.C.R. I-3711.

[32] *Id*, ¶13.

[33] *Id*.

[34] European Commission, *Evaluation Report on the Transfer of Technology Block Exemption Regulation No. 240/96. Technology Transfer Agreements under Article 81*, Brussels, December 2001, available at: http://ec.europa.eu/comm/competition/antitrust/technology_transfer. *See, e.g.*, the Opinion of Advocate General Jacobs in Case C-10/89, *SA CNL-Sucal NV v. HAG GFGFAG*, 1990 E.C.R. I-3711, ¶14 and the Opinion of Advocate General Gulmann in Joined Cases C-241/91P and C-242/91P, *Radio Telefis Eireann (RTE) and Independent Television Publications Ltd (ITP) v. Commission*, 1995 E.C.R. I–74, ¶¶28–31, Keeling, *supra* note 23, at 61–72, and Steven D. Anderman, *EC Competition Law and Intellectual Property: The Regulation of Innovation*, 12–13 (1998).

The specific subject matter and existence/exercise theories have never been much of a safe harbor for IP owners. The Court and the Commission have always narrowly defined the specific subject matter.[35] Some commentators argue that it was defined arbitrarily in such a way as to determine a priori the desired result in a particular case.[36] The case law discussed above shows that there is merit in this criticism. Indeed, neither of the doctrines prevented the ECJ from holding that, under certain circumstances, Article 82 mandates that a holder of a valid IP right is obliged to license it to its competitors.[37] Thus competition concerns are given priority over the need to maintain effective protection of IP rights. This has also been the case in the AZ decision, which creates an important precedent relating to the scrutiny of IP acquisition under the EU competition rules.

2. ACQUIRING IP RIGHTS AS AN ANTITRUST OFFENSE

2.1 Walker Process: the US Approach to Abuse of Regulatory Procedures

The claim that enforcement of a patent procured by fraud could constitute an antitrust offense was accepted by the Supreme Court in *Walker Process*,[38] a few years after it had coined the *Noerr-Pennington* doctrine. Food Machinery sued Walker for patent infringement. Walker denied the infringement and alleged that the patent was fraudulently obtained because Food Machinery failed to disclose its prior public use of the patented innovation. It also claimed that in such a situation the procurement and enforcement of the patent violated §2 of the Sherman Act. The gist of Walker's claim was that since Food

35 Case 15/74, *Centrafarm BV et Adriaan de Peijper v. Sterling Drug Inc.*, 1974 E.C.R. 1147.

36 *See, e.g.*, Karen Banks & Giuliano Marenco, *Intellectual Property and the Community Rules on Free Movement: Discrimination Unearthed*, 15 Eur. L. Rev. 224, 230 (1990), Nicholas Macfarlane, *The Tension between National Intellectual Property Rights and Certain Provisions of EC Law*, 16 Eur. Intell. Prop. Rev. 525, 527 (1994) and Keeling, *supra* note 23, at 65–6.

37 Joined Cases C-241/91P and C-242/91P, *Radio Telefis Eireann (RTE) and Independent Television Publications Ltd (ITP) v. Commission*, 1995 E.C.R. I-734; see also Case C-418/01, *IMS Health GmbH & Co. OHG v. NDC Health GmbH & Co. KG*, 2004 E.C.R. I-5039, and Commission Decision in Case COMP/37.792 – Microsoft. For comment on *Magill* and its accommodation of the concept of specific subject matter *see, e.g.*, Fernando Pombo, *Intellectual Property and Intra-Community Trade,* 1996 Fordham Corp. L. Inst. 491 (Barry Hawk, ed., 1997).

38 *Walker Process Equipment v. Food Machinery & Chemical Corp.*, 382 U.S. 172 (1965).

Machinery obtained its patent by fraud it could not enjoy the limited exception to the prohibition of §2 of the Sherman Act, but had to be held liable for any monopolistic action taken to pursue the fraudulent patent claim.[39] The Court agreed, reasoning that no harm to the patent system could result from imposing antitrust liability for knowingly enforcing a patent obtained by fraud.[40]

The requirements for a *Walker Process* claim have been strictly defined and there are very few appellate cases in which such claims were upheld.[41] The Supreme Court stressed that antitrust violation could only be found when the antitrust plaintiff demonstrates intentional fraud, causation, and other elements of a §2 violation.[42] A *Walker Process* fraud is defined as 'knowingly and willfully misrepresenting facts to the Patent Office'.[43] It can take the form of an affirmative statement or an omission, but it must be material: a *Walker Process* claim requires showing that the PTO would not have issued the patent but for the patentee's misrepresentation or omission.[44] If the standard were lower, the fraud could hardly be said to produce anticompetitive market effects.[45] Misrepresentation also has to be deliberate: good faith is a complete defense to a *Walker Process* claim.[46]

It is not the fraudulent patent itself that creates competitive concerns, but the use of that patent which affects the market in some way. Typically, such anticompetitive use involves filing a patent lawsuit, but under certain conditions threats to enforce a patent obtained by fraud on the PTO can also give rise to liability under *Walker Process*.[47] The antitrust plaintiff must also demonstrate that the patent was employed to produce or preserve monopoly power in a specified market,[48] and that the patent owner has monopoly power, or, if an attempt to monopolize is alleged, dangerous probability of acquiring

---

[39] *Walker Process*, 382 U.S. at 176.

[40] *Walker Process*, 382 U.S. at 177. Two competitors jointly enforcing a fraudulent patent may violate §1; see, e.g., *Beal Corp. Liquidating Trust v. Valleylab, Inc.*, 927 F. Supp. 1350 (D. Colo. 1996).

[41] 1 HOVENKAMP ET AL., *supra* note 1, ¶11.2f.

[42] *Walker Process*, 382 U.S. at 177–8.

[43] *Walker Process*, 382 U.S. at 177–8.

[44] *See, e.g., C.R. Bard, Inc. v. M3 Sys., Inc.*, 157 F.3d 1340, 1365 (Fed. Cir. 1998) and *Nobelpharma Ab v. Implant Innovations*, 141 F.3d 1059, 1071 (Fed. Cir. 1998). (A finding of Walker Process fraud must be based on 'clear showing of reliance, i.e., that the patent would not have issued but for the misrepresentation or omission'.)

[45] 1 HOVENKAMP ET AL., *supra* note 1, ¶¶11.2d.

[46] *Walker Process*, 382 U.S. at 177–8.

[47] *See Unitherm Food Sys., Inc. v. Swift-Eckrich, Inc.*, 375 F.3d 1341, 1357–8 (Fed. Cir. 2004) and *MedImmune, Inc. v. Genentech, Inc.*, 427 F.3d 958, 968 (Fed. Cir. 2005). See also 1 HOVENKAMP ET AL., *supra* note 1, ¶11.2e.

[48] *Bourns, Inc. v. Raychem Corp.*, 331 F.3d 704, 711 (9th Cir. 2003).

such power.[49] Last, but not least, the plaintiff must also prove antitrust injury to have a standing.[50]

Although there are similarities between *Noerr-Pennington* and *Walker Process* type of claims, the latter developed independently from *Noerr-Pennington.*[51] There is no reference to the *Noerr* decision in the *Walker Process* opinion. In *Walker Process*, the argument centered on the relation between antitrust policy and patent law.[52] The question of the relation between *Walker Process* claims and *Noerr-Pennington* immunity has never been addressed by the Supreme Court, but the D.C. Circuit ruled in *Nobelpharma*[53] that *PREI* and *Walker Process* were two alternative legal theories on which a patentee may be stripped of its immunity from the antitrust laws.[54] Under this interpretation, *Walker Process* claims are excluded from the general rules concerning government petitioning established in *Noerr-Pennington.*[55] One reason for the special treatment of patents is the specific circumstances in which patents are issued. Patent examiners spend little time examining patent applications and third parties are given only limited possibility to challenge patent administratively, thus the patent system depends heavily on the candor of the patent applicants. This is also why *Walker Process* claims apply solely to patents and not to any other form of IP.[56]

---

49 *Walker Process*, 382 U.S. at 177–8. *See also* 1 HOVENKAMP ET AL., *supra* note 1, ¶11.4.

50 *See, e.g., SCM Corp. v. Radio Corp. of America*, 407 F.2d 166 (2d Cir. 1969) and *Bourns, Inc. v. Raychem Corp.*, 331 F.3d 704 (9th Cir. 2003) (the antitrust plaintiff that had not yet entered the market when it was threatened with a patent lawsuit did not have a standing to bring a Walker Process claim).

51 Most commentators agree that, in principle, Walker Process claims should be assessed under Noerr before they are allowed to proceed. *See, e.g.*, 1 HOVENKAMP ET AL., *supra* note 1, ¶11.2b, Mark A. Lemley, *Antitrust Counterclaims in Patent and Copyright Infringement Cases*, 3 TEX. INTELL. PROP. L. J. 1, 6–7 (1994), and James B. Kobak, Jr., *Professional Real Estate Investors and the Future of Patent-Antitrust Litigation:* Walker Process *and* Handgards *Meet* Noerr-Pennington, 63 ANTITRUST L. J. 185, 185 (1994). The Ninth Circuit has required the showing that the patent application was a sham to establish a Walker Process claim, *see, e.g. Hydranautics v. FilmTec Corp.*, 70 F.3d 533 (9th Cir. 1995) and *Liberty Lake Invs. v. Magnuson,* 12 F.3d 155, 159 (9th Cir. 1993).

52 *Walker Process*, 382 U.S. at 175–6.

53 *Nobelpharma AB v. Implant Innovations*, 141 F.3d 1059 (Fed. Cir. 1998).

54 *Nobelpharma*, 141 F.3d at 1071.

55 For comment on *Nobelpharma see, e.g.*, 1 HOVENKAMP ET AL., *supra* note 1, ¶11.2b and James B. Kobak Jr., *The Doctrine That Will Not Die: Nobelpharma, Walker Process, and the Patent-Antitrust Counterclaim*, 13 ANTITRUST 47 (1998).

56 *Cf. Clipper Exxpress v. Rocky Mountain Motor Tariff Bureau*, 690 F.2d 1240, 1260–61 (9th Cir. 1981) and 1 HOVENKAMP ET AL., *supra* note 1, ¶ 11.2a.

2.2 The EU Approach to Anticompetitive Acquisitions of IP Rights

Cases in which obtaining an IP right was found to be abusive are scarce in the history of EU antitrust.[57] In *Consten & Grundig*, registration of a trademark with the intention to impede trade between the Member States was held to contribute to an antitrust violation.[58] In *Osram/Airam*, the Commission challenged an acquisition of a trademark by a dominant company. In this case, the Commission objected to registration of a trademark by Osram, one of the major producers of lamps in the EU, after a complaint from Airam, a small Finish lamp producer. Osram objected to the registration of the 'Airam' trademark in Germany, on the ground of possible confusion with its 'Osram' mark. It then defensively registered the mark 'Airam'. The Commission asserted that a dominant company registering a trademark which it knows to be already used by a competitor in another Member State may infringe Article 82, when such conduct may restrict the competitor's ability to compete in the market dominated by the firm concerned. Following the Commission's intervention, the parties reached an agreement whereby Airam was allowed to use its mark in any EU Member State, as long as it used it together with its corporate description, so that the possibility of confusion was eliminated.[59]

Osram/Airam clearly did not present a strong case for antitrust intervention. Osram's behavior, presumably intended solely to protect its trademark from dilution and to maintain its goodwill, did not give rise to significant market foreclosure. Given the developments in EU competition law, it seems unlikely that the Commission would challenge the same conduct these days. The same is true for cases involving registration of a trademark with the intention to prevent parallel trade. In this respect, the free trade concerns have been largely solved by the principle of EU-wide IP right exhaustion.

---

[57] This does not concern acquisition of IPRs as a result of a merger or other business transaction. An acquisition of an exclusive license by a dominant company was found abusive by the Commission in *Tetra Pak* (BTG licence), 1988 O.J. (L 272) 27 (*Tetra Pak I Decision*). The Commission Decision was confirmed by the CFI in Case T-51/89, *Tetra Pak v. Commission,* 1990 E.C.R. II-309 (*Tetra Pak I*). The Court found that although the mere fact that a dominant company acquires an exclusive license does not *per se* constitute an abuse within the meaning of Article 82, the circumstances surrounding the acquisition, and in particular its effects on the structure of competition in the relevant market, may make it abusive. For comment on the case *see* IvoVan Bael & Jean-Francois Bellis, Competition Law of the European Community, at 974–5 (2005).

[58] Joined Cases 56 & 58/64, *Consten & Grundig v. Commission*, 1966 E.C.R. 299, at 343. *See also Bayer/Tanabe, Eighth Report on Competition Policy* (1978), ¶178.

[59] European Commission, *Eleventh Report on Competition Policy* 1981, ¶97 (1982); *see also* Van Bael & Bellis, *supra* note 57, at 973–4.

The most important recent case in which an acquisition of IP rights was challenged as an antitrust offence is the Commission Decision in the AZ case, which raises issues similar to the US *Walker Process* line of case law.[60] As will be seen, however, the standards proposed by the Commission for the assessment of the *Walker Process* type of claim are much different from those adopted in the US. Differences concern in particular the requirements of causation and the effect of the conduct on the market.

In the *AZ* case, the Commission found that AZ abused its dominant position by giving misleading information to several national patent offices in the EU, which resulted in its obtaining unwarranted Supplementary Protection Certificates (SPCs) for omeprazole, the active substance in Losec. SPCs are granted on the basis of Regulation No. 1768/92 (SPC Regulation)[61] and extend up to five years the basic patent protection for the active substances in pharmaceutical products. The duration of the SPC protection depends on the date when 'the first authorization to place the product on the market in the Community' took place.[62] The SPC Regulation was criticized as ambiguous: it is not very clear as to who is eligible for an SPC and what constitutes 'the first authorization to place the product on the market in the Community', which is decisive for the length of an SPC.[63] Putting a new pharmaceutical

---

[60] The only earlier case where abuse of procedures before a national patent office designed to preserve exclusive rights of a dominant company was challenged is Case T-30/89, *Hilti AG v. Commission*, 1991 E.C.R. II-1439. Hilti had a patent covering a cartridge strip for a nail gun in the UK. The original patent granted under the Patent Act 1949 would normally have expired after 16 years in July 1984, but the Patent Act of 1977 extended the term of the patent by four years. All such patents were, during the period of extended validity, subject to a license of right. In the absence of agreement between the licensor and the licensee, the terms of the license were fixed by the patent office. The Commission, following complaints from competing nail producers, found that Hilti violated Article 82 of the EC Treaty *inter alia* by frustrating the grant of patent licenses available under the 1977 Patent Act and requested by the complainants, by trying to fix the royalty so high as to amount to a refusal. The CFI agreed with the Commission, reasoning that 'Hilti was not prepared to grant licences on a voluntary basis and that during the proceedings for the grant of licences of right it demanded a fee approximately six times higher than the figure ultimately appointed by the Comptroller of Patents. A reasonable trader, as Hilti claims to have been, should at least have realized that by demanding such a large fee it was needlessly protracting the proceedings for the grant of licences of right, and such behaviour undeniably constitutes an abuse.'

[61] Council Regulation (EEC) No. 1768/92 of 18 June 1992 concerning the creation of a supplementary protection certificate for medicinal products, 1992 O.J. (L 182) 1.

[62] Article 13(1) of the Regulation 1768/92/EEC.

[63] *See, e.g.*, Herwig von Morze & Peter Hanna, *Critical and Practical Observations Regarding Pharmaceutical Patent Term Restoration in the European*

product on a market requires a number of authorizations from various public authorities. In accordance with the Directive 65/65/EEC,[64] marketing a pharmaceutical product in the EU requires an authorization by a competent national medicinal authority. This is often referred to as 'technical market authorization'. Typically, the authorization decision is notified to the company concerned and published in an official publication.[65] Further, the drug manufacturer has to negotiate pricing and reimbursement schemes in different Member States.

The issue of what constitutes 'first authorization' was of particular importance to AZ: depending on the interpretation of the SPC Regulation, Losec would or would not qualify for SPC protection in some Member States.[66] The first technical marketing authorization for Losec was issued in 1987, in France, but the procedures relating to the placing of the drug on the market were not completed until early 1988. Only in 2003, the ECJ decided that the relevant date for the purpose of the SPC Regulation should be the date of the technical marketing authorization.[67] Before that issue was determined, AZ's strategy was, unsurprisingly, to refer to the latest possible date so as to maximize the length of protection for Losec. That date was the date of 'effective marketing authorization', which is when the decision on price approval was first published in one of the EU Member States. AZ's argument was that only after the price decision is published, as a practical matter, a pharmaceutical product can first be placed on the market in the EU.[68] The date of effective marketing authorization of omeprazole in the EU was 21 March 1988, which is when the list of prices featuring Losec was published in Luxembourg (Luxembourg List).

Communities, 77 J. PAT. & TRADEMARK OFF. SOC'Y 505 (Part I) and 77 J. PAT. & TRADEMARK OFF. SOC'Y 479 (Part II) (1995) and Peter L. Kolker, *The Supplementary Protection Certificate: The European Solution to Patent Term Restoration*, 2 INTELL. PROP. Q. 249 (1997).

64 Council Directive 65/65/EEC of 26 January 1965 on the approximation of provisions laid down by law, regulation or administrative action relating to proprietary medicinal products, 1965 O.J. (L 22) 369, English special edition: Series I Chapter 1965–1966, 24.

65 The relevant regulatory procedures still differ from one state to another, so some of these steps may not be required in all Member States; *see AZ* Decision, ¶146.

66 This concerned Germany, Denmark, and Finland, the countries in which under the special transitional regime SPCs were not available for drugs for which market authorization was obtained prior to 1 January 1988.

67 Case C-127/00, *Hässle AB v. Ratiopharm GmbH*, 2003 E.C.R. I-14781 (the ECJ gave a preliminary ruling on the interpretation of the SPC regulation following a reference by a national court deciding on the validity of an SPC for omeprazole).

68 *AZ* Decision, ¶¶633–4. See also ¶213, citing AZ's submissions to the patent office in the UK.

The Commission alleged that AZ did not advocate its effective marketing authorization theory consistently[69] and that it could not have reasonably relied on the date of the Luxembourg publication in good faith. It found that, in its SPC applications for omeprazole, AZ did not reveal the dates of earlier technical marketing authorizations in France (15 April, 1987) and in Luxembourg (16 November, 1987), though it cited the number of the Luxembourg technical authorization. When national patent offices refused to accept the date of effective marketing authorization and requested AZ to provide the date of the first technical marketing authorization, AZ referred to the date of the Luxembourg technical marketing authorization of 16 November 1987 rather than to the earlier French marketing authorization.

The Commission alleged also that, in the course of court proceedings on the validity of SPCs for omeprazole, AZ concealed the evidence pointing to the conclusion that Losec could have been marketed in Luxembourg before the Luxembourg List was published.[70] It concluded that AZ engaged in a 'pattern of misleading representations as part of its SPC Strategy for omeprazole during two stages with a view to preventing, or at least delaying generic entry'.[71] The Commission stressed that it did not challenge AZ's interpretation of the SPC Regulation, but misleading representations and concealment of certain information by AZ, as a part of its strategy to prevent the generic launch of omeprazole.[72]

The Commission found that AZ obtained SPCs for omeprazole in three Member States where it was not eligible for SPC protection, because of its allegedly misleading submissions to patent offices. Though the SPCs in two of these countries were eventually invalidated, the proceedings before national courts extended beyond the duration of the omeprazole patent.[73] In four other Member States, AZ's misrepresentations gave AZ several extra months of SPC protection.[74] According to the Commission, during that time, generic entry was delayed or at the very least made more difficult, as generic producers were forced to spend time, effort, and money in challenging SPCs before national courts and patent offices in several Member States.[75]

Still the Commission stressed that the finding of an Article 82 violation did not require 'that it is established that the misleading representations were

[69] It seems that AZ did not advocate its 'effective market authorization theory' in its SPC applications filed at around the same time as the SPC applications for omeprazole. *AZ* Decision, ¶¶644–6 and 668.

[70] *AZ* Decision, ¶¶727–35.

[71] *AZ* Decision, ¶773.

[72] *AZ* Decision, ¶¶666–7 and 677.

[73] *AZ* Decision, ¶759–60.

[74] *AZ* Decision, ¶761.

[75] *AZ* Decision, ¶¶762–5. Unlike in the US, where under the Bolar-exemption

relied upon by patent agents, patent offices and courts',[76] or that the effects intended by the dominant company are achieved 'in full'.[77] The Commission asserted that if a dominant company misuses regulatory procedures with an exclusionary intent, it is not necessary to prove that its conduct had actual anti-competitive effects.[78]

This is objectionable. Using antitrust to interfere with the use of regulatory procedures is justified only if such use creates significant market distortions. There is little reason to assume that anticompetitive intentions necessarily lead to market foreclosure if the challenged conduct, the misuse of regulatory procedures, does not directly affect the market.[79] If the patent office had not relied on the misleading information AZ had allegedly submitted, AZ's conduct would not have had exclusionary effects. Moreover, challenging the acquisition of IP rights may undermine the IP regime and have an adverse effect on R&D investments by claimant companies. As such, it should be limited to situations where it is absolutely necessary to prevent consumer harm. Thus, the reliance of the patent office on the misleading information submitted by the dominant company should be a necessary element of an Article 82 violation.

AZ invoked the exercise/existence dichotomy and argued that acquiring SPCs could not violate competition law because it relates to the existence of an IP right, as opposed to the exercise of that right. The Commission agreed that 'mere possession or enforcement of a patent or any other intellectual property right against a competitor does not, in principle, violate Article 82 of the EC Treaty', but rejected the contention that acquisition of an IP right, as a matter of principle, cannot violate Article 82 of the EC Treaty, because it relates to the existence, as opposed to the exercise, of the right.[80] The

---

generic producers are allowed to carry out research before the end of the period of the protection for the original drug, in the EU generic producers could start their scientific and regulatory preparations to prove bioequivalence only upon the expiry of an SPC. The Bolar-type exception has been introduced in the EU pharmaceutical regulation only in 2004 by Directive 2004/27/EC of the European Parliament and of the Council of 31 March 2004 amending Directive 2001/83/EC on the Community code relating to medicinal products for human use, 2004 OJ (L 136) 34. For an overview of the EU pharmaceutical law *see, e.g.*, Manuel Campolini, *Protection of Innovative Medicinal Products and Registration of Generic Products in the European Union: Is the Borderline Shifting? State of Play and the Proposed European Medicine Legislation*, 25 EUR. INTELL. PROP. REV. 91 (2003) and Marcus Hartmann & Florence Hartmann-Vareilles, *Recent Developments in European Pharmaceutical Law: A Legal Point of View*, 39 DRUG INF. J. 193 (2005).

[76] *AZ* Decision, ¶764.

[77] *AZ* Decision, ¶765.

[78] *AZ* Decision, ¶758.

[79] This issue has been discussed in more detail in Section 1.3 above.

[80] *AZ* Decision, ¶741.

Commission reasoned that the exercise/existence dichotomy has been gradually abandoned[81] and replaced by the concept of the subject-matter of the right in question, which reflects the principle that EU law does not affect the property laws of the Member States.[82] It asserted that national property laws are not affected by application of EU competition law to misleading representations made in the context of applications for IP rights,[83] and that the making of misleading representations is not included in the bundle of rights forming part of the subject-matter of an SPC.[84]

By dismissing the existence/exercise doctrine the Commission effectively dismantled the last barrier that secured IP rights from antitrust intervention. This is not to say that this development is a step in the wrong direction. The existence/exercise doctrine has not been useful as a theoretical framework for the application of EU competition law to IP rights. The trouble is that the Commission has not proposed any alternative limiting principle, effectively subjecting both the exercise and the existence of IP rights to full antitrust scrutiny. The Commission's reference to 'mere possession or enforcement' and specific subject-matter of an IP right hardly serves as a safe harbor, as the Commission has never clearly stated what exactly makes the possession or enforcement of an IP right other than 'mere'.

3. DEFENDING IP RIGHTS AS AN ANTITRUST OFFENSE

3.1 The US: Anticompetitive Enforcement of IP Rights

As explained in Chapter 2 above, enforcement of valid IP rights can hardly give rise to liability under §2 of the Sherman Act. Claims involving enforcement of invalid IP rights have been more successful. Since the Ninth Circuit *Handgards*[85] decision in 1979, it is well established that enforcement of an IP right that is known by its owner to be invalid, unenforceable or not infringed

[81] In support of this contention, the Commission cited Case 238/87, *Volvo AB v. Erik Veng (U.K.) Ltd.*, 1988 E.C.R. 6211, ¶8, the first case in which the Court ruled that a refusal to grant a license may, in exceptional circumstances, constitute an abuse of a dominant position in violation of Article 82 of the EC Treaty.

[82] *AZ* Decision, ¶738.

[83] *AZ* Decision, ¶741.

[84] *AZ* Decision, ¶742.

[85] *Handgards, Inc. v. Ethicon, Inc.*, 601 F.2d 986 (9th Cir. 1979), cert. denied, 444 U.S. 1025 (1980) (*Handgards I*); 743 F.2d 1282 (9th Cir. 1984), cert. denied, 469 U.S. 1190 (1985) (*Handgards II*).

may constitute an antitrust offense.[86] As in *Walker Process*, *Handgards* involved allegations that a patentee prosecuted an infringement action knowing the patent was invalid, but, unlike in *Walker Process*, the antitrust suit was brought after the patent case had been tried and lost by the antitrust defendant. In the course of the patent case, one of the patents alleged to be infringed was voluntarily dismissed before the trial, and the other patent was held to be invalid based on evidence of prior public use not disclosed to the Patent Office. The antitrust claim was that the patentee brought ill-founded patent infringement actions in bad faith.[87] The Ninth Circuit stressed that patent owners must be permitted to test the validity of their patents through actions against infringers. Nevertheless, it found that a bad faith patent enforcement suit may be within *Noerr-Pennington*'s sham exception. Good faith is presumed, so that the antitrust plaintiff challenging the validity of the enforcement action bears the burden of proving bad faith by clear and convincing evidence.[88] The *Handgards* Court reasoned that establishing a strong presumption that a patent infringement suit was in good faith was necessary 'to erect such barriers to antitrust suits as are necessary to provide reasonable protection for the honest patentee who brings an infringement action'.[89]

In *Loctite*,[90] the DC Circuit addressed another form of anticompetitive litigation: the situation where an infringement suit was brought against a device that was not infringing. Such litigation may give rise to antitrust liability, but again clear and convincing evidence is required to rebut the presumption that the patent suit was brought in good faith.[91]

The standards applicable to the *Handgards* and *Loctite* types of claims were addressed by the Supreme Court in its *PREI*[92] decision discussed in Chapter 2 above. *PREI* operated a hotel and rented Columbia's copyrighted movies to hotel guests to watch in their rooms; it also sought to develop a market for renting videos to other hotels for the same purpose. Columbia argued that permitting hotel guests to watch movies constituted a 'public performance' in violation of its copyrights. PREI counterclaimed that Columbia's suit was a sham and a monopolization attempt. Columbia's interpretation of the

---

86 *See in general* 1 HOVENKAMP ET AL., *supra* note 1, ¶11.3.

87 *Handgards I*, 601 F.2d at 990.

88 *Handgards I*, 601 F.2d at 994, and *Handgards II*, 743 F.2d at 1289. The Court specifically rejected a 'preponderance standard' as insufficient to make sure that legitimate patent enforcement efforts will not be chilled; see *Handgards I*, 601 F.2d at 996.

89 *Handgards I*, 601 F.2d at 996.

90 *Loctite Corp. v. Ultraseal, Ltd.*, 781 F.2d 861 (Fed. Cir. 1985).

91 *Loctite*, 781 F.2d at 876–7.

92 *Professional Real Estate Investors v. Columbia Pictures Indus.* (*PREI*), 508 U.S. 49 (1993).

Copyright Act was controversial and it eventually lost its copyright case on summary judgment.

In deciding on the PREI's antitrust claim, the Supreme Court rejected the proposition that a sham may be found when the antitrust defendant initiates the infringement suit with 'indifference to outcome' or when it fails to show that it would have brought that suit independently of any 'predatory motive'. An objectively reasonable effort to litigate cannot be a sham regardless of the subjective intent of the party bringing the suit.[93] A lawsuit is not 'objectively baseless' if there is a 'probable cause' to bring a lawsuit,[94] or if the action is 'warranted by existing law', or at the very least is based on a 'good faith argument for the extension, modification or reversal of existing law'.[95] The requirement of objective baselessness is used to filter out antitrust claims that seek to challenge the motivation behind a justified IP enforcement action.[96] The Court reasoned that conditioning the enforcement of a copyright upon a demonstrated lack of anticompetitive intent would upset the notion of copyright as a limited grant of exclusive rights designed to motivate creative activity of authors.[97] In assessing the subjective motivation of the antitrust defendant, the court should focus on whether the suit is a concealed attempt 'to interfere directly with the business relationships of a competitor through the use of governmental process – as opposed to the outcome of that process – as an anticompetitive weapon'.[98]

PREI's definition of a sham lawsuit is substantially more restrictive than the standards established by earlier case law; under the new standard the over-

---

[93] PREI, 508 U.S. at 58–60.

[94] *Id. at* 62–3. It suffices that a probable cause exists when the lawsuit is filed.

[95] *Id. at* 65. The 'probable cause' and the second test for objective baselessness are different standards. It is unclear how these two standards should be reconciled. One way is to assume that the existence of probable cause to institute a lawsuit is an absolute defense for antitrust defendants; in the absence of a probable cause, the antitrust defendant can still be entitled to antitrust immunity under the objective prong if she can demonstrate that her claims, though incorrect, were not frivolous. See Lemley, *supra* note 51, at 3–4 and HOVENKAMP ET AL., *supra* note 1, ¶11.3b.

[96] Courts found that patent litigation was 'objectively baseless' and outside Noerr-Pennington exception for example in *Openlcr.com, Inc. v. Rates Tech.*, 112 F. Supp. 2d 1223, 1233 (D. Colo. 2000) and in *Morton Grove Pharms., Inc. v. Par Pharm. Cos.*, 2006 U.S. Dist. LEXIS 13779 (D. Ill. 2006).

[97] *PREI*, 508 U.S. at 64, citing *Sony Corp. of Am. v. Universal City Studios*, 464 U.S. 417, 429 (1984).

[98] *PREI*, 508 U.S. at 60–61. The Supreme Court did not specify what relevant mental state is required to pass the second prong of the PREI test. The DC Circuit required in this respect a specific intent to bring a baseless suit in order to harass a competitor; *see American Hoist & Derrick Co. v. Sowa & Sons, Inc.*, 725 F.2d 1350, 1368 (Fed. Cir. 1984).

whelming majority of lawsuits are immune from antitrust scrutiny.[99] Since the Supreme Court decision in *PREI*, there has not been a single reported decision in which an IP owner was held liable for enforcing her IP rights.[100]

3.2 The EU Approach to Anticompetitive Enforcement of IP Rights

As explained above, the most common way to attack IP rights in the EU is to claim that a refusal to license a valid IP right constitutes an abuse of a dominant position. By contrast, unlike in the US, there have been few cases where allegations of improper enforcement of IP rights were made. To be sure, these two types of claims have a lot in common. In both situations, the alleged anti-competitive effect results from asserting exclusivity over its IP by a dominant company and the ultimate question is whether it should be allowed to enforce its rights. In *Volvo/Veng*,[101] *IMS*,[102] and *Magill*,[103] the three cases in which the ECJ decided on the circumstances which make a refusal to license an abuse of a dominant position, a request for a license was preceded by an enforcement action on the part of a dominant company to enjoin a rival from using its IP.[104] The key difference is that, in cases involving improper enforcement of an IP right, the allegation is that the right is either invalid or that it was asserted against a competitive activity that was outside the scope of that right. Though to some extent the issue of validity of an IP right or, more precisely, its value has been raised in the context of an objective justification for the refusal to license, the EU refusal to license cases concern valid IP rights.

The question as to whether enforcing an invalid IP right can constitute an antitrust offense was first raised in the AZ case. A part of the Commission's case against AZ was that it made misleading representations in the course of the proceedings before the national courts in order to preserve its SPCs.[105] In the *AZ* Decision, the Commission applied the *ITT Promedia* test to determine

---

99 For comment on *PREI see, e.g.*, 1 PHILIP AREEDA & HERBERT HOVENKAMP, ANTITRUST LAW, ¶205b (2002), Kobak, *supra* note 5, at 187–92, Lemley, *supra* note 51, and 1 HOVENKAMP ET AL., *supra* note 1, ¶11.3.

100 1 HOVENKAMP ET AL., *supra* note 1, ¶11.3b4.

101 Case 238/87, *Volvo AB v. Erik Veng (U.K.) Ltd.*, 1988 ECR 6211.

102 Case C-418/01, *IMS Health GmbH & Co. OHG v. NDC Health GmbH & Co. KG (IMS)*, 2004 ECR I-5039.

103 Case T-69/89, *RTE v. Commission*, 1991 ECR II-485, upheld on appeal by the ECJ in Joined Cases C-241/91 P and C-242/91 P, *RTE and ITP v. Commission*, 1995 ECR I-743.

104 The EU rules applicable to unilateral refusals to license a valid IPR and the differences between the US and EU approaches in this regard are described in more detail in Chapter 2 above

105 *AZ* Decision, ¶¶727–35.

when a court action amounts to an abuse of dominance, namely that the court action cannot be reasonably considered as an attempt to establish the rights of the antitrust defendant and that it forms part of a plan to eliminate competition.[106] The Commission asserted that the conduct of an IP defense can constitute an abuse of dominance if it forms part of a plan to eliminate competition.[107] According to the Commission, AZ's misleading representations before national courts were the implementation of its exclusionary strategy.[108] The anticompetitive effect of AZ's conduct, that is, imposing costs and delays on actual or potential competitors,[109] was not attributable to AZ's defense, but to AZ's misrepresentations in the SPC applications. Generic manufacturers of omeprazole, reasoned the Commission, had no means of entering the market other than engaging in costly litigation. AZ's defense of its SPCs before national courts was the continuation of its abusive conduct, which commenced when it submitted misleading information in its SPC applications.[110]

The Commission reserved the question as to whether the conduct of a defense based on misleading representations could be abusive on its own.[111] It asserted that since AZ knew that Losec could have been launched prior to the 'effective marketing authorization' date, it could not have been said to defend 'rights which it could reasonably have considered to be its own.'[112] This suggests that the Commission takes the view that the first prong of the *ITT Promedia* test requiring that the lawsuit is objectively manifestly meritless is satisfied where a dominant company relies on a legal theory which it knows not to have sufficient support in the facts of the case. This would make the Commission's reasoning similar to the US Supreme Court holding in PREI that a lawsuit is not objectively baseless if the action is based on good faith argument for the extension, modification or reversal of existing law. In this case, the Commission reasoning may have been that AZ was not making a good faith argument for the modification of existing law. Alternatively, the AZ Decision could be understood as establishing the rule that defending an IP right which is known to the antitrust defendant to be invalid makes the lawsuit objectively meritless and, as such, possibly a violation of antitrust laws.

---

106 Case T-111/96, *ITT Promedia NV v. Commission (ITT Promedia)*, 1998 E.C.R. II-2937. The case is discussed in more detail in Chapter 1.

107 *AZ* Decision, ¶¶617 and 737.

108 *AZ* Decision, ¶737.

109 *AZ* Decision, ¶738.

110 *AZ* Decision, ¶738.

111 *AZ* Decision, ¶739.

112 *Id.*

As with the assessment of the submission of misleading information to a patent office by a dominant company, the Commission concluded that the bringing of a meritless lawsuit by a dominant company with an exclusionary purpose violates Article 82, without the need to engage in an inquiry as to whether such conduct had or was likely to have anticompetitive effects.[113] Thus, though the Commission may have used a test akin to the one established by the Supreme Court in *PREI*, this statement makes the EU approach to vexatious litigation substantially different from the analogous US standards. As it has been explained, the fact that the *PREI* criteria are satisfied means only that the act of bringing a lawsuit may be subject to antitrust scrutiny. Condemnation of the challenged conduct under §2 of the Sherman Act would still require the proof that the conduct contributed to creating, enlarging or prolonging monopoly power by impairing the opportunities of rivals.[114] The Commission's focus on anticompetitive motivation behind an IP enforcement action is difficult to understand. As explained above, antitrust intervention is warranted only if vexatious litigation has or is likely to have market-foreclosing effects. An inquiry into the actual anticompetitive effects of the challenged conduct should be part of the antitrust scrutiny of such conduct.

---

[113] *AZ* Decision, ¶758.

[114] *See, e.g., United States v. Grinnell Corp.*, 384 U.S. 563, 570–71 (1966), *United States v. Aluminum Co. of Am.*, 148 F.2d 416, 430 (2d Cir. 1945), *Spectrum Sports v. McQuillan*, 506 U.S. 447, 459 (1993) and *United States v. Microsoft Corp.*, 253 F.3d 34, 58–9 (2d Cir. 2001); see 1 Areeda & Hovenkamp, *supra* note 104, ¶208.2d.

4. Trade secrets and antitrust: an example of the conflicting US and EU approaches*

Application of antitrust rules to trade secrets in the EU and in the United States is the best example of the divergences in the treatment of IP-related market distortions in the two jurisdictions. Both in the US and in the EU, trade secrets are regulated predominantly at the state or national level and 'federal' antitrust rules trump inconsistent trade secret laws. Yet, whereas the US antitrust authorities treat trade secrets with the same deference as IP rights, the position of their EU counterparts is that trade secrets do not deserve the same level of protection as other forms of IP. The differences in the treatment of trade secrets merit a closer look, as they are a very good example of applying antitrust rules in a manner that affects substantive standards for IP protection.

The decisions in which the European Commission has applied competition law to trade secrets have shaped the standards of trade secret protection in the European Union. The Commission has adopted a definition of what constitutes protectable know-how, decided what the acceptable means of its exploitation are, and asserted that trade secrets are not IP. In doing so, it was concerned predominantly with the need to ensure free competition and less with the need to secure the rights of the companies in their know-how. This process, which effectively led to the establishment of trade secret standards for the purpose of application of EU competition law, was erratic and marked by decisions that ignored the standards of trade secret protection at the Member State level. The Commission's refusal to recognize and protect trade secrets, in line with the basic principles of national trade secret laws, considerably undermined these laws and may, in turn, diminish the incentives to innovate and impede the diffusion of new technologies. By contrast, in the United States, the basic principles of trade secret laws have been respected by antitrust enforcers, who have recognized the need to protect trade secrets and afforded them the same treatment as that given to other forms of IP.

---

* An extended version of this chapter was published as *Antitrust and Trade Secrets: The U.S. and the EU Approach*, in 24 SANTA CLARA COMPUTER & HIGH TECH. L. J. 207 (2008).

Although, as discussed in Chapter 2, there are major differences in the approaches of the US and EU antitrust enforcers to IP rights, the differences in the treatment of trade secrets are particularly striking. This, together with the fact that at least some authorities suggest that trade secrets will be treated differently from other forms of IP for the purpose of antitrust enforcement in the EU, is the reason for addressing application of antitrust rules to trade secrets in a separate chapter.

The first part of this chapter briefly discusses the basic principles of trade secret laws, as the necessary background for the analysis of the trade secrets and antitrust intersection. The second part focuses on the application of antitrust rules to trade secrets, including both the rules applicable to anticompetitive agreements and abuses of market power.

1. TRADE SECRETS BASICS

Trade secrets can be broadly defined as confidential information which has commercial value because it is secret. The WTO Agreement on Trade-Related Aspects of Intellectual Property Rights (TRIPS), which comprehensively addresses the issue of trade secret protection,[1] requires the WTO Member States to protect 'undisclosed information' which (1) is secret in the sense that it is not generally known or readily accessible, (2) has commercial value because it is secret, and (3) has been subject to reasonable steps under the circumstances to keep it secret by the person lawfully in control of the information.[2] It is not required that the information is of a technical nature; non-technical information, such as customer lists, sales data, or business strategies, can also be protected as a trade secret. For example, US Courts have held that a recipe for chocolate chip cookies,[3] a pesticide formula,[4] a scheme for an electronic board game,[5] computer hardware design,[6] some elements of

---

1 Article 10bis of the Paris Convention provides for general obligations concerning unfair competition. The first international agreement containing an explicit provision on trade secret protection was the North American Free Trade Agreement (Article 1711), signed in 1993.

2 The definition of 'confidential information' closely resembles the definition of trade secrets in the US Restatement (Third) of Unfair Competition (1995), §38 *et seq*. *See infra* Section 2.1.

3 *Peggy Lawton Kitchens, Inc. v. Hogan*, 18 Mass.App.Ct. 937, 466 N.E.2d 138 (Mass.App., 1984).

4 *Ruckelshaus v. Monsanto Co.* (*Ruckelshaus*), 467 U.S. 986 (1984).

5 *Burten v. Milton Bradley Co.*, 763 F.2d 461 (1st Cir. 1985).

6 *See, e.g., Telex Corp. v. International Business Machines Corp.*, 510 F.2d 894 (10th Cir. 1975), *Data General Corp. v. Digital Computer Controls, Inc.*, 357 A.2d 105, (Del.Ch. 1975); *see also* 2 MELVIN F. JAGER, TRADE SECRETS LAW, §9.2 (2002).

computer software,[7] and information relating to non-technical aspects of business such as customer lists[8] qualify for protection under the trade secret laws.[9] The TRIPS provides that trade secrets are protected against unauthorized disclosure, and acquisition or use that is contrary to honest commercial practices.[10] The notion of unauthorized use typically includes such practices as industrial or commercial espionage, breach of contract, and breach of confidence.[11] It does not extend to the use of protected information by third parties who obtained it in accordance with honest commercial practices. Still, an element of contractual breach is not a prerequisite for liability. A third party who knowingly acquires the information from someone who had earlier misappropriated it is also liable.[12]

All industrialized countries provide for a high level of trade secret protection in line with the principles spelled out in the TRIPS agreement. In the United States, basic principles of trade secret laws developed throughout the nineteenth century were codified in the 1939 Restatement of Torts.[13] The Uniform Trade Secrets Act (UTSA), adopted in 1979, was designed to clarify and harmonize the standards of trade secret protection. The 1995 Restatement (Third) of Unfair Competition was another effort to further high and consistent standards for trade secret protection throughout the United States. The Restatements and the UTSA largely harmonized the common law of trade secrets. The Economic Espionage Act[14] (EEA), adopted in 1996,[15] established

[7] *See, e.g., Telex Corp. v. International Business Machines Corp.*, 367 F. Supp. 258 (D.C. Okl., 1973), *Avtec Sys. v. Peiffer*, 21 F.3d 568, 575 (4th Cir. 1994), *Cisco Sys., Inc. v. Huawei Techs., Co.*, 266 F. Supp. 2d 551; *see also* 2 JAGER, *supra* note 6, §§9.3–9.15.

[8] *See, e.g., Ecolaire Inc. v. Crissman*, 542 F. Supp. 196 (D.C. Pa., 1982) and *American Precision Vibrator Co. v. National Air Vibrator Co.*, 764 S.W.2d 274 (Tex. App. 1988).

[9] *See* 1-1 ROGER M. MILGRIM, MILGRIM ON TRADE SECRETS §1.09 (1984) and 1 JAGER, *supra* note 6, §3.3 and §3.9.

[10] 'A manner contrary to honest commercial practices' is a standard borrowed from Article 10bis of the Paris Convention and defined in FN 10 to the TRIPS Agreement as 'at least practices such as breach of contract, breach of confidence and inducement to breach, and includes the acquisition of undisclosed information by third parties who knew, or were grossly negligent in failing to know, that such practices were involved in the acquisition'.

[11] Article 39 of the TRIPS Agreement, Note 10.

[12] *Id.*

[13] *See, e.g.*, 1 JAGER, *supra* note 6, §3.1 and §3.2.

[14] Pub. L. No. 104-294, §§1831–9, 110 Stat. 3488 (codified at 18 U.S.C. §§1831–9).

[15] For commentary and reasons for the adoption of the EEA *see, e.g.*, James Pooley et al., *Understanding the Economic Espionage Act of 1996*, 5 TEX. INTELL.

a comprehensive and systematic scheme using criminal sanctions to protect trade secrets at the federal level.[16]

Although there are important differences between the UTSA, the Restatement of Unfair Competition, and the EEA, they are all designed to protect information that is (1) valuable in that it confers some sort of competitive advantage, which (2) derives its value from not being publicly known, and (3) with respect to which the holder took reasonable steps to keep it secret. Whereas intellectual property rights (IP rights) are usually limited to a particular type of information,[17] or a particular way information is used or expressed,[18] trade secrets are broadly defined as 'information'. There is no review of novelty or non-obviousness, as in the case of patents, or originality, as under copyright law; it suffices that the information gives a demonstrable competitive advantage.[19] The information must not be readily available and it must be specific enough. General skill and knowledge cannot be protected under trade secret law;[20] readily ascertainable ideas or trivial advances in known formulas or processes are not protectable.[21]

In the EU, there are no harmonized standards for trade secret protection and trade secret laws vary significantly across the EU Member States. Confidential

---

PROP. L. J. 177, Rochelle Cooper Dreyfuss, *Trade Secrets: How Well Should We Be Allowed to Hide Them? The Economic Espionage Act of 1996*, 9 FORDHAM INTELL. PROP. MEDIA & ENT. L. J. 1 (1996), Chris Carr et al., *The Economic Espionage Act: Bear Trap or Mousetrap?*, 8 TEX. INTELL. PROP. L. J. 159 (2000), and Gerald J. Mossinghoff et al., *The Economic Espionage Act: A New Federal Regime of Trade Secrets Protection*, 79 J. PAT. & TRADEMARK OFF. SOC'Y 191 (1997).

[16] The EEA makes trade secrecy misappropriation a federal offense, punishable by fines up to $5,000,000 and imprisonment up to 10 years. Trade secret theft is defined as knowingly engaging in a trade secret conversion, with an intent to benefit someone other than the trade secret owner and with an intent or knowledge that the information will injure an owner of the trade secret; *see* 18 USC §1832. Foreign economic espionage, defined as knowing misappropriation of trade secrets by foreign governments and agents or anyone acting on their behalf, is subject to even more severe penalties: up to 15 years imprisonment and up to $10,000,000 fine. The injured parties do not, however, have a federal cause of action for the loss of a trade secret. *See* 18 USC §1831.

[17] Patents protect only inventions in the field of technology.

[18] Copyright protection extends only to the particular form in which an idea is expressed; ideas or facts as such are not copyrightable. Trademarks give an exclusive right to use a particular sign for a specified type of good or service; protection does not extend, for example, to artistic works where a trademark is employed.

[19] 1-1 MILGRIM, *supra* note 9, §1.03 and §1.08. The information claimed to be a trade secret must also be sufficiently identified. *See, e.g., Nilssen v. Motorola, Inc.*, 963 F. Supp. 664, 672 (N.D. Ill. 1997) and *Basic Am., Inc. v. Shatila*, 992 P.2d 175 (Idaho 1999).

[20] *See* the definition in UTSA; *see also* 1-5 MILGRIM, *supra* note 9, §5.02.

[21] 1-1 MILGRIM, *supra* note 9, §1.03.

information is known under many different names in various EU jurisdictions: 'know-how', 'trade secret', 'confidential information' and 'businesses secret' are among them.[22] Protection is generally afforded to confidential information which has commercial value and whose owner takes reasonable measures to keep it secret.[23] The *de facto* secrecy of information and the owner's continued efforts to maintain this secrecy are the key ingredients of a trade secret. In the absence of secrecy no claim to the information can be made. If any interested party can learn the information without a great deal of sacrifice, the matter is public and cannot be considered a trade secret.[24] It is also usually required that a trade secret holder has the intention to keep the information secret and takes steps to protect secrecy.[25] Secrecy is the source of competitive advantage and it takes precedence over all other conditions of protection.[26] Secrecy alone is not sufficient: there must be a link between secrecy

---

[22] FRANÇOIS DESSEMONTET, THE LEGAL PROTECTION OF KNOW-HOW IN THE UNITED STATES OF AMERICA (1976), and Aldo Frignani, *Know-how and Trade Secrets*, paper presented at IBA/SBL Conference in Paris, Committee X, International Franchising, September 1995, available at: http://www.jus.unitn.it/cardozo/Review/Business/Frignani-1997/ Parigi2.htm.

[23] In the UK, proprietary information is protected if it is used in a trade or business and the owner limits the dissemination of it or at least does not encourage or permit widespread publication, *Lansing Linde Ltd. v. Kerr* [1991] 1 WLR 251. The German Federal Supreme Court (Bundesgerichtshof) defined a trade secret as 'any fact in relation to a business which is not apparent but is known to a narrow circle only, and which according to the manifest intention of the owner of the business, based on a sufficient economic interest, is to be kept secret', BGH GRUR 2003, 356, 358 – Präzissionsmessgeräte. In France it is required that trade secrets have a certain degree of originality and/or commercial value and that they are kept secret from competitors, Court of Appeal in Paris, 13 June 1972; Supreme Court (Cour de cassation), 26 June 1973, Ann. 1974–85.

[24] The IPR Helpdesk sponsored by the European Commission stresses the importance of secrecy in its note on trade secret protection in the European Union. *See* IPR Helpdesk, *The Legal Protection of Trade Secrets*, Section C (2004, updated in June 2006), available at: http://www.ipr-helpdesk.org/docs/docs.EN/ Legalprotectionof TradeSecrets.pdf ('A substantial element of secrecy must exist. Information generally known to the public or inside a particular industry is not typically afforded trade secret protection. While secrecy need not be absolute, it must be sufficient to confer actual or potential economic advantage on one who possesses the information. Thus the requirement of secrecy is satisfied if it would be difficult or costly for others to acquire and exploit the information without resorting to some form of wrongful conduct').

[25] *See* IPR Helpdesk, *supra* note 24, Section B ('the *de facto* secrecy of information and the owner's continued efforts to maintain this secrecy are the key elements of a trade secret').

[26] *See* François Dessemontet, *Protection of Trade Secrets and Confidential Information*, in CARLOS M. CORREA AND ABDULQAWI A. YUSUF (EDS), INTELLECTUAL PROPERTY AND INTERNATIONAL TRADE: THE TRIPS AGREEMENT (1998), at 249.

and economic advantage. The value of trade secrets stems from the fact that they are useful for doing business and not generally known: other companies would have to expend considerable sums of money to obtain the protected information. The fact that competitors are trying to obtain the information at stake may constitute *prima facie* evidence of the information's commercial value.[27] There is also an agreement that a trade secret need not to be patentable. [28]

Trade secret protection has been based on a number of different legal theories: contract, property, fiduciary relationship, and unjust enrichment. In some legal systems, such as in Germany and Japan, protection of trade secrets forms part of the general concept of protection against unfair competition. In other legal systems, such as in the United Kingdom and Australia, trade secrets are treated as a form of confidential information and protected under the laws of confidentiality.[29] It is unclear whether trade secrets can be characterized as property rights in a manner similar to copyrights or patents. Though TRIPS lists trade secrets among other forms of IP, it does not choose between different theoretical approaches to trade secret protection.[30] The case for the proprietary theory is stronger in common law jurisdictions, particularly in the US, where the Supreme Court compared the characteristics and purposes of the law of trade secrets and patent law[31] and held that trade secrets, as intangible property rights, qualified for protection under the Fifth Amendment Taking Clause.[32] By contrast, courts in civil law jurisdictions have been reluctant to recognize proprietary interests in trade secrets.[33] The civil law concept of a

---

[27] DANIEL J. GERVAIS, THE TRIPS AGREEMENT: DRAFTING HISTORY AND ANALYSIS 274–5 (2nd edition, 2003).

[28] Dessemontet, *supra* note 26, at 247–9 (interpreting TRIPS).

[29] *See Protecting Trade Secrets: A Worldwide Survey*, MANAGING INTELL. PROP. 40 (1997–98).

[30] Arguably the reference to the information that is '*legitimately under the control of plaintiffs*' and the fact that trade secrets are listed with other IPRs imply that TRIPS adopts the property rights theory. *See* Dessemontet, *supra* note 26, at 246.

[31] *Kewanee Oil Co. v. Bicron Corp. et al.*, 416 U.S. 470, 480–84 (U.S. 1974)

[32] *Ruckelshaus v. Monsanto*, 467 U.S. 986 (1984). There are more cases in which courts have recognized property rights in trade secrets, *see, e.g.*, *Carpenter v. United States*, 484 U.S. 19, 26 (1987) ('Confidential business information has long been recognized as property') and *Warner-Lambert Co. v. Execuquest Corp.*, 691 N.E.2d 545, 546–7 (Mass. 1998) (trade secrets are property under section 93A of the General Laws of Massachusetts, which requires a loss of property to allow for an injunction).

[33] For example, French courts have held there are no exclusive rights in confidential information. Jean-Pierre Gasnier et al., *France*, in DENNIS CAMPBELL & SUSAN COTTTER (EDS), INTERNATIONAL INTELLECTUAL PROPERTY LAW – EUROPEAN JURISDICTIONS 196 (1995), citing the judgments of the Paris Court of Appeal of 3 July

property right is strictly defined: the right exists, in accordance with the principle of *numerus clausus,* only when is has been created by law.[34] Thus, trade secrets have been described as 'de facto assets' or 'incomplete IP rights' or 'subjective rights' (*subjektive Rechte, droit subjective*).[35]

2. ANTITRUST AND TRADE SECRETS

The problems created by the existence of trade secrets are similar to those resulting from the existence of other forms of IP. Licensing of trade secrets (or know-how), like patent licensing, is generally pro-competitive. It allows dissemination of technology and its fuller exploitation. Unless a know-how license agreement is a mere sham to cover price fixing or territory sharing, just like a patent license it makes it easier for the licensee to enter a new market or to expand in a market in which it is already active. In the case of a patent, the use of a licensed technology by third parties could be enjoined by courts. A know-how license saves the time and money involved in reverse engineering or independent R&D. Trade secrets also create fewer competitive concerns when they are used by a dominant company as in principle they contribute less to the creation or maintenance of market power than other forms of IP.[36] A trade secret holder, unlike a patentee, cannot restrain independent development or reverse engineering. In the United States, these differences have resulted in less vigorous application of antitrust rules to trade secret transactions than to transactions involving patents.[37] In the EU, antitrust enforcers have largely ignored these features of trade secrets and, instead, applied even more stringent rules, reasoning that, due to their uncertain status as property rights, trade secrets do not merit the same level of protection as other forms of IP.

1975 (Gaz. Pal. 1976, 1, 43) and the judgment of the Cour de Cassation of 3 October 1978 (JCP 78 Ed. G., IV, 332). The Italian legal system also does not recognize *erga omnes* rights in confidential information. Giorgio Mondini et al., *Italy*, in DENNIS CAMPBELL & SUSAN COTTTER (EDS), INTERNATIONAL INTELLECTUAL PROPERTY LAW – EUROPEAN JURISDICTIONS 342 (1995).

[34] Carlos M. Correa, *Harmonization of IPRs in Latin America: Is There Still Room for Differentiation?*, 29 N.Y.U. J. INT'L L. & POL. 109, 131–2 (1997).

[35] Stanislaw Soltysiński, *Are Trade Secrets Property?*, 17 INT'L REV. INTELL. PROP. & COMPETITION L. 331, 332 (1986) and Elżbieta Wojcieszko-Gluszko, *Ochrona prawna know-how w prawie polskim na tle prawnoporównawczym*, 154–64, 81 ZESZYTY NAUKOWE UNIWERSYTETU JAGIELLOŃSKIEGO, PRACE Z WYNALAZCZOŚCI I OCHRONY WLASNOŚCI INTELEKTUALNEJ (2002).

[36] 3-10 MILGRIM, *supra* note 9, §10.01 (1)(a)(ii) and (c)(ii).

[37] 2 JAGER, *supra* note 6, §11.2.

2.1 US Antitrust Law and Trade Secrets

Allegations that trade secrets were used to restrain trade were made in the first US reported trade secrets decision: the 1837 Massachusetts Supreme Court ruling in *Vickery v. Welch*.[38] The principal question of law was whether an agreement whereby the seller of a chocolate mill conveyed a secret method of making chocolate on the buyer and agreed not to use the secret method himself was in restraint of trade. The Court decided that it was not, as it was 'of no consequence to the public whether the secret art be used by' the seller or the buyer of the mill.[39] Perhaps more convincingly, holding that confidentiality clauses were not illegal restraint of trade, the Sixth Circuit reasoned that since the public has 'no right to compel publication', it 'loses no right by respecting a restricted disclosure'.[40]

American courts have also found no grounds to interfere with the parties' decision as to the duration of the agreement and an obligation to pay royalties. An obligation to pay royalties even after the licensed know-how has ceased to be secret is valid and can potentially last forever.[41] Thus, unlike patent or copyright licenses, which are strictly limited to the duration of the term of protection, a trade secret license is not subject to any time limitation. In *Listerine*,[42] the court explicitly rejected the argument that the antitrust ban on royalty payments that go beyond the life of a patent or copyright should be extended to know-how licenses.[43] In the case of licenses covering both patent

---

[38] 36 Mass. 523, 19 Pick. 23, 1837 WL 2540 (1837). See *also* 1 JAGER, *supra* note 6, §2.3.

[39] This does not really address the question, as if there was no restraint the secret method of making chocolate could be used by both the seller and the buyer of the mill.

[40] *John D. Park & Sons Co. v. Hartman*, 153 F. 24, 30 (6th Cir., 1907).

[41] *Warner-Lambert Pharmaceutical Co. v. John J. Reynolds, Inc.*, 178 F. Supp. 655 (S.N.Y. 1959) and *Aronson v. Quick Point Pencil Co.*, 440 U.S. 257 (1979). *See also* 2 JAGER, *supra* note 6, §11.7.

[42] *Warner-Lambert Pharmaceutical Co. v. John J. Reynolds, Inc.*, 178 F. Supp. 655, 665–7 (S.N.Y. 1959).

[43] The case concerned a license agreement for the formula of Listerine (antiseptic mouthwash) concluded in 1891. The licensee had paid the licensor over $22 million over 75 years; thereafter the licensee challenged the contract as invalid. The agreement was attacked on the ground that it lacked any future consideration, because the secret formula was disclosed in the *Journal of the American Medical Association* in 1931 and in the course of an FTC action against the licensee. The court upheld the validity of the contract, reasoning that if the parties wished to terminate the royalty payments upon the disclosure of the secret formula they could have provided so in the agreement. The court distinguished the case before it from those concerning patents or copyrights licenses, on the ground that the latter involve exclusive rights that are limited in time and granted in exchange for publication of the information at stake.

and trade secrets, the payment of license fees for expired patents is banned, but the royalties for the use of know-how can continue beyond the life of the licensed patent.[44] The limited exclusionary effect of trade secrets was a significant factor in the antitrust assessment of restrictions in trade secret licenses.[45]

In principle, antitrust analysis of competitive restraints in trade secret licenses does not differ from that found in patent or copyright licenses. The 1995 IP Licensing Guidelines[46] provide that for the purpose of antitrust enforcement all forms of IP, including patents, copyrights and trade secrets, are essentially comparable to other forms of property and that the governing antitrust principles are the same regardless of the type of IP regime at stake.[47] This is a reasonable approach. A trade secret license, just like a patent license, is a transfer of valuable technology allowing for its efficient exploitation, so the economic incentives of the parties to such agreements are essentially the same.[48] In addition, the licensed technology is often a bundle of patents and secret know-how. In such situations, the application of different antitrust standards to patents and trade secrets could impede the transfer of technology.

All in all, trade secrets are treated similarly to other forms of IP rights for the purpose of applying §1 of the Sherman Act. Unlike patents or copyrights,[49]

---

44 *See, e.g.*, *Brulotte v. Thys Co.*, 379 U.S. 29, 32 (U.S., 1964) (regardless of state contract law, a licensing agreement that extends a patent's monopoly beyond the life of the patent involved is a *per se* violation of federal patent law) and *Pitney Bowes, Inc. v. Mestre*, 701 F.2d 1365 (11th Cir., 1983). *See also* 2 JAGER, *supra* note 6, §11.7 and 3-10 MILGRIM, *supra* note 9, §10.01(2)(a)(iii).

45 *See in general* 2 WILLIAM C. HOLMES, INTELLECTUAL PROPERTY AND ANTITRUST LAW, §28.1 (1983) and 3-10 MILGRIM, *supra* note 9, §10.01 (1)(a)(ii).

46 *IP Licensing Guidelines*, ¶2.1.

47 *Id.* 538. The Agencies note that there are 'clear and important differences in the purpose, extent, and duration of protection provided under the intellectual property regimes of patent, copyright, and trade secret', and that these differences 'are taken into account in evaluating specific market circumstances in which transactions occur'.

48 Though unlike in the case of patents the value of the technology at stake is not confirmed by the Patent Office, the commercial value of a trade secret can be inferred from the fact that the licensee is willing to pay for access to the licensed trade secrets.

49 *See, e.g.*, *United States v. Paramount Pictures, Inc.*, 334 U.S. 1312 (1948) (presumption that copyrights confer market power) and *United States v. Loew's, Inc.*, 371 U.S. 38, 45 (1962) ('The requisite economic power is presumed when the tying product is patented or copyrighted'), *International Salt Co., Inc. v. G.S. Suppinger Co.*, 332 U.S. 392 (1947) (presumption that patents confer market power), *United States v. Times-Picayune Pub. Co.*, 345 U.S. 594, 608 (1953) (patents confer monopolistic, albeit lawful, market control). In a more recent decision, the Supreme Court confirmed the presumption in dicta (*Jefferson Parish Hospital District No. 2 v. Hyde*, 466 U.S. 2, 16 (1984), whereas the concurring Justices concluded that there should be no such presumption (id., at 38). Finally, in *Illinois Tool Works Inc. v. Independent Ink, Inc.*, 126 St. Ct. 1281 (U.S. 2006), the Supreme Court unanimously ruled that the fact that a tying

trade secrets have never been presumed to create market power.[50] This has had a significant impact on the assessment of tying arrangements in trade secret licenses.[51] In the 1970s, the DOJ recognized that a trade secret licensor might be able to restrict sales of unpatented product for reasonable periods, even if the same restrictions were at that time considered illegal in patent licenses.[52] Further, contractual clauses extending the duration of royalty payments after the information protected as a trade secret became publicly available were upheld by courts, whereas clauses extending royalty payments beyond the life of a patent in license agreements were held to be an illegal extension of patent monopoly and a violation of antitrust laws.

The right of the owner to assert and defend her trade secret in court has been recognized in the *CVD* case.[53] Enforcement of trade secrets, however, may amount to monopolization if trade secrets are asserted in bad faith, with the knowledge that a trade secret does not exist or that the rights have not been violated.[54] Other elements of monopolization, such as market power in the relevant market, must also be established to succeed on the monopolization claim.[55]

The non-disclosure of trade secrets accompanying patent claims was held not to constitute monopolization in *Christianson v. Colt*.[56] In this case, the Seventh Circuit reversed the district court holding that Colt's insufficient disclosure of information concerning a finished rifle in the patent applications for the rifle's parts allowed it to retain a monopoly over the rifle that extended beyond the life of the patents. The Seventh Circuit pointed out that while information at stake might have been valuable for Colt's rivals, patent law did not oblige Colt to disclose it, as it was not within the scope of invention claimed in the patent application. Thus, the summary judgment on antitrust

---

product is patented does not support the presumption of market power in a patented product.

50 *In re Data General Corp. Antitrust Litigation*, 490 F. Supp. 1089, 1113–14 (D. Cal. 1980) (it has never been held that trade secrets protection is sufficient to create a presumption of economic power) and *3 P.M., Inc. v. Basic Four Corp.*, 591 F. Supp. 1350, 1359 (D. Mich. 1984) (same); *see also* 2 JAGER, *supra* note 6, §11.10.

51 There have been only a few cases where the question of the legality of using a trade secret as the tying product was raised. *See* 2 JAGER, *supra* note 6, §11.10.

52 3-10 MILGRIM, *supra* note 9, §10.01(1)(c)(ii).

53 *CVD, Inc. v. Raytheon Co.* (*CVD*), 769 F.2d 842, 850 (1st Cir. 1985), *cert.* denied, 475 U.S. 1016 (1986).

54 *CVD*, 769 F.2d at 851 and *Christianson v. Colt Industries Operating Corp.* (*Colt II*), 766 F. Supp. 670, 689 (D. Ill. 1991).

55 *CVD*, 769 F.2d at 851 and *Christianson v. Colt Industries Operating Corp.*, 766 F. Supp. 670, 688 (D.D.C. 1991) (*Colt II*).

56 *Christianson v. Colt Industries Operating Corp.* (*Colt I*) 870 F.2d 1292 (7th Cir., 1989), on remand *Colt II.*

claims could not stand.[57] On remand, Christianson argued that Colt's trade secrets were impossible to reverse engineer, thus allowing Colt to perpetuate a commercial monopoly previously protected by a patent. The district court rejected this claim, holding that neither the federal patent regime nor antitrust law mandates striking down trade secrets simply because they are difficult to reverse-engineer.[58]

The use of a trade secret to obtain a competitive advantage, even by a company enjoying monopoly power, does not violate antitrust laws. In a series of cases decided in the late 1970s, American courts rejected the argument that a monopolist should be forced to pre-disclose its new products to facilitate competition in an ancillary market. The problem first arose in the context of changes in IBM's policies in response to increasing competition from 'plug-compatible' manufacturers.[59] IBM began bundling peripheral equipment control functions into mainframe hardware and changed from a full disclosure policy to keeping the operating system software source code secret, as well as limiting and delaying interface disclosures. This strategy was challenged both by antitrust authorities and by IBM's competitors in private litigation.[60] The claim that antitrust laws mandated IBM to disclose its technological changes to its rivals in advance of general release, so that they can make their products compatible with IBM, was firmly rejected; IBM was under no duty to help its rivals survive or expand. IBM's behavior did not completely foreclose rivals since they successfully reverse-engineered IBM's products. Further, depriving IBM of its lead-time would remove its incentive to invent.[61] Notably, the same considerations were important in cases involving compulsory licensing of IP rights.[62]

---

[57] *Colt I*, 870 F.2d at 1303. For discussion of the case *see, e.g.*, 2 HOLMES, *supra* note 45, §11.4 and 2 JAGER, *supra* note 6, §§10.2 and 11.11.

[58] *Colt II*, 766 F.Supp at 690.

[59] In the late 1960s and early 1970s, IBM was a dominant manufacturer of computers in the United States, but its market shares plummeted due to increased competition from peripheral equipment (tape storage drives, disc drives, and add-on memory units that plugged into the standard interfaces used on IBM System 360 and then System 370 mainframes) manufacturers. IBM also faced competition from mainframe producers whose computers could be used interchangeably with IBM computers and were cheaper.

[60] For an overview of the IBM cases, *see* 3 PHILIP AREEDA & HERBERT HOVENKAMP, ANTITRUST LAW §616 (2002).

[61] *ILC Peripherals Leasing Corp. v. International Business Machines Corp.*, 458 F.Supp. 423, 436–7 (D.C. Cal.,1978), *see also California Computer Products, Inc. v. International Business Machines Corp.*, 613 F.2d 727, 744 (9th Cir. 1979), *Memorex Corp. v. International Business Machines* 636 F.2d 1188 (9th Cir 1980), *Telex Corp. v. International Business Machines Corp.*, 510 F.2d 894 (1975), 931–2 (10th Cir. 1975).

[62] *See, e.g., SCM Corp. v. Xerox Corp.*, 463 F.Supp. 983, 1012–13 (D.C. Conn.

In *Berkey Photo*,[63] the Second Circuit further elaborated on antitrust assessment of a refusal to disclose secret information on product development. The case concerned Kodak's simultaneous launch of a 'Pocket Instamatic' camera and a film in a new format, developed specifically to match the camera. Kodak's strategy precluded competitors in the film or camera markets from offering substitute films and cameras, giving Kodak a valuable lead-time advantage. Berkey, one of Kodak's competitors, alleged that Kodak's failure to disclose information on its new offerings was an illegal monopolization or attempted monopolization of amateur camera and film markets. Berkey's theory was that since Kodak was in a position to set industry standards, rivals could not compete effectively without offering products similar to Kodak's. The refusal to pre-disclose information on Kodak's new product allowed it to foster its monopoly power and reap profits from its innovations.[64] This strategy gave Kodak illegitimate advantage in the camera market and foreclosed its rivals from a substantial part of the market, until they were able to produce cameras compatible with the new film format.[65]

The Court agreed that Kodak's control of the film and camera market reached the level of a monopoly.[66] It also held that leveraging monopoly power to gain advantage in a neighboring market is illegal, regardless of whether or not a monopolist is close to gaining control of the neighboring market.[67] Yet, the claim that the lack of pre-disclosure of secret information on new products violated §2 of the Sherman Act failed to convince the Court. The Court asserted that a duty to pre-disclose information on new products cannot be imposed simply because a monopolist is present also in an ancillary market.[68] Preservation of the incentives to innovate was central for the Court's reasoning:

> [i]t is the possibility of success in the marketplace, attributable to superior performance, that provides the incentives on which the proper functioning of our compet-

---

1978); *SCM Corp. v. Xerox Corp.*, 645 F.2d 1195, 1206 (C.A. Conn. 1981), *In re Independent Service Organizations Antitrust Litigation*, 989 F.Supp. 1131, 1138–9 (D. Kan. 1997), *Data Gen. Corp. v. Grumman Systems Support Corp.*, 36 F.3d 1147, 1186–7 (1st Cir. 1994).

[63] *Berkey Photo, Inc. v. Eastman Kodak Co.* (*Berkey Photo*), 603 F.2d 263 (2d Cir. 1979).

[64] *Id.*, at 279.

[65] *Id.*, at 279–80 and 282.

[66] *Id.*, at 273.

[67] *Id.*, at 276; this conclusion is no longer valid given the Supreme Court's ruling in *Spectrum Sports v. McQuillan*, 506 U.S. 447, 459 (1993) (§2 makes the conduct of a single firm unlawful only when it actually monopolizes or dangerously threatens to do so).

[68] *Berkey Photo*, 603 F.2d at 276.

> itive economy rests. If a firm that has engaged in the risks and expenses of research and development were required in all circumstances to share with its rivals the benefits of those endeavors, this incentive would very likely be vitiated.[69]

Thus,

> [w]ithholding from others advance knowledge of one's new products . . . ordinarily constitutes valid competitive conduct. Because, as we have already indicated, a monopolist is permitted, and indeed encouraged, by §2 to compete aggressively on the merits, any success that it may achieve through 'the process of invention and innovation' is clearly tolerated by the antitrust laws.[70]

Since both the camera and the new film format were substantial innovations, the changing of the format was legitimate[71] and Kodak's monopoly power and its ability to set *de facto* industry standards did not create a duty to pre-disclose its new products to competitors.[72]

The key restraint of competition in the IBM and *Berkey Photo* cases was the use of a trade secret to gain advantage in another market.[73] Similar controversies arose in relation to proprietary spare parts designs and the resulting advantage that original equipment producers secured in the aftermarkets. The cases where the US courts considered the claims of independent service providers that a refusal to sell patented parts and to license copyrighted software violated antitrust laws are discussed in Chapter 2 above. It suffices to say that the US courts coined principles which make it highly unlikely for the antitrust plaintiffs to prevail on a claim that an unconditional, unilateral refusal to license a valid IP right constitutes illegal monopolization. Although these cases involved a bundle of rights, including copyrights or patents, there are good reasons to assert that trade secrets should be treated in the same manner as other forms of IP for the purpose of applying §2 of the Sherman Act. The fact that a trade secret owner takes advantage of lead-time after a new product is introduced on the market is not a ground for a valid antitrust claim. Difficulty in reverse engineering does not support the finding of an illegal restraint of trade. Forced disclosure of trade secrets undermines the private incentives to innovate in the same way as compulsory licensing does. The continued existence of a trade secret does not necessarily preclude the

---

69 *Id.*, at 281.

70 *Id.*, at 281.

71 *Id.*, at 282–3.

72 *Id.*, at 281. For a comment on cases involving disclosure of innovations *see* 1 HERBERT HOVENKAMP ET AL., IP AND ANTITRUST: AN ANALYSIS OF ANTITRUST PRINCIPLES APPLIED TO INTELLECTUAL PROPERTY LAW, ¶12.4 (2002).

73 *See Berkey Photo*, 603 F.2d at 275–6.

prospective licensee from competing with the goods, services or processes of the trade secret owner.[74] There is an additional argument for caution when it comes to compulsory licensing of trade secrets: the continuing existence of trade secrets depends in part on how licensees behave and, in particular, whether they take appropriate measures to guard trade secrets.[75]

2.2 The EU: Regulating Trade Secrets through Antitrust Law?

The history of European competition law touching IP rights has been turbulent.[76] At first, national IP rules were considered a nuisance when they were used to limit competition across frontiers between resellers of identical products. The EU antitrust enforcers viewed IP rights as *ex post* barriers to entry, rather than *ex ante* incentives to invest in R&D.[77] There was also little doubt that the competition rules may override IP rights.[78]

From the mid-1980s, with the judgments in *Café Hag II*[79] and *Ideal Standard*,[80] IP rights gained recognition in EU law and new EU legislation governing IP innovations emerged. On the competition law side, block exemption regulations for patent licenses were adopted in 1984[81] and for pure

---

74 3-10 MILGRIM, *supra* note 9, §10.01(2)(j).

75 1 HOVENKAMP ET AL., *supra* note 72, ¶13.3.e, note 111.1. The authors note that in *Telecomm Technical Services, Inc. v. Siemens Rolm Communications, Inc.*, 150 F.Supp. 2d 1365, 1370 (N.D. Ga. 2000), the district court held that the per se legality rule established by the DC Circuit in *In re Independent Service Organizations Antitrust Litigation*, 203 F.3d 1322, 1326 (Fed. Cir. 2000) does not extend to trade secrets. There does not seem to be any broader authority to support this line of reasoning; indeed the Intel case referred to above largely concerned trade secrets.

76 For an overview of historical attitude of the Commission and EU courts towards licensing *see, e.g.*, VALENTINE KORAH, IPRS AND EC COMPETITION RULES, 25–43 (2006) and Ian S. Forrester, *European Competition Law and IP*, Remarks at the Twelfth St Gallen International Competition Law Forum (April 2005).

77 KORAH, *supra* note 76, at 25.

78 The examples of this policy include the ECJ judgments in Joint cases 56&58/64 *Établissements Consten S.à.R.L. and Grundig-Verkaufs-GmbH v. Commission*, 1966 E.C.R. 299 and Case 40/70 *Sirena S.r.l. v. Eda S.r.l. and others*, 1971 E.C.R. 69. For an overview *see, e.g.*, KORAH, *supra* note 76, at 1–20, and DAVID T. KEELING, INTELLECTUAL PROPERTY RIGHTS IN EU LAW, VOL. 1: FREE MOVEMENT AND COMPETITION LAW 22–9 (2003).

79 Case C-10/89, *SA CNL-Sucal NV v. HAG GFAG*, 1990 E.C.R. I-3711.

80 Case C-9/93, *IHT Internationale Heiztechnik GmbH and Uwe Danzinger v. Ideal-Standard GmbH and Wabco Standard GmbH*, 1994 E.C.R. 2789.

81 Commission Regulation 2349/84/EEC of 23 July 1984 on the Application of Article 85(3) of the Treaty to Certain Categories of Patent Licensing Agreements, 1984 O.J. (L 219) 15, corrected by 1985 O.J. (L 13) 34.

know-how and mixed patent-and-know-how licenses in 1988.[82] The recognition of the need to protect IP resulted in the adoption of standards for IP protection at the EU level and the establishment of unitary trademark and design rights at the EU level. At the same time, a new source of tension between IP rights and antitrust law emerged: the alleged conflict between IP law and the rules concerning abuse of dominance. Although similar traits can be found in the developments at the intersection of trade secret and antitrust law, trade secrets have been treated particularly harshly by the EU antitrust enforcers, who, in the absence of harmonized trade secret laws, decide from case to case what qualifies for protection as a trade secret.

2.2.1 Article 81: from troubled beginnings to recognition

Trade secrets have had a thorny way to their recognition by the European Commission's Directorate General for Competition. In *Reuter/BASF*,[83] the first decision addressing trade secret protection, the Commission questioned the validity of a non-compete clause and a know-how assignment agreement under Article 81(1). Dr Reuter, a research chemist, sold Elastomer, a polyurethanes company, together with all related know-how and technology, including documents containing most of the scientific and technical data and know-how possessed by Elastomer AG, to one of BASF's subsidiaries. The know-how agreement imposed an eight-year non-compete obligation on Dr Reuter; it also provided that Dr Reuter was not to divulge to any third party any protected or unprotected know-how and experience in the relevant field.

The Commission decided that the restrictions on using know-how and the non-compete agreement violated Article 81(1). It reasoned that the post-transfer ban on use had to be limited in time since the transfer of legally unprotected know-how confers no exclusive rights on the purchaser. Under no circumstances could an obligation to keep know-how secret from third parties be used to prevent Dr Reuter, after the expiry of the reasonable term of a non-compete clause, from competing with BASF and developing the transferred know-how. The Commission also challenged the obligation of secrecy towards third parties, asserting that, in view of the rapid development of technology in polyurethane chemistry, it may be questioned whether such know-how has at the present time sufficient economic value to justify its continued protection by an obligation of secrecy. The condemnation of the non-disclosure clause shows the Commission's hostility to trade secrets. This decision effectively questioned the validity of know-how assignment and licensing agreements.

---

[82] Commission Regulation 556/89/EEC of 30 November 1988 on the Application of Article 85(3) of the Treaty to Certain Categories of Know-How Licensing Agreements, 1989 O.J. (L 61) 1.

[83] 1976 O.J. (L 254) 40.

The *Reuter/BASF* decision was soon reversed.[84] Two years later, in *Campari*[85] the Commission confirmed the validity of an exclusive know-how license, noting that licensors had to be allowed to impose confidentiality obligations or else secret know-how would not be passed on for use by other companies. Later on, the Commission conceded that licensing was desirable, and acknowledged that know-how had to be guarded by contractual arrangements if its owner were not to lose the benefits of innovation.[86] In 1984, the Commission granted a group exemption for patent licenses.[87] Mixed patent-and-know-how licenses were also covered as long as know-how permitted better exploitation of the licensed patents and the licensed patents were necessary in implementing the licensed technology.[88] The block exemption was very narrow and did not include pure know-how and other licenses. This was a major problem: there was evidence that US firms were hesitant to grant technology licenses in Europe due to doubts as to the validity of know-how licenses under EU competition law.[89]

The European Court of Justice (ECJ) addressed some of these concerns in its 1986 *Pronuptia* judgment.[90] The case involved franchise agreements setting up a chain of wedding gown stores. The franchisees were given the exclusive right to use the Pronuptia mark in specific territories. They were obliged to equip their shops in accordance with the specification of the franchisor, not to move their location, and to obtain 80 percent of their merchandise from the franchisor. The ECJ noted the importance of trade secrets and stressed that:

> franchisor must be able to communicate his know-how to the franchisees and provide them with the necessary assistance in order to enable them to apply his methods, without running the risk that that know-how and assistance might benefit

---

84 VALENTINE KORAH, TECHNOLOGY TRANSFER AGREEMENTS AND THE EC COMPETITION RULES 13–14 (1996).

85 *Re the Agreement of David Campari Milano SpA*, 1978 O.J. (L 70) 69.

86 VALENTINE KORAH, KNOW-HOW LICENSING AGREEMENTS AND THE EEC COMPETITION RULES 10–11 (1989). This was part of a more general tendency for more favorable treatment of IPRs.

87 Commission Regulation No 2349/84 on the application of Article 85(3) of the Treaty to certain categories of patent licensing agreements, 1985 O.J. (L 280) 32.

88 In *Boussois/Interpane*, 1987 O.J. (L 50) 3, the Commission made it clear that a mixed license was not covered if the licensed know-how dominated the technology and did not merely permit better exploitation of the licensed patents. The Commission eventually granted an individual exemption in this case.

89 STEVEN ANDERMAN, EC COMPETITION LAW AND IPRS. THE REGULATION OF INNOVATION (1998) 78–9.

90 Case 161/84, *Pronuptia de Paris GmbH v. Pronuptia de Paris Irmgard Schillgallis*, 1986 E.C.R. 353.

> competitor, even indirectly. It follows that provisions which are essential in order to avoid that risk do not constitute restrictions on competition for the purposes of Article [81(1)].[91]

Consequently, restrictions designed to protect know-how, such as non-compete clauses, restrictions on the transferability of the franchisee's business, or obligations to use the know-how provided by the franchisor, were found to be in line with Article 81(1).[92]

Following suit, the Commission recognized the need for a more coherent policy with respect to know-how licensing and adopted a number of decisions confirming the legality of some common restrictions contained in such agreements.[93] In *Rich Products/Jus-rol*,[94] the Commission acknowledged the existence of the exclusive right which the owner enjoys over its know-how and held that the obligation not to use the licensed know-how for ten years following the termination of the agreement was not in violation of Article 81(1), as long as know-how did not become a part of the public domain. It also found that the obligation to keep the licensed know-how secret, a non-exclusive grant-back clause, and the obligation not to grant sub-licenses were outside the scope of Article 81(1).[95]

The Commission fully recognized the need to protect know-how in its 1989 Know-How Block Exemption Regulation, observing that:[96]

> [t]he increasing economic importance of non-patented technical information (e.g. descriptions of manufacturing processes, recipes, formulae, designs or drawings), commonly termed 'know-how', the large number of agreements currently being concluded by undertakings including public research facilities solely for the

---

91 *Id.* ¶16.

92 *Id.* ¶¶16–20. Conversely, restrictions that the Court deemed unnecessary for the protection of know-how or for the maintenance of the network's identity and reputation were held to violate competition law, and as such to be unenforceable. *Id.* ¶¶23–5.

93 These included the *Boussois/Interpane* decision cited above, as well as decisions in *Mitchell Cotts/Sofiltra*, 1987 O.J. (L 41) 31, *Rich Products/Jus-rol*, 1988 O.J. (L 69) 21, *Delta Chemie*, 1988 O.J. (L 309) 34 and *Transocean Marine Paint*, 1988 O.J. (L 351) 40.

94 *Rich Products/Jus-rol*, 1988 O.J. (L 69) 21.

95 For comment on the case, *see e.g.* J. Kodwo Bentil, *Favourable EEC Attitude Towards Exclusive Know How Licensing Agreements: The Jus-Rol Case*, 11 EUR. INTELL. PROP. REV. 291 (1989).

96 Commission Regulation No. 556/89 on the application of Article 85(3) of the Treaty to certain categories of know-how licensing agreements (Know-How Block Exemption Regulation), 1989 O.J. (L 61) 1. The Regulation is discussed in detail e.g. by KORAH, *supra* note 86, and D.R. Price, *The Secret of the Know-How Block Exemption*, 10 EUR. COMPETITION L. REV. 273 (1989).

> exploitation of such information (so-called 'pure' know-how licensing agreements) and the fact that the transfer of know-how is, in practice, frequently irreversible make it necessary to provide greater legal certainty with regard to the status of such agreements under the competition rules, thus encouraging the dissemination of technical knowledge in the Community.[97]

In the absence of applicable Community laws, the regulation defined 'know-how' as substantial, secret and identified technical information. 'Secret' means that the know-how package is not generally known or easily accessible. The regulation specifically states that the term should not be construed narrowly so as to require every element to be totally unknown or unobtainable outside the licensor's business. 'Substantial' means that the know-how must be important for the whole or a significant part of a manufacturing process or a product or service, or for the development thereof. The licensed know-how must be useful in improving the competitive position of the licensee.[98] Thus, 'know-how' is limited to technical information. 'Identified' means that the know-how must be described or recorded so that it is possible to verify that it fulfills the criteria of secrecy and substantiality.[99] The definition is quite limited when compared with the definitions of a trade secret used in national laws. It appears that the Commission was anxious to make sure that the block exemption would otherwise encourage cartels to operate customer/market-sharing under the auspices of a license of trivial know-how.[100]

The Know-How Block Exemption Regulation treated know-how licenses essentially in the same manner as patent licenses were treated under the 1984 Patent Block Exemption Regulation.[101] However, unlike in the case of patent licenses, the exemption for territorial restrictions in know-how licenses was limited to ten years from the day the first license agreement was signed (the same restriction did not apply to patent licenses). The Commission explained that this was necessary since it would be difficult to determine when the licensed know-how ceases to be secret otherwise.[102]

---

[97] Recital (1) of the Know-How Block Exemption Regulation.

[98] The requirement of substantiality is not very strictly defined, it suffices that the licensed know-how can 'reasonably be expected at the date of the conclusion of the agreement to be capable of improving the competitive position of the licensee, for example by helping him to enter a new market or giving him an advantage in competition with other manufacturers or providers of services who do not have access to the licensed secret know-how or other comparable secret know-how'. Article 1(7) of the Know-How Block Exemption Regulation.

[99] Article 1(7) of the Know-How Block Exemption Regulation.

[100] Price, *supra* note 96, at 275.

[101] KORAH, *supra* note 86, at 51.

[102] Recital 7 of Regulation 556/89.

Both the Know-How Block Exemption Regulation and the Patent Block-Exemption Regulation were formalistic, narrow, and overly restrictive. As discussed in Chapter 2 above, the more IP-friendly and economics-based approach which prevailed in the 1990s resulted in the adoption of the Technology Transfer Block Exemption Regulation (TTBER) in 1996[103] and further liberalization of the rules on the transfer of technology in the 2004 TTBER.[104] The 1996 TTBER removed disparities between the old patent and know-how block exemptions,[105] and covered bilateral agreements for pure patent licensing, pure know-how licensing, mixed licenses of patents[106] and know-how and ancillary provisions regarding IP rights other than patents. The 2004 TTBER further extended the scope of the exemption to software licenses and industrial design licenses.

In the first draft of the 2004 TTBER, the Commission narrowed the scope of know-how definition by requiring that the information must be 'indispensable' rather than just 'useful' for the manufacture or supply of the contract products. Following an outcry from industry and the legal scholars, the Commission withdrew this idea and the 2004 TTBER did not introduce significant changes to the definition of know-how, as compared with the 1988 and 1996 regulations.[107] In the 2004 TTBER, the Commission acknowledges the

---

[103] Commission Regulation No. 240/96 of 31 January 1996 on the application of Article 85(3) of the Treaty to certain categories of technology transfer agreements, 1996 O.J. (L 31) 2.

[104] Commission Regulation No. 772/2004 on the application of Article 81(3) of the Treaty to categories of technology transfer agreements, 2004 O.J. (L 123) 11.

[105] There was an overlap as to the mixed patent-and-know-how agreements between the two technology transfer regulations, which meant that in the case of mixed patent-and-know-how agreements companies were unsure as to which regulation applied. *See, e.g.*, KORAH, *supra* note 86, at 79–80, and Chris Mitropoulos, *Technology Transfer: the New Regulation*, 2 EC COMPETITION POLICY NEWSLETTER, No. 1, Spring 1996.

[106] Patent applications, utility models, and supplementary protection certificates (SPCs) for pharmaceutical products were treated like patents.

[107] TTBER, Article 1(i). Section 47 of the Technology Transfer Guidelines offers further guidance on the notion of 'substantial', as follows: '[t]he information must significantly contribute to or facilitate the production of the contract products. In cases where the licensed know-how relates to a product as opposed to a process, this condition implies that the know-how is useful for the production of the contract product. This condition is not satisfied where the contract product can be produced on the basis of freely available technology. However, the condition does not require that the contract product is of higher value than products produced with freely available technology. In the case of process technologies, this condition implies that the know-how is useful in the sense that it can reasonably be expected at the date of conclusion of the agreement to be capable of significantly improving the competitive position of the licensee, for instance by reducing his production costs.' Know-how is defined in similar manner in

status of know-how as IP: the regulation defines IP rights as including 'industrial property rights, know-how, copyright and neighbouring rights'.[108] Unlike the 1988 and 1996 regulations, the new TTBER allows exemption for territorial restrictions in know-how licenses until the licensed know-how is no longer secret, or, in the event that secrecy has been compromised by the license, for the length of the agreement.

It is fair to say that the 2004 TTBER and the Technology Transfer Guidelines treat know-how as a form of IP; anticompetitive restraints in patent and know-how licenses are assessed broadly in the same manner. Still it is unclear why the Commission insists on having a rather narrow definition of know-how specifically for the purpose of applying competition law. The argument that the know-how licenses could be used to cover cartel arrangements is not very convincing. Most cartel arrangements are clandestine. Typically, rather than trying to cover their agreement by disguised licenses, cartel participants concentrate on keeping the paper-trail to a minimum. If the concern really is sham know-how licenses, a provision excluding such arrangements from the block exemption could be included in the TTBER, instead of the definition of know-how which has the undesirable effect of limiting the legal certainty when it comes to licensing a large body of information which is eligible for protection as trade secrets in the Member States.

2.2.2 Trade secrets and Article 82: the confusing message of Microsoft

Since the early 1990s there have been a few cases in which a refusal to license an IP right was held to be anticompetitive and a compulsory license was ordered as a remedy. These cases have been analyzed extensively in Chapter 2. The *Microsoft* case is the first instance where Article 82 has been applied to trade secrets. The facts of the case and its legal implications are discussed in Chapter 2; the focus here is solely on the issues relating to the application of the antitrust rules to trade secrets.

In *Microsoft*, the Commission held and the CFI confirmed that Microsoft's refusal to provide interoperability information violated Article 82 of the EC Treaty. The interoperability information Microsoft was obliged to disclose was highly valuable, proprietary, and confidential technical information, which clearly qualified for protection under trade secret laws and was arguably covered by other forms of IP. The Commission essentially asserted that the interoperability information was not truly valuable or innovative because it did not qualify for patent protection, and even if it did the licensees would be able

Article 2(10) of the Commission Regulation 2659/2000 of 29 November 2000 on the application of Article 81(3) of the Treaty to categories of research and development agreements, OJ 2000 (L 304) 7.

[108] TTBER, Article 1(g).

to find means of implementing the licensed technology so as to avoid the techniques over which Microsoft held patent protection. On appeal, the Commission argued that trade secrets cannot be equated with 'intellectual property rights created by law' and that the case law on compulsory licensing does not as such apply to trade secrets.[109] The CFI upheld the *Microsoft* decision, but did not decide whether trade secrets should benefit from the same level of deference as other forms of IP.[110] It did, however, hold that the specific features of trade secrets do not warrant affording them a higher degree of protection than that given to proprietary information protected by other forms of IP rights.[111]

The implementation of the Commission's decision has created further questions as to exactly how much protection Microsoft's trade secrets should be given. The Commission intended that the open source community benefit from the technology disclosed by Microsoft,[112] yet, open source software cannot be based on technology supplied under a traditional software license, which requires the licensee to protect trade secrets. To solve this problem, the Commission required Microsoft not to charge royalties for interoperability information lacking 'significant innovation'.[113] In addition, the Commission required Microsoft to allow the publication of the software source code developed by the licensees and based on Microsoft's interface documentation, as long as the latter does not 'embody innovation'.[114] If no 'innovation' is involved, third party software developers should be allowed to access Microsoft's trade secrets without giving Microsoft the possibility of ensuring that its trade secrets are kept confidential through licensing terms, as is the case for licensees. This effectively destroys Microsoft's trade secrets not embodying innovation.[115]

---

[109] Case T-201/04, *Microsoft v. Commission*, ¶280 (*Microsoft* judgment), 2007 E.C.R. II-3601.

[110] *Microsoft* judgment, ¶¶283–90.

[111] *Microsoft* judgment, ¶¶692–5.

[112] See European Commission, 'Competition: Commission to market test new proposals from Microsoft on interoperability', Press Release IP/05/673, 6 June 2005, at http://europa.eu/rapid/pressReleasesAction.do?reference=IP/05/673&format=HTML&aged=1&language=EN&guiLanguage=en.

[113] Microsoft can charge non-nominal prices only for protocol technology that is innovative. *See* European Commission, 'Competition: Statement of Objections to Microsoft for non-compliance with March 2004 decision – frequently asked questions', MEMO/07/90, 1 March 2007, at http://europa.eu/rapid/pressReleasesAction.do?reference=MEMO/07/90.

[114] *See* European Commission, supra note 113.

[115] Microsoft challenged this interpretation before the CFI. *See* Notice for the O.J. on Case T-313/05 *Microsoft Corporation v. Commission*, 2005 O.J. (C 257) 16.

Thus, the Commission created two categories of trade secrets: those 'embodying innovation', which deserve some level of deference from antitrust enforcers, and those that are not innovative enough and which must fully give way to antitrust laws. It was not entirely clear what is the required standard of innovativeness and how it relates to the national trade secret and patent laws or the TTBER definition of know-how.

Inevitably, this became the source of another dispute between the Commission and Microsoft. In March 2007, nearly three years after the adoption of the *Microsoft* decision, the Commission issued a Statement of Objections alleging that Microsoft failed to comply with its decision by charging unreasonable prices for the interoperability information.[116] The Commission concluded that there was no significant innovation in Microsoft's unpatented protocols and, consequently, that license prices proposed by Microsoft were unreasonable.[117] According to the Commission, the protocols did not involve significant innovations because 'all of the described features were considered either to have been Microsoft implementations of prior developments by others, or to have been anticipated by prior developments and to be immediately obvious minor extensions to that prior work.'[118] Thus it seems that the Commission's required standard of innovativeness is akin to that required to obtain a patent. Consequently, 'know-how' which merits protection when Article 81 is applied to it does not necessarily merit protection if it is owned by a dominant company whose behavior is subject to Article 82.

Eventually, following a prolonged dispute, Microsoft and the Commission agreed on a compromise solution, allowing open source software developers to access and use the interoperability information and setting the royalties at a nominal one-off payment of 10,000 for a license excluding patented information and 0.4 per cent for a worldwide license including patents. The fact that the Commission allowed Microsoft to charge royalties for the licensed trade secrets indicates that it had acknowledged that trade secrets could not be subject to expropriation without the right to compensation. Still, the theories advanced by the Commission in the course of litigation and the implementation of the Microsoft decision significantly undermined the position of trade secrets. After *Microsoft*, it is far from clear to what extent dominant

---

[116] European Commission, 'Competition: Commission warns Microsoft of further penalties over unreasonable pricing as interoperability information lacks significant innovation', Press Release IP/07/269, 1 March 2007, at http://europa.eu/rapid/pressReleasesAction.do?reference=IP/07/269.

[117] *Id.*

[118] *Id.*

companies can rely on trade secrets to effectively protect their proprietary information in the European Union.

The Commission's position on trade secrets is difficult to justify given that patents, copyrights, designs, and other IP rights may be used to protect some or all aspects of a secret technology. Forced sharing of proprietary technology undermines the incentives to innovate regardless of whether that technology is protected by a patent or under trade secret laws. Further, ordering disclosure not only destroys trade secrets but also precludes the proprietor from obtaining a patent on the invention at stake and eliminates the incentives to innovate. To be sure, trade secrets may give rise to competitive concerns just as other forms of IP do and by no means should trade secret holders enjoy immunity from antitrust scrutiny. Still, the fact that trade secrets provide an important incentive for private investments in developing new products implies that antitrust enforcers should treat them with a similar level of deference to that afforded to other forms of IP. Furthermore, the specific features of trade secrets, such as the ease of misappropriation and the relatively limited scope of protection they afford, should be taken into account for the purpose of application of antitrust rules.

The Commission disregards special features of trade secrets such as the ease of misappropriation, the need to protect secrecy and the fact that their existence does not preclude competitors from developing or reverse-engineering the information at stake. It has also chosen to ignore the economic effects of reverse engineering in its analysis of refusals to provide interoperability information and competitive concerns resulting from trade secrets. The divergence in the treatment of patents and trade secrets in the *Microsoft* case is particularly striking, considering that, as explained above, for the purpose of applying Article 81, the Commission does not make any significant distinction between patent and know-how licenses. It appears that in that case the Commission took the absence of the EU standards of trade secret protection as an invitation to coin trade secret protection standards as it sees fit when applying antitrust laws to a particular situation. The results of this approach are not only at odds with national and international standards of trade secret protection but also internally incoherent.

All in all, the *Microsoft* case shows that antitrust authorities are not best placed to fashion IP protection standards. This results in legal uncertainty and undermines IP protection laws.

Index